smile:) the story of Lily Allen

smile:) the story of Lily Allen

Bella Wolfson

OMNIBUS PRESS

London / New York / Paris / Sydney / Copenhagen / Berlin / Madrid / Tokyo

Exclusive Distributors
Music Sales Limited,
14/15 Berners Street,
London, W1T 3LJ.

Music Sales Corporation,
257 Park Avenue South,
New York, NY 10010, USA.

Macmillan Distribution Services,
56 Parkwest Drive
Derrimut, Vic 3030,
Australia.

Every effort has been made to trace the copyright holders of the photographs in this book but one or
two were unreachable. We would be grateful if the photographers concerned would contact us.

Typeset by Phoenix Photosetting, Chatham, Kent
Printed in the EU

A catalogue record for this book is available from the British Library.

Visit Omnibus Press on the web at www.omnibuspress.com

CHAPTER ONE

"Ever since I can remember, I bin poppin' my collar."
An early quote on Lily Allen's now somewhat legendary
MySpace page.

May 2, 1985: a manic-looking man with wild eyes and a colourful vocabulary is driving his wife, who is quite calm considering the circumstances, from their council flat in Bury Place, Bloomsbury, to Hammersmith Hospital in West London. The man is Keith Allen, comedian, actor, *Comic Strip* regular and at this moment, panicking future father. The woman is Alison Owen, a dynamic up-and-coming producer with a young daughter from a previous relationship. They are about to welcome their first child together, and in so doing, welcome a character into their world who would match their chaos and throw in a truckload of drama, emotion, laughter, destruction, notoriety and unshakeable love.

Alison bedded down in the maternity ward, produced a book from her bag and, serenely, began to read. She'd done this before and knew what to expect. Keith was already technically a parent twice over as a result of a couple of one-night stands, but this was the first time he would really become a *parent*, present from the moment of his child's birth. As a result he was not quite so serene.

He tried to calm down by looking out of the window. Despite its name Hammersmith Hospital is not in Thames-side Hammersmith but on the northern reaches of Shepherd's Bush, and it was a far from idyllic view, dominated by the imposing walls of one of the capital's biggest prisons, Wormwood Scrubs. Keith was, as he explains in his book *Grow Up*, "trying to locate the exact cell I'd been in all those years before while waiting to be shipped off to Borstal" when Alison's contractions started.

"All of a sudden the top of Lily's head appeared, all of a rush to get the fuck out of there and get off to some party..." The newborn Lily was rather green and, as her father poetically recalls, "covered in all this white shit". But she was a beautiful baby with a glossy thatch of dark hair, perfect pale skin and big, knowing brown eyes.

Thus did Lily Rose Beatrice Allen make her first appearance into the world she would, in about two decades' time, hold in the palm of her hand. She would be a tough yet tender Taurean, always something of a contradiction; she would grow up loving her home comforts but she faced a fragmented upbringing and a career that ensured she would be forever on the road; she would prove a vital (sometimes reluctant) female role model but would often admit to feeling threatened by other women; she'd develop into a girl whose street style and intermittent mockney airs would bemuse critics and clash with her middle-class roots and turbulent private school education. A natural-born rebel with, as far as her far from conservative parents were concerned, little to rebel against, she would rebel against the world, and sometimes herself and her own better judgement. And, for better or worse, she would always be utterly her father's daughter, *and* her mother's, in very different ways – while always remaining very much her own person. Lily would also become a compelling natural diarist and documenter of London in her blogs and her song-writing (let's face it, if Samuel Pepys were alive today, he'd have a MySpace blog himself – although he'd have to wait for his potential readers to finish reading Lily Allen's before they got to his own posts), and it seems right that the baby Lily would live the first few years of her life in the heart of the city, moments from the British Museum (and the shoppers' heaven that is Oxford Street).

Lily Rose, known to all now except her bank as simply 'Lily', by all accounts owes her pretty name to a less than romantic source. If legend is correct, Keith chose to name his daughter after The Lilywhites, a nickname for Fulham FC, his favourite team. Fortunately Lily is also a fan, not that she had a huge amount of choice – after Keith left the family when Lily was five, football matches would represent essential if awkward bonding time for Keith and Lily, although she would always feel as if she was being treated like a boy. It was just as much, if not more, fun when he occasionally took her with him on film shoots. She observed with no small interest how her dad would be treated when he was filming, she saw how he had his own trailer and how a car would pick him up when he was needed. She liked the look of that. Being famous didn't look like a bad life at all.

Once in the public eye herself, she would be defined in many people's eyes by her father's apparent influence but, according to Lily herself, he was rarely around as much as she'd have liked him to be. Maybe her fierce independence and embracing of other cultural references in her music and persona would be her way of ensuring that there'd at least be a part of her that was defined by elements she chose, not by the world she was born into.

But there were elements of her family's world that would inevitably shape her own path and sense of self: a love for bucking trends, giving authority the finger and also adhering to family traditions such as attending the Glastonbury Festival each year with a collective 'family' of fellow bon viveurs. One thing was for sure, Lily's parents were determined their children should fit round them, not the other way around. This was partly because that's what 'groovy' liberated parents did, but in another way the Eighties was very much the 'me' generation: Thatcher was in government, and people were encouraged to make it on their own terms and live their lives to the full – if they wanted something, they had to push forward and grab it, kids in tow or not. But this would at least amount to an interesting journey for the children. This would be no 'normal' childhood, whatever 'normal' is.

TV presenter Miquita Oliver, Lily's best friend since the age of two, had a similar experience, which may be why they bonded so fiercely. Miquita, born the year before Lily, grew up with former Rip Rig and Panic singer and single mum Andrea Oliver, who counted Neneh Cherry as a bosom buddy and Slits bassist Tessa Pollitt as a sister-in-law.

As a result Miquita, Lily and Tessa's daughter Phoebe would grow up amid a whirlwind of creativity, open-minded, artistic individuals and bohemian parties in the former punk squatland of Ladbroke Grove.

The three girls would also appear in the Portobello Panto, a West London festive institution at the Tabernacle in Notting Hill, started by Keith Allen's actor brother Kevin, and recently revived by Lily's sister Sarah. Lily would later complain that she always had to play "a frog or a boy, Phoebe and Miquita would get the beautiful parts".

"The performer genes have definitely been hogged by two other members of my family," quipped Sarah in an interview after she relaunched the panto in 2005 with her childhood pal Ruby Platts-Mills. "Lily and [brother] Alfie were in it as kids, but I was just becoming a teenager and feeling self-conscious. As a kid it was fun because you got the sense of it being a little bit grown-up and naughty. You felt you were being allowed into the grown-up world."

This sort of free, homespun bohemian environment would make an impression on the children developing within it, although they wouldn't realise the full effect until they started mixing with other people who didn't grow up in quite the same way. Miquita said in an interview: "Until I met Simon [her former *Popworld* TV co-presenter Simon Amstell], I thought everybody grew up around brilliant actors, musicians, stylists and characters. It was only when he told me about his suburban upbringing in Ilford that I realised not everyone did."

Lily would be whisked to her first Glastonbury within weeks of her birth, no less; "this gleaming white baby being carried over a sea of mud", remembers Alison. And while you might think that at least as a baby Lily might have been kept away from any nefarious festival activities, you couldn't be more wrong. It was pretty handy having her around when it came to making a bit of extra dosh, as far as Keith was concerned. A cute baby was the perfect foil, not to mention a fine marketing tool "for my 'out the back of the van' beer and amyl nitrate business, like the homeless lads do with dogs".

He explains: "Lil sat next to the stall gurgling in a pushchair while I cranked up the sales patter and knocked out the lager. It wasn't long before Lily and I were surrounded by a pile of semi-conscious revellers on all fours picking up bits of their shattered minds." At this point Glastonbury was still seen as quite hippyish, the atmosphere taking precedence over what might have been happening onstage. The line-up was relatively alternative (Echo & The Bunnymen, Boomtown Rats, Aswad). This year at least, all the rock fans were gearing up to catch the likes of Status Quo and Queen at Live Aid instead.

Appropriately for a girl who would spend her adult life very much on display, even her conception was ceremoniously marked. After her parents wed at what is now the Union Chapel in Islington on July 21, 1984 (although, says Keith, the "'I Do's' should have been 'I Don'ts',") the newly-weds left their drunken reception for a honeymoon in the auspiciously named Hope Cove in Devon, where they picnicked and made love on the sand. The mood was only slightly broken when Keith started shovelling up the sand from underneath Alison's bottom and pouring it into a wine bottle.

"This is going on our mantelpiece so everyone will see the very sand on which we had our first married fuck," he enthused to his wife, reminiscing in later years: "The bottle did indeed take pride of place on the mantelpiece in Bury Place, and took extra significance when we discovered that our daughter had been conceived there."

"We didn't have much money, but it was a really exciting time," Alison told *Times* journalist Beverley D'Silva. "London was fun, Keith was in the *Comic Strip* and it was the birth of Channel 4. I was finding my feet, working in the booming pop-video industry. My first child, Sarah, was five when Lily was born. I was about 23."

Alison had first attracted Keith's attention in the early Eighties when she was a young student at University College London, having come to the capital after leaving her home-town of Portsmouth with barely any money. She was a punk, complete with an impressive pink Mohican (then-struggling comic Keith was more taken with the size of her vast bosom, however), hanging out at trendy West London clubs with socialites such as Bella Freud and Rose Boyt, who had taken her under their wing. She was young, small and clearly had an air of vulnerability that mingled with her bubbly, feisty nature; people – Keith included – wanted to take care of her (he mentioned he wanted to protect her from himself. That didn't last long, naturally). In her arsenal she also had a very young child, Sarah, and she made full use of her single mother status in cleverly ensuring she secured herself grants galore from her college. (The posher students also wasted no time in borrowing the baby in order to appear like wholesome 'earth mother' types.)

The money Alison cannily managed to accrue secured her a sizeable flat in Bury Place, Bloomsbury, the place where, once Keith and she officially became an item, they would live as a family, trying all manner of schemes (making and selling sandwiches, selling cans of Red Stripe at parties, hawking poppers at festivals) to stay afloat as their brood started to grow. A year after the arrival of Lily, Alfie was born, also in Hammersmith Hospital. And he would be described just as beautifully by his dad: "Like a deflated crisp packet." Poor Alfie. Well, it could only get better.

While Keith attempted to be a model father-to-be during Alison's pregnancy, bustling about doing the shopping and generally getting on her nerves, it wasn't long after she came home with Lily that his nesting instincts dissolved, allowing his wild old ways to re-emerge. In a similar way to how Lily would channel her break-ups and frustrations into creative energy and song-writing in later years, Keith would do the same in this situation. A new baby, a new home life, a new lover, these provided "the emotional backdrop to writing *The Yob*".

The Yob, about a pretentious director whose brain transforms into that of a football hooligan after a psychic teleportation experiment gone wrong, was a *Comic Strip* episode that would be unveiled three years hence, featuring pop-reggae band UB40 and, interestingly, Lily and Alfie as toddlers, as well as big sister Sarah. But for every TV success and acting part Keith took, there would be a period of 'resting' to balance it out. What didn't rest or diminish was Keith's capacity for going out and having a good time. Alison juggled caring for the kids with temping jobs on music videos to stay afloat but it was far from plain sailing, and it was about to get harder.

In 1990, Keith, close pals with the Manchester scene – including the Happy Mondays and New Order – bagged the opportunity to co-write the lyrics to England's World Cup anthem 'World In Motion' with New Order's Bernard Sumner. But while professionally this could only be a good thing, personally Keith was struggling to stay committed to family life. The prodigiously fecund Allen had had another fling, this time with former singer and psychic counseller Anjel Tabatha, which produced a daughter, Galoushka, in 1990. To make things even more complicated, by the time Galoushka was born, Anjel alleged, he'd already started an affair behind both Alison *and* Anjel's backs with the TV producer Nira Park (*Spaced, Shaun Of The Dead*).

Keith felt his marriage to Alison was sadly "spiritually over long before" he'd hooked up with Nira (who, bright, high-powered producer or nay, first caught his eye when she happened to be dressed as a maid. Men are simple souls…) and he decided he wanted to move into her home in Gospel Oak, North London. The kids were on holiday in Malaga, Spain with their nanny when Keith felt he had to break the news and talk to them about the future. He wept for the duration of the flight. As soon as they returned to England, he prepared for his personal exodus.

"I remember the day dad left, and us all saying goodbye to him in the hall of our flat in Bloomsbury," remembers Lily in an interview. "I just remember there being a thing of 'does that mean dad's never going to be around?' Then of course dad did go, and didn't come back for a while. He was there, but he wasn't, as well. It was the Nineties, you know…"

The Nineties would be a wild, cocaine-fuelled decade for many in London's media circle, and Keith Allen was at the very heart of it. Keith and his Glasto-going pal Joe Strummer (Lily's unofficial 'godfather' – her real godfather is video director Roger Pomphrey) had already been drinking up a storm in Soho's legendary Colony Room and Gaz's Rockin' Blues, a basement club at the St Moritz on Wardour Street, run by John Mayall's son Gaz. ("Lily's dad," chuckles a Gaz's regular of the time. "He was an *enfant terrible*. He was always around, being naughty, getting involved in all sorts of things. They'd go to parties and be very wild in their middle-agedness…")

But it was when Keith met the Brit-art superstar Damien Hirst in the Groucho Club that the debauched "hedonist years" really kicked off. "I think Damien, me and later [Blur bassist] Alex James upset many, many people we probably shouldn't have…" he confessed. It didn't leave much room for his kids, unless they chose to force their way into the circle themselves when they were old enough, which Lily did, earning a Groucho membership herself at just 17.

A music industry executive who partied with Keith in the Nineties admitted that these were "wild times, Keith was a nutter. I can't believe the things we did. There'd be parties with mountains of coke, mad times. I'm amazed Alfie and Lily turned out... well, turned out at all."

The madness aside, the effect of the divorce was certainly devastating to Lily and Alfie. Alfie started showing more and more signs of attention deficit disorder, deliberately winding Keith up whenever they were together in order to extract more attention from him. But as a result, Lily would become withdrawn and sullen as her brother became the centre of her parents' focus.

The kids would sometimes have to be in the care of nannies if Alison was out working or shopping, and this didn't always go down well with Lily. But she made sure she was always one step ahead of her folks, always aware of where they were and what they were doing at any given time. "She can track me down anywhere," says Alison. "I'll be in Harvey Nichols and somebody will hold out a phone and say: 'Lily Allen for you'. She could always find her dad, too. I'd hear her imperious little voice on the phone when she was six, telling a waiter: 'If he's not in his room, I suggest you try the bar.'"

Lily would become intensely watchful of her mother, who had to work harder than ever after the split, concerned about her state and picking up on every vibe when she was around. "She was a delightful child, always exuberant and outgoing," Alison told *Times* writer Beverley D'Silva. "But after I split with Keith, she became introverted, more difficult to get on with. It was hard for her.

"She became 'caretakery', checking I was OK all the time. I was distraught, really frightened. And Lily was so perceptive; she felt every ounce of my depression and distress, and that was awful."

"I did probably lack a bit of the tender loving care that most kids get if their mum's home all the time," admits Lily to *The Guardian*. "I suppose all I wanted was someone to put their arms around me and give me a big hug, and that never really came. It's not that my mum didn't love us though, she was working incredibly hard to get a roof over our heads."

As a result Lily understandably must have felt she had to harden up, and she became more self-sufficient. She didn't need to go to her mum as much as she might have done, primarily because she felt she'd be better off sorting out her problems on her own, rather than focusing on the time and the hugs she thought she was missing out on. But it is sad to note that in years to come, when Lily was 22, she would shrug off Alison's attempts to cuddle her. "I had to share my mum's bed recently and she woke up and gave me a hug, and I said, 'Get off me, I'm 22 and I don't want you to hug me any more.' She started crying and I thought: 'Oh, grow up.'"

In 1991 it became clear that Alison's grafting was paying off – she had her first major breakthrough with the award-winning TV series *Teenage Health Freak*, which featured *Blackadder* star Tony Robinson, and she produced her first movie, *Hear My Song*, which would win a British Comedy Award, not to mention Golden Globe and Bafta nominations. This obviously didn't immediately guarantee a life of ease, despite how it may have appeared on the outside, but it was an encouraging sign.

Hear My Song was shot in Leixlip, County Kildare, and Alison whisked her kids over to the Emerald Isle with her while she worked, planting Lily and Alfie in the Montessori school Scoil Bhride, just a field away from where she was working. Alison remembers this era as "strange, fraught, but quite magical" and it certainly saw Lily develop a strong affection for Ireland.

Scoil Bhride was where Lily would make friends with Poppy Lloyd, a "mental but lovely girl" who introduced Lily to plenty of alternative music including the Irish punk band Sultans Of Ping FC. No surprise that Poppy would later become a club DJ, as would her brother Lester, who Lily also met when she was seven. He would be little more than 'Poppy's brother' to Lily until, years later, the pair bumped into each other as teenagers in London and hit it off in a big way. He'd even inspire a song – *the* song. But we'll come to that later…

After returning to England, and in the wake of *Hear My Song*'s success, Alison had been wooed by a comedian who was at the top of his game and not daunted by the prospect of taking on three awkward children. In early 1992, Alison started seeing Harry Enfield. Despite his own behaviour, Keith was not happy to hear the news. Particularly as it came, in gloating form, from Lily.

"The split wasn't so easy to deal with when Alison found someone else," Keith admits in *Grow Up*. "I took the kids to get a pizza and they took great delight in breaking the news. Lily, especially, wanted to shock me. It was an annoyingly familiar trait. She was changing from an angelic little girl into me...

'Dad, Mum's got a new boyfriend and he's famous.'

'So am I.'

'You're not.'

'Yes I fucking am.'

'Don't you want to know his name?'

'No I do not.

'It's Harry Enfield,' she said triumphantly, thrilled at the effect her announcement had on her dad, who'd hurt her and her family so keenly with his own actions. She added a final cheeky sting before happily biting into her pizza: "I told you he's more famous than you."

CHAPTER TWO

'Since you've gone I feel like I've gotten older'
Lyric from 'I Could Say'.

The new family moved in to a four-bedroom house off Uxbridge Road in Shepherd's Bush before dispatching to Harry's "disgustingly nice" pad in Primrose Hill, and, as Keith bitterly observed, "The superstar comedian Harry got himself a ready-made family."

"It was a happy time when mum was with Harry," remembers Lily. "It wasn't so much him, but we lived in a nice, big house in Primrose Hill. We had Chinese in Hampstead every Sunday and a nice car…"

Keith inevitably wasn't amused that his kids also found Harry very funny, which was a temporary tonic for Alison as well despite Lily later insinuating that Harry suffered from depression himself. Keith was also suspicious of Enfield's 'war fixation' – giving Alfie Airfix kits of warplanes and encouraging the children to watch *Colditz*. But Lily didn't mind at all; she adored "arcane subjects, like the Second World War, Greek mythology, 18th-century aristocracy". Another strike for Enfield.

The only thing that made Allen senior happy on this subject was that he knew how difficult his kids were; knowing they had "inherited his devilishness" and would be winding up their new stepfather was good enough for him.

It would take a Zen Buddhist monk not to get irritated by Lily and Alfie's naughtiness – they always shared a cast-iron bond but the battling between them was unrelenting. Harry would even base one of his popular sketches on it: the characters and scenarios of the fighting children. The familiar-sounding 'Lulu and Harry', played by Kathy Burke and Harry himself on *Harry Enfield And Chums*, were directly inspired by Lily and Alfie's endless bickering, screaming, misbehaving and manipulating.

Alison was getting busier and busier as the Nineties marched on: she produced star-studded *The Young Americans* (starring Harvey Keitel and Thandie Newton and even Keith Allen himself as a gangster – no hard feelings then) and she collaborated with her new beau, Harry, by producing the hilarious and poignant portrait of two radio DJs past their prime, *Smashie And Nicey – The End Of An Era* in 1994, which won her a Silver Rose at Montreux and another Bafta nomination.

But it would soon be the end of an era for Alison and Harry – after three years together their relationship was becoming increasingly strained, taking a turn for the worse when Alfie's chaotic behaviour started spiralling into violence. He was expelled from every school he was sent to and Harry's suggestion that Alison send him to his own boarding school (where he himself was miserable and only lasted two years) was not popular.

Not long before the split, Harry publicly said that Alison and the kids had "made a new man out of me. I suddenly feel anything is possible. I just think Alison, Sarah, Lily and Alf are rather nice to put up with me so I couldn't be nasty to them – they might get up and go."

But just three months later, according to Keith, the relationship was over officially when Harry kicked down the bathroom door while Alison was doing coke inside with a pal. "It was a very druggy scene," confirmed a former friend of the couple's. "There was a lot of coke, it wasn't great."

On the outside, Alison seemed to be holding things together remarkably, but the external, polished façade belied what was beneath. "Men loved her," said a former colleague. "She was this little bubbly blonde woman, so together, and she seemed able to just handle anything

– bringing up all these kids, and really building up an impressive career at the same time. And she'd have these passionate relationships.

"She always had lots of entertaining stories from being on set, it was a bit *Ab Fab*… and she'd joke about her kids, it was affectionate but it was unlike most middle-class parents who go on about their kids and how amazing they are. Yes, she was always very up."

Lily remembers that during the time Harry and Alison were an item, her mum had been drinking and taking cocaine more frequently, which caused her to be "in and out of rehab… so out of her head half the time she'd forget I was there". After Harry and Alison finally called it quits, Alison would be admitted to a clinic again, depressed and in need of help.

Lily: "I would go there on Family Day and listen to people talk about their heroin overdose and awful things, so I knew what was bad and what to avoid. I don't know anyone who isn't a drug-taker, in recovery from drugs or on prescription drugs. I knew all about it early on."

It was this prior knowledge, and the cavalier way in which drugs were used around her from such an early age, that ensured she would more than likely try them herself before long, but she chose to start off with a drug that better suited her character. Coke made people aggressive, energetic, loud, arrogant and unstoppable – perfect for the go-getting, cut-throat media circle. But Lily, perhaps understandably, wanted to escape from that and turn inward. What better drug to choose than introspective, soporific marijuana? In her teens she would snuggle up in her room, roll a joint and listen to the stack of records 'Uncle' Joe Strummer had lent her. (No surprise that there was plenty of reggae and rockabilly in there, as well as records by his old mates and contemporaries Ian Dury & The Blockheads, The Specials and The Slits, musical and lyrical influences she cites to this day. Joe Strummer would always be a special figure in Lily's life, and the fact he came from a background that fans found dubious for a punk icon – he was famously a diplomat's son – must have resonated with Lily when her own background was brought up again and again in later years.)

"I smoked my first spliff when I was 15. (Mum's) a busybody, and I hated that when I was younger, and smoked a lot of weed. But I can see myself turning into that. I love her but I don't want to be her."

Lily started to define herself early after being taken on set and to parties by her high-flying mother. She grew up quickly, knew how to talk to adults at parties and became, by her own admission, "precocious and pretentious. I remember thinking, 'I just want to be older so that everyone listens to me and takes me seriously.'"

(Apparently Lily wasn't the only one maturing at an alarming rate. "Alfie's got a huge penis," she obligingly told gay magazine *Attitude* in later years. "I would often be in the bath in the morning and Alfie would get up with his morning boner and come in for a wee. I'd just be like: 'That is the most disgusting thing I have ever seen!' He'd even poo in front of me, it's disgusting. I'd never poo in front of my brother! Wee, yes definitely...")

Courtney Love remembered being amazed by the 11-year-old Lily who was acting all grown up at the Groucho Club. She reminded Love of Drew Barrymore who'd had a similar turbulent childhood, desperate to be an adult. "She wasn't bratty, she was a really nice kid. I remember like I remember Drew before I was friends with her – she was sort of like 40 when she was 11." (The feeling of admiration was clearly not mutual however: Lily would say of Love in 2007: "One night with her made me realise why Kurt Cobain killed himself." And that's before we even get to the undignified spat they had on Twitter in 2010...)

That year at Glastonbury, Lily started becoming more aware than ever of drug culture – how could she not when Happy Mondays' pill-head Bez had started to hang around the campfire with Keith, Joe Strummer and Sean Ryder? That year Keith Allen was up for some serious showing off and put on Lily's pink and green shell suit (even style icon Lily had a shell-suit moment) and a leather biker's cap, and pretended to be a 'gay Welsh taxi driver' (he claims this is where *Little Britain* got the idea for the 'only gay in the village' act). Lily was getting increasingly cross as she saw the "seams of her shell-suit bursting because of her MDMA-stoked buffoon father," writes Keith.

Another character that would hang around with Joe and Keith was a "GHB (drug)-guzzling youth-botherer and qualified potter" (who knew the two could go together?) called Pockets, aka Dave Girwan. He was known as 'Pockets' because, you guessed it, he had a proliferation of pockets on his clothes and seemed to be able to produce anything from them at any time – a torch, string, wire, needle and thread, cuddly toy, you name it. He was also a sofa-surfer of no fixed abode, and thus needed to travel light. Pockets was Joe's right-hand man, but after Strummer passed away in 2002, and Lily later became famous herself, she would take him on as her own man Friday.

"(Festivals) were more about hanging out with family and friends, sitting round the campfire singing songs," said Lily in an interview with *The Telegraph*. "It's people from all different walks of life hanging out together, and everyone gets really drunk. I don't think festivals would be very good without drink. But then I didn't drink when I was five and I found them quite fun…

"(Joe) had a thing about him where he could be really out of his mind but still really cool…"

When she wasn't at festivals hanging out with loved ones and rolling her eyes at her hedonistic dad, her opportunities to join her mother at work were a vital respite to her time at school.

"Lily's naturally outspoken but, because I was the loud one at home, she became disruptive at school," Lily's sister Sarah told *Grazia* magazine. "My relationship with Lily back then was strained – I was a crazy teenager, and that must have affected Lily. I had a big gang of friends but Lily was more of a loner. She had no one to talk to about getting her first period or (later) breaking up with her first boyfriend. Would it have been different if we'd been closer? Probably."

"Everyone thought I was a bit of a joke," insists Lily. "I was very much like my dad, wanting attention, fighting and being very aggressive."

At least she could leave her frustrations behind when she was hanging out on film sets. It was like another world, and she would often receive more of an education from travelling with her mum than she would at any of the 13 schools she attended throughout her childhood, and her experience and experimentation with sex and drugs from a relatively early age, she feels, stood her in good stead. She got them "out of the way", while others would waste time discovering them for the first time in their late teens and early twenties.

"I was very unhappy at school," she told her father's old drinking buddy Damien Hirst in *Interview* magazine, in which celebrities interview other celebrities. "I didn't get on with people my age. Adults were far more interesting. I think I spent too much time with adults, and I just thought kids were stupid."

Once Alison started working on the low-budget movie division within Working Title films, she whisked Lily over to Toronto for a shoot, where she got to know Gwyneth Paltrow and had her first Domino's pizza. It's hard to know which Lily found more exciting, but being a down-to-earth girl not given to getting star-struck, it might well have been the pizza. (In later years, when Gwyneth came to London to visit, Lily gave her the grand tour of their house, deliberately walking in on big sister Sarah and her boyfriend having sex. Blushes all round, thanks to impish Lily.)

Back at school, or should that be 'schools', Lily was getting her kicks where she could. Her mother strived to send her to the best schools she could afford, often "crying on the phone for money for school fees to Keith", according to one former colleague. Yes, she sent Lily to Chelsea's super-strict Hill House school (previous alumni includes Prince Charles), Somerset's Millfield prep school (she only liked it because she was good at hockey), Cavendish in Camden and later the liberal, progressive Bedales (her favourite), but she didn't last long in any of them. "She worked so hard to pay for our education," remembers Lily. "It was pointless; none of us have any qualifications."

At Bedales at least, Lily had Joe Strummer's daughters Jazz and Lola looking out for her, and so many famous people sent their kids there, there was never any danger of any unwanted attention from that point of view. Another self-styled 'freakish' personality who attended Bedales at the same time as Lily was the singer Patrick Wolf, who would later boast that Bedales took all the "freaks" that other schools wouldn't be able to deal with. ("Freaks" who fortunately had parents with the dosh to pay for a Bedales education anyway, which included bread-baking, harp-playing and sailing small Celtic boats that they had crafted themselves down the river. "Freaks" at state schools, on the other hand, just had to put up with being stared at or bullied, and keep their harp-playing ambitions to themselves.)

For all Bedales' grooviness, Lily generally didn't get on with the other girls, refusing to join the cliques that invariably spring up at school, and she became a loner, skipping off to take ecstasy or sleep with boys.

She was finally asked to leave one school when she turned up wearing a T-shirt that proclaimed 'I am a naughty girl', Paula Yates (who once teased the press with her 'Little Miss Naughty' T-shirt) eat your heart out.

"I couldn't come out of myself at home, so I used to do it at school. I wanted to get attention," she once said. She also watched the behaviour of her West London childhood family friends, many of whom went to the rougher, more street-wise Holland Park Comprehensive, and tried to emulate it in a bid to shrug off her parents' aspirational media middle-classness. "I saw that behaviour and I probably used to take part in it to a certain extent... I never stabbed anyone but I probably gave the impression I would."

"I was doing things with boys that I shouldn't have been doing at such a young age... I was doing blow jobs," she told *Rolling Stone*. "(My parents) didn't care... They're products of the Sixties, they're bang up for a bit of that."

Her former Hill House classmates remember her as a "crazy little girl, naughty, emotional, quite the attention-seeker", but obviously popular, even if she didn't realise it herself. Hill House was the sort of place where kids say 'yah' without a trace of irony, in contrast to Lily's intermittent glottal stops and dropped 'h's. Hill House students would go on three-week-long school trips hiking in Switzerland, on one of which Harry Enfield visited her on. Which put the kybosh on all the kids who didn't believe her when she said her stepdad was Harry Enfield.

"I found it hard at those posh schools because everybody else was much richer," said Lily. "They'd be picked up in helicopters and Rolls-Royces, and I'd be picked up by Hippie Dave in a VW camper with flowers painted on it..." Nothing wrong with that.

But it was back in her early years at Cavendish in Camden, a private Catholic girls school, that Lily would find her voice, literally, as an 11-year-old. (Lily wasn't actually brought up as a Catholic. Alison had, according to Lily, "lied on the form and said I had had my communion. And then we had to go to church and eat the body of Christ and drink the wine and I thought I was going to hell. And my mum said, 'Darling, if you feel that guilty about it, you're definitely a Catholic'.)

She didn't particularly enjoy it there; as usual, she felt alienated or threatened by the other girls, but she would have an epiphany, thanks to a certain teacher, that would inform the rest of her life.

Canadian soprano Rachel Santesso came to teach music at the school in the mid-Nineties, taking over the school choir. Lily was, she observed, "a grouchy little lump, a tough little thing sitting apart from the others", but she saw sadness as well as potential aggression, and was curious to find a way to bring her out of herself.

After hearing Lily absent-mindedly but very sweetly singing Oasis' 'Wonderwall' as she wandered out of class, she decided to call her up to sing it in front of the class the next day, complimenting her in front of her classmates. This made a huge impression on Lily and gave her a great deal of confidence. "Lily still stands out as an exceptionally talented child," confirms Santesso. "Enormous talent for words."

The lyric, 'Maybe you're going to be the one that saves me', from 'Wonderwall', might be appropriate under the circumstances. The then troubled, uber-busy Alison admits she had no idea her frustrated daughter had such hidden talents – it took a teacher, an objective outsider, to bring out her potential and see what was there in Lily to be tapped. Thanks to Santesso, a lot of Lily's pent-up anger as a child subsided: she'd finally found something she could do, and that people would respect her for.

"I didn't see Lily's talents emerging," confessed Alison. "I knew she was mega-bright, but it didn't translate in academic terms. When she started singing and went to number one, I'd say: 'I'm very proud, but who'd have known?' And people would say: 'We knew. She's been like a superstar from the age of two.'"

This new-found attention would certainly make a change from Lily's usual experiences performing in school shows – at least one of which was a stark reminder of her days as a tot performing in the Portobello Panto, watching the 'pretty' parts go to her friends.

"We did a play of *The Railway Children*, the other girls got the best girl parts and the best songs, and I got given the part of Bert, the stationmaster's son…" Not exactly the part of every girl's dreams. But some gentle coaxing from Rachel Santesso ensured that this would change, at Cavendish at least. At an upcoming school show, she persuaded Lily to sing a song. Lily was keen to stick to 'Wonderwall', but Santesso felt the poignant 'Baby Mine', from *Dumbo The Elephant*, would be more fitting. It was all about how if 'they knew the sweet little you, they'd end up loving you too'. Naturally there was not a dry eye in the house once everyone had heard Lily's lilting, Blossom Dearie-esque trill. And for Lily, it was enough to know she had proved herself to her doubters. "They knew me as angry little Lily and everyone cried, but in a good way: 'She's finally got something!'" says Lily, and Santesso confirmed: "I swear to God, I knew then she was going to be a singer."

"I must have been a puddle on the floor," remembers Alison. "She'd kept it a secret and presented it like a gift. Singing and music became her thing then."

Musically, and personally, 1997 was a significant year for the nascent star – it was the first year she visited her true alma mater, her Lourdes – Glastonbury – without her father, allegedly trying ecstasy for the first time at the age of 12. She also saw the Chemical Brothers perform, little realising that she was watching her future boyfriend Ed Simons.

"Big, big night," she recalled. "Jo Whiley poured a bottle of water over my head, cos I was steaming." She didn't know whether she dared to dream of getting up there and singing herself as a professional singer, lapping up the applause and good vibes, making her family proud, being listened to at last, and on a grand scale (not to mention being able to use the good toilets backstage). Maybe one day...

CHAPTER THREE

'Education is great for some people, but for me it just wasn't.'
Lily Allen to Jo Whiley (Radio 1).

Despite finding an inspiring ally in Rachel Santesso, Lily didn't last long at Cavendish School – apart from anything else she had a problem with its religious stance. "They told me gays were bad, adultery was bad and drugs were bad," she told *Word* magazine. "At the same time, all my mum's friends were gay, my dad was having various affairs and there were drugs in the house when I was a kid – so it was a bit cruel," but her new-found love of music continued apace.

She was experimenting with different instruments, reaching grade five on the piano and playing violin, guitar and trumpet, but now she was trying things out as a singer, freeing up her voice with jazz improvisation, "my teacher playing the piano and me singing along". Lily might not have been a committed student in the conventional sense, but she dedicated herself to her new passion and achieved grade eight singing. This would prove more useful in strengthening the gift that would make her fortune than anything else she might have picked up in class. Most importantly, the progress she was making was totally independent of her parents, and the fact she found it so hard to connect with other children her age meant she had more time to focus and work out what she wanted to do.

"She'd been slogging it out, singing for ages," says an old Bedales classmate. "She was doing that in her teens, and she is very talented. Loads of people have copied her since."

A couple of years after her first singing triumph at Cavendish, she would have a bit of competition from an unlikely source – her dad. It was 1998 and Keith was preparing for his wedding to Nira Park after being talked into proposing by Lily (she wanted to be a bridesmaid). His debauched and extended stag included, of course, the drinking dream team that was Damien Hirst and Alex James and it was during this stag that the idea for 'Fat Les' was born. They decided to write an alternative anthem for the World Cup that year, which would become the hit 'Vindaloo'. (The name 'Fat Les' was inspired, if that's the right word, by a phone call Keith received from a TV executive he wisely chose not to name in *Grow Up*, after which Alex sniffed, 'Oh, not that fat les.')

The video, intended as a pastiche of The Verve's 'Bittersweet Symphony', featured various British celebrities (including Matt Lucas, Marcus Brigstocke, Edward Tudor Pole from Ten Pole Tudor, in a nod to Keith's punk roots, and Keith himself marching about shouting like a hyperactive schoolboy alongside a Richard Ashcroft lookalike, shoulder-barging his way down the street) and a lairy-looking cross-section of Londoners marching through town. The song reached number two in the charts, in competition with the official song 'England United'. No prizes for guessing which was more likely to be chanted in the playground or by the football crowd though.

Despite the fact Keith Allen believes most of Lily and Alfie's schoolmates were fans of his musical project, Lily claims she still had to explain who her dad was (the penny would usually drop when she mentioned the old Listerine ads, in which he played the evil fairy), and his claim that "kids find Fat Les cool" didn't wash with Lily, who admits the video alone makes her "cringe".

Fun times were to be had as a result of this unlikely but quite brilliantly opportunistic chart success. Lily's first experience of *Top Of The Pops* would be as a result of Fat Les. After performing on the chart show, they went to the BBC after-party, with Lily in tow. She was spotted slouching in a corner, taking it all in, drinking vodka and gazing at her exuberant dad as he gleefully held court. "With his track record, he could hardly complain," she smirked to a concerned reveller who asked if her dad knew she was drinking. She was "sweet but very confident and precocious, like one of those stage-school kids. You could tell she felt comfortable in her father's world and wanted to be part of it."

Christmas '98 would see Fat Les release another single, 'Naughty Christmas (Goblin In The Office)' – a homage to office parties; that common touch clearly handed down from father to daughter, considering some of Lily's own observational, funny, downright rude lyrics about sex. It featured Lisa Moorish, and Alex James cheerfully assured *NME* that the song would be "obviously shit". But 1998 was also a big year for Alison; she produced *Elizabeth*, a movie starring Cate Blanchett. It was subsequently nominated in seven Academy Award categories. (It won just one, for make-up, but it also won five Baftas.)

Elizabeth was a lavishly beautiful portrayal of Elizabeth I that also starred Kathy Burke, John Gielgud and, more surprisingly, Eric Cantona. Alison also managed to sneak her kids into the picture as background artists (you can spot Lily in one of the movie stills on the film database IMDB, dressed as a lady-in-waiting, standing next to Kelly Macdonald, a rare fringe-free shot.) Lily and Alfie fitted in well, but Sarah, at 17, found the experience "hideous. I'd wake up with knots in my stomach. It wasn't a speaking part, but I hated every minute of it."

For Alison, *Elizabeth* was work, pure and simple, but when awards season swung around the following year, well, "It all got rather stupid," she says. "I had designers ringing me up to offer me dresses. Harry Winston gave me diamonds. Then there was that whole roller-coaster machine of publicity…" All things her youngest daughter would become very used to in time. But at this point, this was all new and strange and hard to fathom. As were Hollywood's double standards.

"Mum's done amazingly well, but I do feel protective of her," says Lily. "When she got nominated for an Oscar for *Elizabeth* she went to Hollywood and they had this big dinner. Yet Mum, who was the main producer, got sat on a table away from the director, Shekhar Kapur, and Cate Blanchett, whom she cast in the film. They were seated with executives who hadn't worked on it.

"I wrote a letter about how fucking angry I was. Now some of the top producers call mum and say: 'Love your daughter's album!' They're all sycophants in that industry, so it's worked out quite well for her." Lily makes no secret of the fact she feels that, far from having been given a leg-up by her parents, the reverse is in fact more accurate now. "I didn't have attention as a kid, when I went out it was: 'This is Lily, Keith's daughter.' Not any more. Now it's: 'This is Keith, Lily's dad.'"

Despite the continuous accusations of nepotism levelled at Lily as a result of her parents, on reflection it is probably more likely that Alfie's career, not Lily's, has been more directly helped by his parentage, or at least was pushed in the right direction. And why not? He's simply in the family business, and he's clearly a talented actor. No one gets cross when they see signs on shop-fronts proclaiming 'Smith & Son, Grocers'…

Alfie performed in a one-off Channel 4 comedy production, *You Are Here*, in 1998, co-written by Matt Lucas and David Walliams, who both starred in Keith's video for 'Vindaloo', and Keith was involved in the production himself. Alfie then starred in *Agent Cody Banks 2: Destination London*, directed by his uncle Kevin Allen and co-starring Keith, and then after this auspicious start safely among his kith and kin, Alfie moved onwards and upwards, bagging a role in the film *Atonement* alongside Keira Knightley and the lead role in a prestigious stage production of *Equus*. But it seems Lily is the one doomed to bear the brunt of the 'celebrity child' syndrome, even though her own arc is less directly linked to her parents than Alfie's.

Admittedly, Lily's professional vocal debut would come via her dad, albeit by accident, when she was 16; in 2001 Keith wrote a song for football movie *Mike Bassett: England Manager* called 'On Me 'Ead Not Off Me 'Ead'. Atomic Kitten were slated to record the vocals for it, but when one Kitten failed to show, Lily, who had just come along to hang out at the studio, was encouraged by Keith to step in and, of course, she gave a pitch-perfect performance, and was praised for having the "strongest vocal, patching it all up", according to a witness in the studio.

After such an impressive debut, Keith also ensured his little girl's distinctive, marshmallow light voice would be featured on the next Fat Les production: 'Who Invented Fish And Chips?' Perhaps understandably, Lily doesn't go on about that too much. (Lyrics include: 'Who invented fish and chips?/Who invented poo?' No danger of giving 'What's Going On?' or 'Blowing In The Wind' a run for their money in the lyrical stakes, but still, it was another vital experience of being in a studio for Lily.)

Before these opportunities came along, Lily was spending her mid-teens absorbing music (which at this stage consisted of a lot of ragga and jungle) and escaping her often confusing situation as often as possible, sneaking out and going to raves and "doing naughty things at festivals". The part of those nights she looks back on with the most fondness would be the moment at which her body finally rejected the amount of booze she'd ingested. Yes, her favourite part of the night was having a good barf. "I always used to really enjoy being sick, because you'd feel like a new person."

But Lily would swing from phases of being a party animal to feeling desolate – she finally left school once and for all at 15, and, as Alison remembers, "was really depressed, staying in bed all day. When people's kids go into depression, if they haven't experienced it themselves, they think it's forever. But I could say: 'This is not the end, things will get better.'" It wouldn't be the last time Lily would want to hide from the world and retreat into her thoughts. But alongside music, one of the only things that would give her some relief from her own head was a big night out.

She received arguably her first serious wake-up call far from home, however, during the same year she ditched school. Alison had planned a holiday for her and her kids in the Nineties party Mecca Ibiza, and Lily couldn't wait. Up to now (despite having been away to Italy and France with her dad and Nira), the idea of a 'holiday' meant staying in a "poxy" Romany caravan – complete with horse – with her dad. (It's not surprising the caravan holidays remain worryingly fresh in her mind though; on one occasion the caravan crashed when the horse suddenly reared up, startled at the sight of a van. The kids were relatively unscathed but Keith lost four teeth.)

Ibiza and Lily proved a dangerous combination. Lily loved it so much she begged her mum to let her stay on for another week if she stayed with 'friends'. Alison reluctantly agreed and flew home with the rest of her brood while Lily checked into a Welsh-run hostel in San Antoni de Portmany on her own, getting ready for some serious thrill-seeking without the burden of anyone else around her telling her what to do. After all, Alfie was still "extremely demanding", Sarah she described as a "fucking nightmare, taking loads of drugs", and she felt awkward around her popular, pretty, blonde, confident sister. (Lily also felt like the odd one out being the only one with Keith's short stature and dark, Welsh colouring – Alfie had also inherited Alison's natural flaxen hair and pale skin.)

Lily might not have been a shrinking violet herself in the past but she saw her lone stay in rave-capital Ibiza as "her turn" to really run wild. At an age when most 15-year-olds were sitting their mock-GCSEs, this one had left all of that behind, her time was her own, and frankly 'education' was all around her – she was living it.

A 'week' turned into a month. And she certainly made the most of the time. She picked up a job at a record shop called Plastic Fantastic to fund herself, sold ecstasy (and, by her own admission, spent way too much time "trying out her own merchandise"), went clubbing (where, on one occasion, she "snogged a 35-year-old stripper called Cheryl"), smoked, drank, topped up her tan and made extra money handing out nightclub flyers in her bikini, hanging out of the back of a limousine. "I was a bit of a lost soul," she would later confess.

The holiday finally fell apart for Lily when, at a nightclub, some sleazy men started to round in on her. Fortunately there was another man nearby who was not interested in taking advantage, quite the opposite. He stepped in and saved her, Lily has said. Love him or hate him, George Lamb, now a TV presenter and radio DJ, is clearly a good man to have around in a crisis. She'd also just been thrown out of her hostel, and was facing a night sleeping on the beach. Lamb wasn't having that. He took her back to his hotel, let her sleep on the sofa, and then took her mobile phone and rang up her mum to explain what had happened, and assured her that he was going to put her wayward daughter on a plane the next day, and pay for it.

Lily and George, six years Lily's senior, had plenty in common. He had been spending the previous year or so putting out dance records and flyering for the Ministry of Sound before getting into club promotion and A&R, managing the drum and bass outfit Audio Bullys. (On this particular visit to Ibiza he had been hired by the Ministry of Sound to drive DJs around.) Clearly, both George and Lily loved music and clubbing, but the similarities ran deeper than that, not least because Lamb's own dad, like Lily's, is an actor, in this case the *EastEnders* actor Larry Lamb, who has since starred in the hit series *Gavin and Stacey*. He also, like Lily, went to a progressive boarding school, where, like Bedales, "it was about developing as a person: no school uniform, no religion, teachers by their first name, vegetarian…"

While his own experience might have been very different from Lily's, and his father might have had a different reputation to that of Keith Allen, George will have still been aware of the ups and downs of a more bohemian, unpredictable background, one that might overshadow your own ambitions if you weren't careful. It also meant a "conventional" job was not a given, and dreams of a less average occupation were never dismissed as impossible.

After Lily returned to England, much to her exasperated family's relief, she stayed in touch with her quasi-big brother George. They had bonded after he took her under his wing, and she had expressed to him her love of music, her determination to sing and her songwriting ideas ("I wanted to write about my world in an entertaining way"). George agreed to manage her as an artist and try to help her get a record deal.

Exciting times lay ahead for both of them, but one thing that concerned Lily's loved ones was that despite the month of carnage in Ibiza, she hadn't got her partying urges out of her system. Far from it, she was going out to clubs and bars just as much, maybe staying a little more in control, seeing as she was in her home town once again, but she was still causing heartache for her parents, particularly as her new party companions were the people Keith himself was hanging out with. People at least 20 years older than Lily.

"I had a talk with my dad when I was about 15," she explained in an interview. "I was going from being a little girl to a woman, I suppose, and I think he found that really difficult to deal with. Especially as I've always hung out with older people, so suddenly I'd be turning up at Groucho's and hanging out with people he knew. He started shouting at me about it – 'You can't behave like this' – and I sort of said to him, 'Look, you weren't around to tell me how to behave in the beginning, you can't suddenly do that now.'"

At least Keith could rest easy that one person she started to hang out with was a little closer to her age. While out and about in London Lily randomly bumped into none other than Lester Lloyd – the brother of her childhood friend Poppy in Ireland. They were amazed by the coincidence and hit it off immediately. Lester, then 20, was struck by Lily's quirky prettiness, attitude and wit, and Lily similarly felt a strong sense of connection with him.

After spotting each other again at a nightclub, the pair realised they were going out to the same venues, had the same taste in music and DJs, and they started to meet up regularly at Notting Hill Arts Club. Now, Lily is an expert flirt, and Lester was a willing victim. For all Lily's bravado, she longed for love with an older, protective man she could share everything with, listen to records with, eat takeaways in front of the TV with and cuddle up to. It wasn't long before they were truly under each other's spell, sealing their romance in an appropriate way – their first proper kiss was when they huddled up together while queuing to get into a club in the rain. Lily had found a kindred spirit, and she adored his family too. When she visited the Lloyds in Ireland, she was moved to tears by how cosy and affectionate their home life was – it simply made her ever more aware of how different her own upbringing had been. Lester and his family, in Lily's eyes, became a paragon of stability, and his presence filled a void and satisfied a need for affection from any other source, including her own loved ones. She looked to Lester to give her everything she needed.

CHAPTER FOUR

"Take the highs with the lows dear/ You'll get what you're given/ And everything's gonna be alright."

Lily Allen − 'Take What You Take'.

Lester and Lily's mutual love of music and clubbing (not to mention pills and weed) bonded them ever closer. Over the next year, they'd go to festivals together, including Glastonbury (where Alfie unfortunately went into their tent while they were in a somewhat compromising position. Who knows whether he's even recovered but Lily and Lester thought it was hilarious).

Lester would also stay over at Lily's family home, where they'd have sex as quietly as they could on the top bunk as Alfie snoozed below. They'd also smoke secret spliffs in her bedroom, covering each other's mouths before blowing the smoke out of the window in an attempt to hide the smell from Alison. They were just like naughty kids. Because, in Lily's case at least, she *was* a naughty kid.

George Lamb meanwhile was encouraging Lily to get into the studio and record some demos, but his well-meant attempts to effect a record deal for his wayward protégée were coming up against brick walls. Lily's aesthetic was not that of a 'pop star', supposedly, in the same way that another more alternative artist, Ian Dury, didn't look like a typical pop star. Their influences and ideas proved they were both artists who were unlikely to play the game, and lyrically both had fresh, cheeky approaches to their chosen subjects, which were far from traditional chart fodder for a start. But while society seems to congratulate a man for being subversive and provocative, the idea of a young girl boasting the same attitude didn't seem to be quite so welcome.

Still, George watched Lily work up her song ideas, which at this stage were about her family members, her beloved West London, going out… and she knew musically what she wanted to reflect too, making mix tapes of what she was listening to in order to focus on the sounds she wanted, and show potential producers what she was after. "The music was wonderful," remembers George, "but for whatever reason then we couldn't get her a record deal."

Lily has long since had to fight against assumptions that her dad used his influence to get her started, but she insists, "If there's one famous dad that's going to go against you, it's my dad. The people that got me into the studio were people I met in Ibiza (George Lamb)." George also urged her to develop her song-writing. "There's no money in it if you don't write your own songs," he warned. Not that it's even possible to imagine Lily becoming a pop puppet, content to warble someone else's anodyne songs about being someone's 'baby', but she'd been writing her own songs anyway, most of which a typical girly pop star wouldn't know how to approach, let alone write.

One of Lily's bugbears – a source of endless inspiration for her writing – was her family. She longed for some unity and togetherness, and was concerned about the half-siblings she knew she had, thanks to her father's one-night stands, but didn't really know well. Keith was happier not knowing about his illegitimate kids, Kevin and Grace, but Lily felt very differently. Lily, then 16, managed to track down her half-brother Kevin Marshall, the boy who used to come round to play when they were little. He was languishing in Feltham Young Offenders Institute after being convicted of stealing cars. Kevin was conceived after a fling between Keith and an 18-year-old Anglo-Caribbean girl, after they flirted at a shebeen in Ladbroke Grove. "It was to be her child, not mine," insisted

Keith. "After that I neither saw nor heard from her, she got on with her life and I got on with mine."

Lily bought Kevin a present, a tracksuit and trainers, and went on her own to the Institute to surprise him. "I was so happy," he said. "She said she wanted us to be more of a family and that she didn't want to see me in places like this again."

After spending time reconnecting with Kevin, Lily's mind was ablaze, she was thrilled to have been able to hang out with her flesh and blood, and equally devastated that he'd fallen off the rails, spending six months of his young life locked up, and not for the last time either – he'd later serve another stint behind bars at Wandsworth for dealing cannabis. Lily wrote a song, 'Nasty Business', about Kevin's situation, which has not been released.

Lily's ideas and development as a writer were very much her own, but despite her understandable concerns to distance her nascent musical journey from her father, Keith did help by spending time booking studio time and encouraging her in her early years. Maybe it was his way of making up for not being there when she was younger. Lester Lloyd has insisted that, looking back, Keith was instrumental in keeping Lily going and setting her on the right path professionally. Naturally, like any parent, he wanted to help where he could, and he also had contacts at Warner Brothers' imprint London Records, the label that gave Lily a short-lived deal in 2002. But, contacts or no contacts, a record company isn't going to spend good money on someone who doesn't have their own talent and presence. And, as *The Guardian* observed, "She only became successful after her father's involvement in her career ended."

The label was intrigued by what Lily could potentially do and signed her. Lily was over the moon. She spent the night after signing the deal getting wasted in the West End with Lester on champagne, ecstasy and weed, puking out of the cab window in Piccadilly Circus on the way home.

Keith Allen was excited for his daughter, and he and his mate Pablo Cook, who was in Joe Strummer's post-Clash band The Mescaleros, wanted to get involved. London Records' first idea for Lily was to record some folk songs with Pablo, who helped write some of the material that would later turn up on Lily's debut release (including 'Friday Night'). Keith loved nothing more than tinkering about in the studio with Pablo and Lily. There was a festive feel in the air, Christmas was just two days away and dreams were being realised for Lily in the bosom of her family and family friends. While folk wasn't exactly what Lily wanted to do, this was a great opportunity and while she did her best to hide it under a stroppy teenage front, being in the studio felt right.

Keith also brought in pals he thought might be able to help or lend something to the sound, including Blockheads' bassist Norman Watt Roy and former Ian Dury aide Derek 'The Draw' Hussey on harmonica. There was more weed being smoked than commitment to the cause (unless the cause was weed-smoking) however but, at this stage, the recording sessions were fairly loose.

"Pabs was the technical maestro," remembers Keith, "laying down beats and operating the desk, and I chipped in with the tunes and melodies. Lily would wander in, sit down and build up a spliff.

'Right, what do you want me to do?'

'Well, some singing might be a start.'

"Once the mouth opened, the argumentative youth who reminded one too much of the person who stole your phone was transformed into an angel. Lily had a voice that could shatter hearts...'"

Hearts would shatter that night for another reason altogether. After a successful day in the studio, Keith received a phone call to say that Joe Strummer, his and Pablo's close friend and Lily's musical mentor, had died of a heart attack at just 50.

Ironically it wasn't until the funeral the following week, in the Clash-heartland of Ladbroke Grove, that Lily would finally realise who 'Uncle' Joe actually was – the lead singer of The Clash. She just thought he was a popular friend of her family's, she didn't realise why men stopped him in Portobello to say hello, why he was treated with such reverence or why wherever he seemed to be would always be the epicentre of cool, other than the fact he was a warm, open-minded adventurer.

But at the funeral, the penny dropped, and she saw many of the people whose faces she had only seen on record sleeves lent to her by Strummer – the Blockheads, still reeling from the death of their own frontman Ian Dury two years before, were pall-bearers. Madness, Courtney Love (who apparently "threw herself onto the coffin" in a fit of histrionics) and Chrissie Hynde were in attendance, as were, of course, the surviving members of The Clash: Mick Jones, Paul Simonon and Topper Headon. It was the end of an era for music, for the Allens, and for Glastonbury. "I don't actually like going to Glastonbury now that he's gone," Lily said. "Because he's the one thing that held all of that stuff together and made it nice. Rather than just a bunch of drug addicts."

Lily wasn't completely into the idea of the folk project she was supposed to be developing with Pablo, although she was aware she had to play the game to get her feet under the record industry table. Thanks to her love of multicultural Portobello, and Strummer's record collection, she was much more interested in black music, hip-hop, reggae and dancehall, and wanted to have the opportunity to fuse her own music with those influences while still remaining authentic. She claimed to be jealous of MIA for nailing the Jamaican dancehall sound, using the effects and tricks so beloved by reggae stars, but it was through groups like The Specials and Madness that she knew white artists could successfully attach themselves to reggae too and produce effective music.

But her plans would not see the light of day on London Records' watch at least. The executive that was initially interested left, she was dropped and the folk songs shelved. They had momentarily toyed with the idea of putting her in a girl band, but they could see it wouldn't work.

"It was a total waste of time," Lily told *The Times* in 2010. "I didn't have a relationship with anyone there. My dad was writing all the songs for me and it got to a pretty miserable point where the record company didn't like the songs and it all just sort of fizzled out.

"I was trapped in a record deal that I couldn't get out of and I had to hire lawyers that were working for me on a 'no win no fee' basis. You know, when Warner are threatening to countersue you for a million and a half pounds and you're 16 and just want to be a singer, it's quite stressful. Dad wasn't around to help me then."

A label insider apparently said, simply: "We couldn't see her developing into the full package. We wanted pretty girls who were instantly marketable." Nice. And, clearly, wrong. While no one could deny the popularity and 'marketability' of identikit girl pop stars with weedy voices but the right kind of hair, face and body, there was a gap in the market for someone a bit more real. Needless to say they must now feel similar to how Decca felt after turning down The Beatles.

Music industry stalwart Simon Napier-Bell discusses this very issue in his book *Black Vinyl White Powder,* a dissection of the pop industry. "Some people in A&R departments kid themselves that they're looking for musical artists but they're not. They're looking for marketable faces with which to exploit copyrights. It's not an artistic disaster, just a shift in emphasis…"

It felt like a disaster to Lily of course, but London Records' lack of vision fortunately didn't halt her in her tracks completely, although there was a considerable pause in her progress as a result of the shock and disappointment of having the rug pulled from under her dreams. She'd walked away from the deal with some money, but she slumped temporarily into a miasma of marijuana, daytime TV, internet shopping and mood swings, to Alison's exasperation.

Lily: "I had loads of money cos I'd had a record deal that came to a standstill and I took them to court so I had this bank account full of cash. And all my dealers knew about it as well. So I didn't even have to go to the bank to get money out. They'd come over and I'd write cheques. Dreadful…" she told *The List.*

Lily describes a typical day, during this stagnant period: "I'd get up in the morning and have nothing to do, so I thought, 'Fuck it, might as well smoke a joint'. Then I'd sit on the bed and probably go to sleep for a couple more hours. Wake up. *Neighbours.* Listen to music in the afternoons: ragga, drum'n'bass, jungle. Sometimes I'd get *The Racing Post* in the morning and sit in my bed watching Channel 4 Racing smoking weed all day… I used to smoke about a quarter (ounce, 7g) of hash a day, pretty much. Terrible."

When the money started running low, Lily decided to have a rummage through Alison's handbag, her eyes lighting up when she spotted her credit card. She sneaked it out of her mum's purse and sloped over to the sofa, home alone, and switched on the internet. The online shopping possibilities were, to Lily, seemingly endless.

"In her adolescence we had a lot of screaming fights and, shall we say, 'selective borrowing' of my credit card," recalls Alison. "She was addicted to internet shopping and she'd go on ordering binges. Weird things would turn up: balloon-makers, popcorn machines. She'd always shop for other people – she loves to give. I had to explain there were boundaries, even if the things were for me."

Alison kept close tabs on what Lily was spending, and made sure every penny was paid back later on. But the situation at the time became so desperate, and Lily's attitude so obstreperous, that Alison finally kicked her out of the house. For Lily, this would simply mark the beginning of another short-lived period of lazy indulgence…

"She wouldn't have me there any more," admits Lily. "So I moved in with my godfather and it was pretty much the same. They were away quite a lot so I had the run of this big house to myself. And lots of mates. And a wine cellar…"

None of this could last, of course, and it soon hit home that Lily was wasting her time, her teens and her talent when she could be trying again for another deal, making and honing more demos, writing and earning her own money. She and Lester decided to move into a place of their own – at least now if they wanted to stay in bed smoking now and again, they didn't have anyone to answer to.

Lily needed to pull in some cash to pay the rent, not to mention pay for records, nights out, drugs and the Nike trainers and cute prom dresses she loved. She tried various jobs, working severally as a barmaid, a PR girl and a florist. (Her top tip: "Don't mix country flowers with exotic foliage, it's a common mistake.") She enjoyed floristry more than the other jobs because, as she rather dramatically told her friend Miquita in an interview, "Flowers don't talk." "Wow, Lily…" replied Miquita, slightly sarcastically. "Wow…" When you're a pop star, there aren't many people prepared to keep your feet on the ground and point out when you're being a bit mawkish or just need a bit of earthing. Miquita, however, amusingly seems to have taken on that role with Lily.

(Lily's love of fresh flowers would always be there, even if later down the line she'd be arranging flowers that had been sent to her by fans, admirers, industry bigwigs. But, because of her insomnia, she'd sometimes get up at 2am and drive to New Covent Garden market in South London and buy up fresh flowers from there to brighten up her flat.)

Therapeutic as it may have been creating beautiful bouquets every day, the cold, relentless early starts didn't mix well with Lily's nocturnal partying. She didn't take kindly to having to buy up flowers and be told what to do at 4am, when she'd rather be in bed. Still, she knew it was a means to an end, and stuck it out for a few more months as she tried to find the right manager, and the right deal. But it would be another three years of making demos and sending them out before she managed to attract the attention of the right label, and her confidence was still dented after being dumped by London Records.

Life at home with Lester was also far from plain sailing – the pair shared a passionate relationship that had been taken to a new level of commitment when they chose to move in together, but Lily still felt insecure. It was her first proper relationship and she'd thrown herself in headlong with total trust, but it was possible that old subconscious memories of being left behind by her father were affecting how she felt with Lester. Their relationship became increasingly blighted by petty rows. Lily thought he was the love of her life, but whenever the couple argued, it would generally stem from Lily's own insecurities and irrational feelings. Lester has always insisted he was totally in love and would never have been unfaithful to her, but the cracks were starting to show after nightly fighting. Lily was suffering from depression, struggling to get herself out of bed on some days, and had also been undergoing cognitive behavioural therapy to combat her anger issues. She needed her boyfriend's support but it was too much for Lester to deal with, and after feeling he was under constant attack, he decided he needed space. He organised an extended holiday to Thailand with friends (which, admittedly, was probably not going to make Lily feel any more secure).

Lester and Lily spoke almost every day during his break, but the conversations were monopolised by her fears and questioning, she needed constant reassurance that they were still a couple, that he was still hers. She was panicking, feeling lost, and her fears connected to her relationship were just the tip of the iceberg. She couldn't find her focus, nor could she be certain a record label would ever want to touch her again, she'd upset her mum and on top of everything, she'd had her driving licence revoked after a drinking session. Keith reckons these were important rites of passage she had to get through and get through on her own. But the split from Lester, the 'love of her life', was the final blow. Bereft, she desperately tried to lure him back, but to no avail. She felt the one thing that still belonged to her had gone.

Alison: "When Lily split from Lester, it was the only time I've been seriously worried about her. She was on the verge of being suicidal. Being with him was probably the first time she was really happy. She was mad about him."

Alison's fears would be confirmed. One morning, Lily's big, brown eyes would open to see, not the inside of her girly, messy bedroom at her mum's, but the clinical white of a hospital room, her stomach and head feeling strange, her arm connected to a drip. She'd made an attempt on her life the night before, taking 35 sleeping pills. At just 18 she felt too tired emotionally to carry on, she just wanted to fall asleep and never wake up.

"I'd fallen in love, that was holding me together and once he left me I was like, 'Well this is just the end now'. I was coming down off all the drugs I'd been taking for years and felt really alone. I remember thinking, 'I just don't have the energy any more to try.'"

She was given a charcoal-based liquid to drink, which detoxified her stomach and absorbed the sedatives in her system. "A psychiatrist came round and said, 'Basically this is an attention thing and she'll get over it.' But it triggered me to sort my life out."

Not straight away, however. Once she had recovered from the overdose and Alison had taken her home to keep an eye on her, Lily would try, unsuccessfully, to slit her wrists on two occasions, sinking into her grief at the end of her first relationship, unaware of the devastation she was causing her loved ones. "I took her to casualty twice," remembers Alison. "The third time it happened, when I brought her home she immediately ran off saying: 'I'm going to kill myself.' At that point, I thought: 'I can't cope.' I took her to the Priory, where they could keep a 24-hour watch on her."

The Priory, a haven for celebrities with 'exhaustion', addicts with means and burnt-out high-flyers, was a place Lily was very well acquainted with after visiting Alison there on numerous occasions. Lily herself spent four weeks in the Priory's care and beautiful surroundings, looking inward, looking forward, meditating and healing, waking up and going to bed every day at the same time. It was a world away from the chaotic, structureless lifestyle she had slipped into. Lily connected with the therapist she had been assigned, and, as her mother recalls, this month was "a turning point" – before long, Lily would be on track.

However, as soon as she left, the first thing she did was contact Lester, trying again to persuade him to give their relationship another try, "which shows how stupid we can all be", she said in hindsight. He was largely unaware of the details of her breakdown, only learning about it several years down the line – when the rest of the world had heard about it, and him, as well. "I felt awful about it," he said. "She's a sweet girl and I loved her. We just fell out of love. It was brilliant while it lasted."

At least this latest knock-back didn't see Lily spiralling back into destruction again. On the contrary, she was able to get her life in perspective, see how irrational she'd been in the past, and smile about it. What's more, being in rehab had given her the boost of confidence and space to get creative and start writing songs again. Writing is used in therapy to get certain emotions out of a patient's system, and now Lily had a much more cathartic, and lasting, way to get Lester out of her head and consolidate her feelings – she'd write a song about it. Needless to say, it wasn't a love song, but at least it wasn't a sad song – and it would end up making up for any pain Lester caused her, many times over.

CHAPTER 5

"It was amazing. I'd never seen anything move from nothing to something so quickly."

> Lily Allen collaborator Future Cut's Darren Lewis on
> how rapidly their tracks went from concept to reality.

Lily assimilated herself back into everyday life with gusto, enjoying cosy family meals at Alison's house in Islington, seeing her friends and checking out plenty of live music, particularly at Holloway Road's former indie hotspot and pub Nambucca (destroyed by fire in 2008). Keith and Nira had moved to a house in nearby Fairmead Road, just a stone's throw from the venue. It made sense for Lily to kill two birds with one stone and tie in her visits to Dad with a jaunt to Nambucca to see what was going on inside.

Nambucca used to be a straight-up London boozer, but as it started to fall into decline, a young group of middle-class kids who'd come to London to study or make their mark as musicians or artists took over the running of it, staying upstairs in cockroach-infested, liberated boho heaven and putting on DJ and gig nights for their friends. It was the perfect breeding ground for the kind of talent that would turn indie-pop on its head without being alternative to the point of obscurity – acts like

The Holloways, Kid Harpoon and Florence And The Machine would form, develop and flourish within those walls like hothouse flowers before relative stardom beckoned.

Lily would meet the likes of Kate Nash at Nambucca, promoter and 'middle man' Tom Frog, and she would rub shoulders with models and slumming-it socialites like Daisy Lowe and Alice Dellal too, slinking about waiting to pounce on DJs and little boy lost guitarists. In the dark, chaotic upstairs rooms things could get a little lawless, and some young, naïve members of the Holloway scene started dabbling in heroin.

"I was like, actually, you're all losers and you're all taking ketamine and turning into heroin addicts and I don't want to be your friend any more," Lily would later tell *OMM's* Miranda Sawyer. "But I never burn my bridges with people, I just step forward to something else." But drugs aside, Nambucca itself was a hugely positive, vital part of London's independent music scene, and even if you weren't playing there, you never knew who you were going to meet.

Back in Soho, Gaz's Rockin' Blues and the Groucho still held their place in Lily's heart too, and she'd often bump into her dad in the latter, or members of the Ladbroke Grove scene in the former. But the Groucho, that old Allen family favourite and playpen for rich kids (of all ages), would be the site of Alfie's 18th birthday party in September 2004, and Lily took the opportunity to make it a night not only her brother, but her dad, would never forget, no matter how he might try to.

Lily was confused and put out by Keith's seeming lack of interest in his first two kids, Kevin and Grace, and Lily managed to persuade both of them to come to Alfie's party without telling Keith. She wanted to get a reaction out of him, and kept calling him all day to make sure he was definitely coming down, which raised his suspicions. He was used to his daughter being much more blasé – and anyway, it was Alfie's birthday, why wouldn't he be there?

When he arrived, unsure of what Lily had cooked up, he saw her, grinning at him. He stared around the room, and saw a tall, good looking, mixed-race youth he semi-recognised. When he turned around, Lily was by his side with a young woman who looked very like her. The penny dropped, and he tried to leave. Not the response Lily had hoped for.

Keith did feel a pang of remorse about Kevin, but Grace at least had been brought into the world, he maintains, as a companion to the mother's first child, and both parents had been quite happy to keep the one-night stand as exactly that. Grace's upbringing had been relatively privileged and nothing was ever expected of Keith, although Grace wasn't happy about the fact he was so disinterested in her. It wasn't all about money.

Meanwhile Lily was still struggling to find the right manager and get herself signed, but most labels were concerned by her boozy lifestyle and quirky ideas. "They're all pussies in the record industry, they thought I was a risk," she would later tell Miranda Sawyer, an early supporter of Lily. "It's annoying when people assume that you're handed something on a plate, when it's actually completely the opposite."

But a chain of events would soon pluck her from the mire and help lead Lily from struggle to stardom. George Lamb, Lily's first manager, had introduced her to the DJs and drum 'n' bass producers Future Cut – Darren Lewis and Tunde Babalola – in 2004. They clicked with Lily and spent some time with her, listening to her ideas and the music she loved, ranging from the Manchester sound of 808 State and the Stone Roses to hip-hop to jazz to punk – it was obvious that if they pooled their creative resources and holed up together, something good would come out of it.

Lily was also trying out a third manager, Adrian Jolly, with whom she was getting on well, and it wouldn't be long before they were all one big happy family – Lily and Adrian joining Empire Management, the company that also managed Future Cut, and the company that would help launch Lily into a very starry stratosphere in the crucial first two years of her career.

In the autumn of 2005, Adrian managed to finally land Lily the deal she was waiting for with EMI/Parlophone offshoot Regal Recordings (a "small development deal" for an advance of £25,000). EMI might have left Lily to it, more concerned with the output of bigger names on their roster such as Coldplay, Kylie and Gorillaz, but they were right to trust their instincts on Lily Allen. Who knew this scruffy-haired, Chopper-bike-riding girl in trainers and the kind of 'Creole' gipsy earrings you'd find in Argos would score Regal their first ever number one single?

Lily was still an unknown quantity, and the label started off by trying to team her up with tried-and-tested songwriters like Cathy Dennis, who wrote Kylie Minogue's smash hit 'Can't Get You Out Of My Head', and had her own pop success with 'Touch Me' in 1991. But frustrating as it was to have to go through the motions of showing willing, Lily did try to play ball. She didn't want her sound and image to be contrived, but she knew if she didn't play the game she might get dropped. Lily just had to keep on keeping on with her own progress, with co-writers of her own choice, until Regal was convinced. The aim was to make something 'organic' and unlike anything else that was popular at that time. While she liked the electro pop of Rachel Stevens and Madonna, she had other ideas for her first record.

Lily and Future Cut had already started working on some songs together and producing some of the tracks she had recorded with Pablo Cook. Their creative workspace for this mission would not be in London, but Manchester, where Tunde and Darren first met, and a place culturally close to Lily's heart as well – not just because of the rich heritage of music there, but because The Happy Mondays, specifically the spiral-eyed dancer and maraca-shaker Bez, had become part of that Glastonbury 'family' she was so used to seeing every year around the campfire since childhood.

Bez had agreed to put Lily up when she stayed in Manchester, and she was subjected to some typical Bez antics while she was there. Lily agreed to babysit his two kids, Arlo and Jack, when he had to go to London for a night. He instructed her to just put them in a cab to school the next day and make sure they had their lunchboxes. But 'one night' turned into a week: "He ended up in Dublin or something." But Bez would always be a support to Lily: even if his antics were somewhat unpredictable, he was always generous. In just a couple of years, he'd be dancing down the front at Lily's sold-out gigs, pouring pints for her fans at the front of the audience and making everyone feel welcome.

Lily, Tunde and Darren worked quickly from the basement of an old office building, and Lily had to try hard not to let it show that she was actually a little nervous of them. They were knowledgeable and charismatic, and they took their mission seriously, questioned her intensely on what she wanted to do, and went through what seemed like hundreds of seven-inch singles for suitable samples (decent musicians were too expensive at this stage) as Lily improvised melodies and ad-libbed with the thoughts and concepts she had in her head. There were plenty banked up from personal experiences.

From this point forth, simply improvising in the studio became Lily's trademark – she would never prepare before going in, and that was how she liked to work. Lily also planned to give her label an album of 12 singles as opposed to the usual LP that featured some singles among album tracks. This album, Lily's debut, was going to be all killer, no filler.

Future Cut used the digital studio programme Logic on a Mac in their small studio space to start recording and producing Lily's songs. It seems appropriate that an artist so associated with new media and the rapid results it garners would be working with these tools. Tunde: "We can have a song written – some of Lily's are good examples – in minutes or hours because (of Logic). We can build tracks as fast as we can think of the ideas. These days, you don't need a huge studio to have a big hit."

Key to the success of these songs was the inspired use of samples, carefully chosen to reflect the music Lily was so interested in. There were flashes of reggae, New Orleans piano hooks from Professor Longhair meshed against broken beats ('Knock 'Em Out', a song about being hassled by blokes in bars), there was a sprinkling of calypso and Latin-tinged reggae thanks to a sample from Tommy McCook's 'Reggae Merenge' in the anti-love song to London 'LDN' (text-speak for London), and a sample from a Jackie Mittoo track, 'Loving You', on Lily's 'Shame For You', a vengeful break-up song with a sinister, slow reggae groove and a snippet of melody pinched from Dawn Penn's 'You Don't Love Me'. 'Don't take me on,' Lily cautions in the song, rather appropriately: as a former studio executive observed in later years, "Not just Lily but the people around Lily are very, very tough."

Last but not least, from the combined magic of a sample of Soul Brothers' 1969 track 'Free Soul', produced by Coxsone Dodd, and the still hot ashes of her failed romance and breakdown, the song 'Smile' appeared.

Musically 'Smile' was so sunny and upbeat that the song started to lack edge. Future Cut's Darren Lewis turned to Lily and asked if she could "twist the lyrics a bit". And so a ditty about smiling after adversity turned into what many would construe as the perfect 'revenge song'. Lily tried out a few possibilities, channelling a little more vitriol each time until she came up with: 'When I see you cry, it makes me smile...' The melody was so summery and her voice so sugar-sweet that if you didn't listen carefully to the lyrics, you'd never notice the dark heart of this bright, bouncy track.

'LDN' would also share the same sweet/sour tang – a sparkling, euphoric melody and lyrics that starkly point out that nothing in the gritty metropolis is as it seems: "When you look with your eyes, everything seems nice/but when you look twice, you realise it's all lies." And the singer of these songs is also a contradiction, multi-faceted, not all she appears. She's not as sweet as she seems, but she's not as hard as she seems, neither as 'street' as she appears, nor as 'posh'.

Song by song, with Lily's estuary voice (she'd sometimes say she was singing 'in character') against the samples that perfectly reflected the West London she knew and loved – family parties, Portobello, Carnival – Lily's quintessentially London sound was crackling into life... in Manchester.

In the midst of all this industriousness, Lily decided to set up a MySpace site for her music in November 2005, just three months after Sheffield's big success story the Arctic Monkeys set theirs up, becoming a runaway success before the music press even got a sniff of them.

Lily was turned on to the site by fellow West London urchin Lady Sovereign after they'd been chatting about their respective music in a bar (Lily would later be compared to the Sov in her first mention in *NME* in February 2006, which didn't go down too well). Lily set up a personal site first of all, but when she realised she could have a page that featured her music, she deactivated the first account and set up a new one: myspace.com/lilymusic. Unlike the Arctic Monkeys, Lily started using the blog frequently for personal missives rather than just gig announcements, interacted directly with fans and, as her Myspace fan base started to snowball, she sent out her now notorious mix-tapes, before she had anything official of her own to release.

As well as her own demos, these mix-tapes contained plenty of songs she just loved or found influential, and by sharing them with some of her fans, she was promoting other people's music as well as her own – from Dizzee Rascal to Vanessa Paradis to Cutty Ranks to Lee Dorsey and Ludacris. Because things were still relatively small scale, she had no idea of the legal implications of what she was doing – technically distributing other people's music for free – and it would only come back to haunt her several years down the line. But in the meantime, this was a snappy way of offering something as a gift to fans, a sweetener, and a hint of what to expect, not to mention something to focus Lily's own mind. "It was something for me to do because the writing wasn't happening. Every night I'd spray the covers and they were individually numbered. And it was free. I hand-wrote everyone's addresses on the front and put them in the post and that got people talking. I'm not very good at articulating what I want with music, so it was really helpful to have the mix-tape and say 'OK this is the kind of music I like, these are my influences.'"

Her love of reggae and calypso, worked into her demos through sampling, hadn't gone unnoticed by the reggae fraternity, sparking the curiosity in particular of the legendary dub producer and DJ Neil Fraser, better known as the Mad Professor. He was impressed that these influences were being utilised and channelled, as pseudo R&B and American-style pop had been the order of the day for so long. What Lily was doing was also drawing attention to the original songs and artists that were being sampled. "I thought, 'There's a smart girl!'" said Fraser. "She came at a time when no one was doing reggae, and definitely no one was doing calypso. The time to jump on anything is when no one else is doing it, that's what the real smart ones do. I could see it was working for her, although she only really scratched the surface.

"The UK has a good history of reggae, the punky thing, then the dub thing, but for some reason a lot of the young girl pop stars don't look that way, they look to America. But if you asked them to go through their parents' collections, they'd find some reggae hits in there. Sometimes when someone reinterprets or samples it's not as good as the original, but who cares? Some people didn't even know the originals anyway.

"Lily would have grown up around those influences and the slang thing. Her music, especially the early stuff, is also a reflection of what London has become, a rapid melting pot."

Aside from airing her demos, Lily loved being able to air her opinions on MySpace; it made a change from the artists of the past, who seemed enigmatically hidden behind a wall constructed by their label or their PR. She liked the fact it also gave ordinary people the opportunity to share their own views on music, rather than just listening to the perceived 'tastemakers'. This was the way forward musically, and Lily was soon on the crest of the MySpace wave. It was all the more significant to her because of the 'popularity' side of it. It was all about how many 'friends' you have, how many people have signed up to check out your music and your updates and show support. There was a delicious irony in this – Lily always felt somewhat friendless at school, and now things were very different. The more she blogged and the more she put in musically, the more her profile grew, again, largely before the press or even her own label had cottoned on. Some weeks after Lily had set herself up on the site, someone from Regal told her she should check out this web phenomenon called MySpace. "Already done it," she retorted. Lily was way ahead of them.

Hundreds of 'friends' rapidly turned into thousands, and Lily became more bolstered and confident every time she opened her computer and saw words of encouragement and signs that her demos were being listened to and her blogs being read. Alison remembers walking upstairs to go to bed and looking in on Lily just as she was shutting the lid of her laptop: "She said: 'Well, I've got the most friends in Great Britain.' This little girl who found making friends quite difficult finally had the most friends in the whole country." And she hadn't even had anything officially released yet.

The speed of the technology she was using to make her music and promote herself would reflect the speed at which she would, from this point, seal her future as a serious artist. After her final session with Future Cut, the last song they recorded together would be whacked straight up onto her MySpace player as soon as it was made.

"It was the last session we had with Lily before the album release," explains Darren Lewis in an interview. "We'd done what we wanted to do with the album, and had a day left. Tunde and I knocked up a beat in a few minutes using an old reggae track we'd written a while ago. Then we noticed it fitted really well with 50 Cent's 'Window Shopper'.

"Lily was in the studio the next day and we had a little time before she had to catch the train back to London. We suggested it might be a laugh to make a cover version of 50 Cent's track and she came up with the line, "Nan, you're a window shopper".

"When we had the track, she put it on her page as an MP3, and within minutes people were coming back with comments on it. It was amazing. I'd never seen anything move from nothing to something so quickly. Including the night before and her coming in, the whole thing took no more than three hours before she published it. We were getting so much feedback that it went from being a bit of fun to a double A-side for the second single ('LDN')."

After a few hours of going through 50 Cent's lyrics and matching them with cheekily granny-specific fare, no doubt pausing only for a few giggling fits on the way, 'Nan, You're A Window Shopper' was born – a perfect pastiche of 50 Cent's original track, with Fiddy's lyrics: 'When we got the tops down, you can hear the system thump/When we rollin', rollin', rollin'…' transformed into: 'You've got a leak in your colostomy bag /Yeah, it's got a hole in, hole in, hole in…'

Fortunately for Lily, thanks to her nan not knowing how to use the internet, and the track not ending up on the resulting album, this not particularly flattering portrait of her grandmother was kept away from her. Ignorance is indeed bliss.

Of course, poetic licence often dictates and the lyrics could as well have been drawn from any batty old woman, rather than specifically Keith's dear old mum, Mary. But lines such as, "It's funny how I come round your house and I'm 20/And I still have to wear all of the presents you sent me…" do sound as if it's Lily's own slightly sullen experience talking.

Another member of Lily's family who would be written about in sniggeringly unflattering terms would be her little brother, Alfie, just a couple of months later. He unfortunately did know how to use the internet, and was livid when this 'tribute' came to light. 'Alfie', based on a sample of Sandie Shaw's Sixties Eurovision hit 'Puppet On A String', was written by Lily and Greg Kurstin, a friend of Mark Ronson. It's time to rewind a little…

After returning to chilly London from even chillier Manchester, Lily was hanging out at all her favourite haunts again as winter edged slowly towards spring, going with her dad to the football and meeting his new girlfriend, Tamzin Malleson, at their home in Stroud ("I liked her, which I didn't expect," she wrote in her blog) and going to the Notting Hill Arts Club. Lily had been seeing the DJ and promoter Seb Chew, who ran a popular club night called YoYo there, and Seb, a slightly rotund, balding older man (exactly Lily's type, as it happens) with glasses and plenty of connections, would prove to be another link in the chain to Lily's success.

Seb Chew was pals with the young producer and DJ Mark Ronson, a hipster of wealthy parentage who had spent rather too much time DJ-ing at celebrity parties (including Tom Cruise and Katie Holmes') and was kicking back a little, keen to improve his image and make things a little more hip again. The very solution to his problem was just around the corner.

Lily had already met Mark at the club, and she immediately made an impression on him, literally. "I'd just bought this really nice leather jacket. It was the most I had ever spent on a piece of clothing, and I was wearing it only for the second time," he told *The Independent's* Guy Adams. "Lily came up with this pin badge and stuck it into that jacket, right into the most expensive thing I owned. I was like 'What did you just do?' and she just shrugged and said, 'It's cool.'"

Mark clearly forgave Lily as he agreed to meet her and Seb for lunch at the uber-popular West London haunt Paradise By Way Of Kensal Green. Lily managed to restrain herself from ruining any of his clothes, but she did press one of her precious demo CDs into his hands. He later admitted it took him a couple of months to sit down and actually listen to it; it was nothing more than "my friend's girlfriend's tape". But as soon as he did listen, he knew it was gold dust.

CHAPTER SIX

"I love being me at the minute."

Lily's blog post, March 26, 2006.

A couple of months passed with no word from Ronson, and Lily almost gave up on him completely. But her heart leapt when, one afternoon, she opened her emails to find one from him, asking if he could play 'Smile' from her demo on his New York* radio show.

It hadn't escaped his notice that she was becoming more popular by the day – Lily had made sure that demos were in the hands of the right people and, on March 12, Gilles Peterson gave 'LDN' a spin on Radio 1, Lily's favourite station. A couple of weeks later, Jo Whiley played one of her songs on her Radio 1 show too, causing the total plays on her MySpace player to suddenly leap up, and Lily was keeping tabs on all of it.

Mark Ronson had started to take a keen interest in the girl that once ruined his most expensive jacket, and by the end of March 2006, Lily

---

* Mark was practically a New Yorker despite being born in London's glamorous St John's Wood – he was schooled in New York and had been hanging out with fellow hipster kids in the Big Apple such as Sean Lennon since he was 13.

would be jetting over to New York with Mark to work on ideas together. Lily would even sing on one of his inspired cover versions – Kaiser Chiefs' 'Oh My God'. But sadly the song they would write together, 'Littlest Things', for Lily's album would be a lonesome lament about the break-up of a relationship: that of Seb and Lily's.

"It's my 'Dry Your Eyes'," she told Irish site *HotPress*. "My childhood wasn't by any means the worst in the world, but I never really had a chance to talk about it with anyone. About the bad bits I mean. I was kind of a loner and never had constant best friends throughout my life. So that lyric (in 'Littlest Things') is a reference to finally trusting someone."

Lily's devoted and ever-growing following on MySpace were privy to her heartbreak before 'Littlest Things' was even written. "What a shit week eh?" she wrote in February. "As if Mondays aren't crap enough as it is, when they're followed by Valentine's Day it makes things so much worse…"

She would then complain that "Monday was spent being really quite hysterical when the grim reality of being single hit me, and hard… Apologies to Seb my darling ex boyfriend for having to put up with teary phone calls every half an hour, desperately begging him to take me back…"

Her heartbroken inability to accept the demise of a relationship echoed how she tried her damnedest to persuade Lester Lloyd to take her back (and possibly reminded her of how abandoned she felt when the first man in her life – Keith – walked out). Luckily now she was ensconced in the realities of being a signed artist with a record to complete, which tethered her to earth, but she was very hurt and, perhaps against her better judgment, went back to Seb's club night YoYo and, by her own admission, "got pretty pissed off and gave a lot of people a hard time. I'm SORRY".

Daytimes were at least spent having meetings with "music industry heads" and re-recording her vocals in a "posh studio" ("I could smoke in the studio and no one could say shit, plus you get free tea and biscuits and proper food…"), which proved adequate distraction, but night times were harder to get through. Lily would crawl into bed with her laptop, check her MySpace site, respond to her 'friends' and then switch on the

TV, tune into the Winter Olympics and half-focus on the curling, ski jumps and glittering costumes of the figure skaters as she fell asleep.

This month was quite a watershed for Lily – not only from the point of view of her break-up with Seb, or because she was on the brink of being a star, but also because she finally felt sick of living with her family. The contrast between her increasingly high-flying life and coming home to her bickering siblings and girlhood bedroom was starting to grate. After a "posh lunch" with one of her new managers, her mood plummeted when she arrived back home to find her sister Sarah "and her friend Kate were here being dumb, and driving me up the wall with their pointless, meaningless conversations and general existence", she wrote rather testily in her blog, before admitting, "I think it's time I left home, flee the nest once and for all…"

The following day, March 18, Lily would be out of London, away from all that reminded her of her domestic ennui. She'd think about leaving her mum's when she got back, but now she was going to work – and play – with Mark Ronson and Greg Kurstin in LA and then New York. But the excitement that had been building on MySpace in the meantime was a double-edged sword – Lily had been retreating to MySpace and her blog the way others would turn to friends or family. She had become addicted to the adoration of her ever-growing fan base, the constant comments of reassurance, the compliments that just kept on coming. She loved nothing more than, at the end of the day, to open her laptop, log on and drink in the admiration. But when she reached America she realised there was a price to pay – writer's block. She had completely distracted herself, after nights in front of the screen, refreshing her page over and over again for new messages from her fans.

It was, she admits, "a really bad time for it to happen. Everyone was getting excited on the back of the MySpace site and the album wasn't finished." Fortunately, Mark and Greg were able to stoke her creativity and bring her musically back to life. "I finished the second half of the album in, like, two weeks," she told the music site *Pitchfork*.

Lily got herself settled in a hotel in LA not far from Los Feliz, which, naturally, had the ubiquitous pool, but she was so self-conscious about her figure in comparison to the classic skinny, pneumatic and often surgically enhanced LA babes she imagined would be down there, she

51

stayed in her room watching TV when she wasn't working or venturing out to the odd gig. She popped out to see her "fellow countrymen" the Mystery Jets at The Troubadour, and managed to make an enemy of Californian girl group The Like by calling them "stupid bitches" in her blog after spotting them making fun of one of their fans. Lily was also highly suspicious of how friendly everyone was, and admitted in her blog that already she "missed home".

At least Kurstin, who had previously worked with Kylie Minogue, Natasha Bedingfield, Sia and Britney to name a few vital female artists, got on well with Lily, and made her feel comfortable. Greg was impressed by how open she was to his ideas and suggestions. The pair had first met in the UK, when Greg was over working on other projects. "Her A&R guy asked if I wanted to meet her. I checked out a mix CD of a few of her songs and I liked what she was doing," he told *Mix Online*, "So we met up in the studio and we ended up writing a song together, 'Everything's Just Wonderful.' I listened back to it and decided I really liked it, so we took it from there.

"For the songs we did together for her first record, I had a few tracks that I had started," he continues. "I'd play her ideas, and she'd say, 'Oh, I like that,' or, 'What if we changed that this way,' and she'd start writing lyrics and then I'd develop the track more. The song 'Alfie' we created from scratch. We listened to a few songs for inspiration, then I built the track quickly in Logic."

It didn't take long to put something together, and they resisted the (expensive) temptation to noodle over finer points in Echo Studio for hours on end. They whipped up three songs in as many days – 'Everything's Just Wonderful', 'Not Big' and 'Alfie' and Lily was feeling positive. "It's going well so far," she blogged, "I seem to have got my confidence back, since all you MySpacers have been showing me so much support."

She uploaded 'Everything's Just Wonderful' straight onto the player, replacing 'Knock Em Out', just, she teased, to make sure they didn't get too comfortable, and also to make sure they got off their "lazy arses" and bought the record when it came out.

And so we come back to the story of the song 'Alfie'. Again, Lily was just singing about what she knew and what was on her mind, ideas and lyrics she'd been mulling over for the past year that were finally transmuting into complete songs. 'Alfie' was an affectionate message from a concerned big sister to her wayward little brother who was smoking too much grass, playing too many computer games, and spending too much time in his bedroom masturbating when he could be out doing something with his life and carving out his future.

The song developed into a cartoony, retro merry-go-round, cheerful, funny and sweet. But when 'Alfie' made it onto Lily's MySpace player, the star of the song was not amused. And it was only going to get worse – the song was included on the album, to be released as a single, and soon the whole world would be privy to her little brother's less than savoury habits. For now it was just Lily's MySpace friends – which was bad enough as there were now tens of thousands of them, and they were growing by the day.

"When I wrote 'Alfie' nobody really knew who I was," Lily tells *Pitchfork*. "At first he was really upset about it, because he thought that I was just pointing out all of his bad points and attacking him. I thought it was really flattering. I thought he'd be really, really happy because it proved to him how much I loved him, that I care about him, and I want him to do something with his life.

"I suppose his paranoia – induced by smoking so much weed – made him think, 'Why are you trying to be mean?'" Hm. Maybe... either that or it was because he was a self-conscious 19-year-old who was embarrassed by being made to look a bit disgusting in front of quite a lot of people? Lily reassured her concerned fans by insisting: "Alfie will get back at me, don't you worry." She also promised she wouldn't be writing about family again. At least not until she started work on her next album, for which she'd write about her mum, her dad, her sister... Well, they say you should write what you know.

Lily rationalises further: "It's not so much him disliking the song as not wanting to be reminded of my success. It's that thought of, 'If she's doing really well then I must be doing really shit'. It probably isn't great for your own self-esteem or confidence." Either way, he seems to quite like it now and sees it as the compliment it was intended to be.

After her whirlwind LA experience with Greg, Lily packed her bags again and flew over to New York to work with Mark Ronson. Mark paid for Lily's flights with air miles and put her up at the Holiday Inn in Chinatown. "It was at the height of the SARS epidemic, and she ended up checking out and sleeping at a friend's," he remembers. "But she was too shy to tell me..." (Lily however blogged that there had been a confusion with her booking so she stayed with her godmother, the singer Angela McCluskey.)

The best thing about the trip was that they could work from Mark's studio, and their time was their own. Lily was still thinking about Seb, and missing him, and it made sense that her next song should be about him. 'Littlest Things', a poignant paean to happier times with Seb, would be based musically on the theme tune to the Seventies soft-core porn flick *Emmanuelle*, all swooping strings and sentimental piano flourishes, which went perfectly with Lily's heartbroken words that proved she was far from over him: "There's no one in the world that could replace you"...

"We spent a day together and worked on a couple of things, and went to record shops where I played samples to her," says Mark. "Then I wrote the piano and guitar bit to 'Littlest Things', and she sat down and scribbled for about an hour and finished the lyrics. We went into the booth to record the song.

"She originally wanted to do a Mike Skinner thing, rapping the verse and singing the chorus. But I asked her to sing it all, and she just made up the whole melody on the spot, and sang this amazing solo. At that moment I realised that this girl has a really special gift."

"It must have been quite awkward for Mark because Seb was his friend," adds Lily, of the lyrics to 'Littlest Things'. "But being fresh out of a relationship I wanted to write about what was on my mind. Mark came up with the music first, then I came up with the words and we fitted it all together into a melody. That's the way I normally make songs – I write everything in the studio – and it obviously means that producers are very important to me. It's a complete joint effort." Also credited for songwriting are the singer Santi White and the *Emmanuelle* composers Pierre Bachelet and Herve Roy.

While Lily was in New York working on tracks and going through her own personal catharsis in the process, she got wind that her demo tracks had ended up on Limewire, the free file-sharing site. She mock-chastised her fans on her blog, before conceding, "I haven't got a problem with it, so long as a few of you buy the album, the main thing is that you're enjoying yourselves…" It was an issue that would concern her more in time, when there was more at stake. But right now she had enough to think about, between recording, visiting hip-hop record shops with Mark and meeting new people. Mark even persuaded her to stand in for him on his East Village Radio show on April 1. "Thanks Mark," she blogged, "for letting me totally embarrass myself in front of the whole of New York's trendy East Village…"

Before she left, Lily even managed to squeeze in some session work for Robbie Williams. Mark Ronson recommended her for some backing vocals on two tracks he would be producing: 'Lovelight' and Manu Chao song 'King Of The Bongo'. Her voice, more obvious on 'King Of The Bongo', is unmistakably Lily, complete with mockneyfied vowels (something Mark encouraged Lily to exaggerate).

Working with Robbie gave Lily her first real glimpse into the puffed up, pompous side of fame that she was not interested in at all. She said later Robbie was totally "affected by it", lording it over his entourage; he even had someone put sweetener in his tea and stir it in front of him rather than do it himself. His album *Rudebox,* released in October 2006, was not a success (copies of the unwanted CD were crushed and used to pave motorways in China). Lily's own album, released just a few months before his, would be a smash hit, however. So, as Lily would cheekily quip, "that worked out well for Robbie, me being a number one artist and all…"

After a thoroughly successful trip to the States – album finished, record shops raided and a bit of extra exposure into the bargain – Lily returned home, desperate for a well-earned rest. She'd missed London terribly, exciting as it all had been. But getting back home was far from restful.

Lily, laden with three suitcases and bags of records, hailed a cab as she came out of the airport, rain teeming down, a classic April shower. Negotiating the tube on a night like this was out of the question.

But when she finally reached her mum's house in Islington, she realised her family were all out – they'd gone to Manchester for the weekend. Lily wouldn't have minded a quiet night in on her own, but that wasn't to be. After rummaging madly through her bags and pockets as the meter was running on the taxi, she remembered she had left her house keys with her sister Sarah. Who was, of course, in Manchester. "The only person whose number I know off by heart is my darling ex-boyfriend's," blogged Lily. " So I jump back in the cab and head into town to meet him, thanks for saving me, Seb." Seb was still the knight in shining armour (or rather, leisure-wear and trendy spectacles) for Lily. Even if he was just helping out a mate, it was another opportunity for our love-sick heroine to see him again after penning the tenderly exposed song 'Littlest Things' for him.

The following week, life was getting back to normal, or rather this new version of normal for Lily – meeting people from her label and management, discussing possibilities for her first live concerts, and planning the video for 'LDN'. The promo they would make the following week, which featured Lily zooming around London on a Chopper bike wearing a yellow furry coat, is not the one that would eventually be used, but needless to say Lily played her part with gusto and ended up completely whacked by the end of the day. She must have cursed that opening line, 'Riding through the city on my bike all day' after several hours of pedalling on demand. (It was, of course, a nod to the time the police [or 'filth'] really did take away her licence, as she describes in the song.)

By the end of the day, after sweating her way around town in her too-warm but beautifully bright attire, it was agreed that Lily had earned a day off to catch up on rest. No such luck. "My dad calls me to tell me his missus (Tamzin) had gone into labour at 5am," she writes. And as if that wasn't enough, after trying to get some sleep for a couple of hours, she received a panicked call from her sister telling her Alison had been rushed to hospital after an allergic reaction to an antibiotic. Lily stayed by Alison's bedside until 2am, when doctors allowed her to take her home (presumably in a car, not on her bike).

After her supposed 'day off', Lily would be back on the Chopper bike, back in the coat and ready to film once again. The video, which starts with Lily leaving her mum's house, soon sees her wheeling around Soho Square, having tea and cake in the legendary cake shop Maison Bertaux, perusing the view from Primrose Hill, getting the tube at Ladbroke Grove and whizzing up towards Buckingham Palace, then past the Thames.

On the last day of shooting, the crew filmed the segment in Soho Square, "where I used to play as a kid". The director checked with the park keeper that it was OK to film in the square, among the flower-beds, and they all seemed set for their final day of filming. But unfortunately, chaos was about to ensue, and whatever they'd planned to film in the garden of Soho Square itself would never see the light of day.

"I'm wearing these trousers under my dress cos it's fucking freezing," explains Lily, "and the director asked me to take them off cause you could see them in the shot. I told him to fuck off, or take his shirt off so he could see how he liked it, so he did (well, down to his vest anyway).

"I kept my part of the bargain by taking my tracksuit bottoms off when this park guy comes running out of his shed with a RAKE telling us in an Eastern European voice: "Get out! I no agree to make sex movie in my garden!"

After an exhausting day (cake at Maison Bertaux somewhat making up for it), Lily headed back home, changed and went out to catch up with some friends for dinner, but the day's events were not over yet, and when she wrote it up on her blog that night, she couldn't resist a little political joke when she heard that her new baby sister, Teddie, had been born, two days after Tamzin had gone into labour: "Must've been New Labour..."

To sate the Lily Allen fans desperate to get their hands on a release, 'LDN' was rush-released as a limited edition 7" in April, and Lily herself wasted no time in organizing her friends to get down to Rough Trade on Portobello and buy it. She even bought a copy herself, pretending to be a regular punter. Well, it had to be done.

That week would be another big one for Lily – although increasingly it would seem that every week something momentous would happen. London was bathed in sunshine and blossoms, it was the threshold of May, and all in the same week, Lily was similarly in full bloom, on the brink of her 21st birthday. To add to the excitement, 500 of her limited-edition singles were being released and Lily would play her first proper show, appropriately, at Seb's night YoYo at the Notting Hill Arts Club. While taking a break from her rehearsals at The Premises studios in Hackney, Lily would have her first 'famous' moment – or so she thought. Either way, it was flattering.

"This guy stopped me in the hall, 'Are you Lily Allen?' 'Er, yeah, why?' "I play in Babyshambles, we really like your stuff, you should do a show with us sometime." Lily admits, flattered as she was, she was tempted to lock away her expensive new equipment while taking a break when she realised the louche and unpredictable bandmates of Pete Doherty were lurking about – Lily still wasn't convinced they hadn't just sent this friendly musician to distract her while they pilfered her gear.

Several more days of rehearsals would follow, the last of which Keith would pop down and sit in on, before taking her for a drink. "Dad came down to watch and gave me my birthday present," said Lily. "A beautiful gold bracelet. He can't make it for my actual birthday." After dinner with one of the musicians in her newly assembled group, she proceeded to "get banned from this club" for misbehaving. Like father like daughter.

In between being naughty and practising for her first performance – something she was dreading – hunting for pretty dresses in Selfridges ("I might even be able to get the record company to pick up the bill, he he…") and making sure she had her favourite Nikes at the ready, she squeezed in a meeting with the video director Sophie Muller with a view to work with her on the promo of 'Smile', her next single. She also took a jaunt to Brick Lane's 93 Feet East venue to support her pal Jack Penate (bumping into Lester Lloyd, the very subject of 'Smile', while she was there – "bit of a shock"). Life was moving at rapid-fire pace. Just weeks later Lily's first promo would be done and dusted. Lily's summary: "It's really sick and twisted but funny and sweet at the same time, so it suits the song and me perfectly…"

Anyone would think Lily would have had enough to think about but no, she wanted to send out another mix-tape: this one included tracks such as 'Friday Night', 'Alfie', 'Oh My God', the Mark Ronson cover, and 'Nan, You're A Window Shopper' interspersed with St Etienne ('Only Love Can Break Your Heart', the only track of theirs she really liked), Black Grape, Jay-Z, Jefferson Airplane, The Kinks, who shared her romantic London-centric focus, and T-Rex.

She enlisted the help of Alfie, asking him to spray-paint the covers for the mix-tapes. Perhaps predictably, this little project did not end well.

Alfie, still smarting from hearing 'Alfie', demanding she took it off her MySpace player, sullenly agreed to help when money was offered, but left most of the job to one of his friends, refusing to muck in. Lily flatly told him she wouldn't give him any money if he wasn't going to do his bit, which was fair enough, but Alfie took exception to being told what to do, lost his rag and tried to grab the mix-tapes and throw them onto the fire. Lily snatched them back and threw them into her room but she couldn't have prepared herself for what her darling little brother was about to do next, just to spite her.

"He opened the front door and threw my laptop into the street," she blogged. "I cried and cried…" Her laptop was her pride and joy, it was practically surgically attached to her most of the time, and it was very much the secret of her success, being, as she by now surely was, the queen of MySpace. Saying that, she later admitted she was more upset about losing the stickers she had adorned her laptop with – fortunately she had funds enough to buy another laptop… but she'd never get those stickers back.

Still, once the tears had dried and she'd stormed away from the house – anything to get away from Alfie in one of his moods – a burger with Seb and some friends lifted her spirits, and she soon started smiling again and looking ahead to her gig.

Despite being temporarily laptopless, the blogging continued apace – there was always someone else's computer. The moral to this tale, she concluded, was that "It doesn't matter how many friends or plays you get on MySpace, little brothers are still shits."

A classic image of Lily Allen during her breakthrough year, 2006. (*Dean Chalkley*)

Schoolgirl Lily recording music at Millfield School in Somerset, with Ben Knopfler, son of Dire Straits' Mark Knopfler, and Ben Harknet. (*Rex Features*)

Always camera-ready, Lily Allen (9) & Alfie Allen (8) go go-kart racing with their dad Keith (not pictured) 1994.

(*Rex Features*)

All grown up: Lily and Alfie hang out at her after-show party in a junk yard under the Westway, London, May 2006. (*Richard Young / Rex Features*)

Lily Allen and Keith Allen head up the red carpet together for the BRIT Awards 2007, the night Lily nearly chose not to attend. (*Gareth Cattermole / Getty Images*)

o that's where she gets that smile from… Lily and her nother, the producer Alison Owen. (*Richard Young / Rex Features*)

Lily Allen and her half-sister Teddie Allen at Radio 1's Big Weekend, May 10 2009 in Swindon, England. (*Dave Hogan / Getty Images*)

Another classic Lily Allen pose, a photo posted by her on her now legendary Myspace page. *(Rex Features)*

Lily gets bouncy at the Big Day Out festival in Sydney, Australia. January 2007. *(Newspix/Rex Features)*

Lily the Pink – her short-lived but much-photographed pink hair-do steals the show, alongside uber-producer and sometime collaborator Mark Ronson. *(David Fisher/Rex Features)*

Lily Allen and Debbie Harry of Blondie perform on the NBC *Today Show* summer concert series in Rockefeller Center, New York, on May 25, 2007.

(Bryan Bedder / Getty Images)

You know you've made it when you've been immortalis on *The Simpsons*: The Lily Allen Simpsons character is displayed at the UK premiere of *The Simpsons Movie* at The O2, Greenwich on July 25, 2007 in London.

(Claire Greenway / Getty Images)

Lily Allen and the rapper Common. Lily lent her marshmallow-light vocals to Common's track 'Drivin' Me Wild' in 2007, but the video shoot was not a happy experience… *(Lester Cohen / WireImage)*

You might be more likely to see her with an iPod than a ghetto blaster these days… (*Dean Chalkley*)

Can't believe her luck – Lily on her promotional tour of *Alright, Still*, in Australia, wearing her trademark ballgown/trainers combo. (*Jim Trifyllis/Newspix/Rex Features*)

CHAPTER 7

" 'Am I nervous? Yes, I'd be stupid not to be,' she says, not sounding nervous
in the slightest."
Lily Allen talks to Miranda Sawyer before her first gig,
May 2006, Observer Music Monthly.

The snowballing response on Lily's MySpace page thanks to her
constant interaction with fans gave her label more confidence in
her music and her as an artist. This 'emotional connection' with the star
would make a huge difference to sales, although the higher her profile
became, the less convinced the MySpace massive were that it was Lily
herself blogging and responding to messages – but it *was* her, every day
she spent at least two happy hours poring over every response. Even
when she became a bona fide 'celebrity' she admitted she liked nothing
more than getting online after a gig and seeing "thousands of people
telling you how brilliant you are". The flipside of this was that those who
chose to criticise her or just send weird messages, the pond-life of the
internet, would wield a great deal of power over Lily's feelings, and she
found it hard to throw off the darker side.

However, the main result of this online phenomenon was her
burgeoning fame. Even before her gig or album release – which had

now been brought forward to July (as opposed to January 2007) due to the massive demand and Lily being more than ready – more and more respected publications were contacting her label for interviews. The problem was that while the word on the street was that Lily Allen was the one to watch, the press department at Universal, with whom she had signed a publishing deal, had no idea who she was. They had bigger fish to fry, it seemed, and they were missing out on a jewel they had right under their noses. *Pitchfork* admitted it took a while for them to even respond to their requests for an interview with Lily, and the influential but now sadly defunct *Observer Music Monthly* had the same issue.

OMM writer Miranda Sawyer was bored of the current fare of popstrels, and loudly exclaimed to the rest of the office that they could let her know when a 'real' pop star came along. Blatantly manufactured pop bands of the most one-dimensional variety held sway thanks to the ever nascent *Pop Idol / Popstars / X-Factor* TV talent phenomena. Madonna still had an iron grip on the charts and 2006 was also a good year for Girls Aloud and James Blunt. There was also an Emma Bunton comeback.

Where were the home-grown individuals this country was once so good at spawning? That's what Miranda wanted to know. And it was only when a work experience girl at *OMM* flagged up an artist called Lily Allen, whom she'd heard about on MySpace, that Miranda's ears pricked up. The MySpace revolution was something the magazine was planning on covering, and Lily appeared to be at the forefront of this – but she was deserving of coverage in her own right. Fresh, funny, bright and photogenic, she'd be perfect on the cover. *OMM* got on the phone to Polygram to set up an interview. And no one knew who she was. Polygram's Murray Chalmers, now her press agent, was becoming increasingly bemused as to why more and more phone calls were coming in enquiring about this girl who, up to now, he had been blissfully unaware of.

Lily Allen told *Pitchfork* (after they finally had their call answered): "It took like four or five phone calls from the *Observer Music Monthly* magazine. They were like, 'We're writing an article about MySpace and we want to do a thing on Lily.' Murray was like, 'OK, this is stupid. Now five people have called about this Lily girl, who the hell is she?'" Needless to say, this soon changed. Now he probably struggles to remember life when he *didn't* know who Lily Allen was.

As the calls rolled in, more people from within Lily's record company were intrigued to come down to her gig and see her for themselves, which isn't always a given. Her four-week Thursday night residency at Notting Hill Arts Club's YoYo night was about to kick off on May 4, just two nights after her 21st. This was, as Lily rightly titled it, 'Lily Week.'

The week began on May Bank Holiday with Lily's 21st birthday party at her house; she'd already put out a jokey announcement on her blog that she wanted lots of presents, and her friends and family didn't disappoint: "all really good ones" confirmed Lily. Champagne flowed, a special birthday cake took pride of place courtesy of Alison and mini hamburgers were munched; Lily had even hired caterers to take care of the food so she could get down to the best part — eating it — without having to worry about rushing to the oven every five minutes to check on the nibbles.

The next day, Lily's birthday proper, Lily went out for a Thai curry with Adrian, her manager, before meandering down Portobello, killing time before her birthday drinks at the Electric Brasserie. Her friends, who "know how demanding I am on the present front", decided to tease Lily by handing over her "gift" — the biographies of Daniella Westbrook and Jade Goody. After allowing Lily to try to work out what they were playing at, they gave her the real present: "A beautiful Diane Von Furstenburg dress that I'd had my eye on, thanks guys," she blogged. "From there I went to, wait for it, NOBU (I've made it)..." The days that a trip to Nobu would be seen as a novelty for Lily were soon over — for the tabloids the words 'Lily Allen' and 'Nobu' are never far away from each other. The hifalutin Japanese restaurant in Mayfair soon became her favourite eaterie, and why not? Before long, she'd certainly be able to afford it.

On the next day, the Wednesday, Lily met up with *OMM* for her interview (she revealed she loved sleeping, making roasts and reading *The Other Boleyn Girl*, and told them she'd never fallen off a bar stool but she had weed on her own shoes). This was also the day of that memorable cover shoot on Primrose Hill, where Lily, radiant, messy of hair and dressed in a bright red ball-gown, had another taste of fame, one that she would have to get used to, and one that she would have a complicated, confusing relationship with the more her star ascended:

"We noticed a guy with a huge lens taking pictures, I looked behind me scanning for a glimpse of… who could it be? Kate, Sienna, Donna Air, Kerry McFadden? No. It was I he was snapping, very strange indeed, good though, I won't lie, I loved it. Sick I know, but I did…" (She nervously waited for the piece to come out – and when it did, a few weeks later, she was so proud she persuaded Seb to take a picture of her in the newsagents next to the magazine before snapping it up. "I really enjoyed the end product, friends kept saying, 'If I didn't know you were such a twat, I'd think you were quite cool.'")

Lily would be buzzing by the end of the photo shoot, not only from the focus and limelight being lavished on the girl who once felt so bereft of attention, but also because she was inching ever closer to the big night, her first gig, the following night. "Shit, shit, shit," she wrote on the day of the gig. "What am I doing? I can't play a gig."

Thanks to having close friends promoting her residency, namely Seb, the first night was given a suitably Lily-themed slant in every way, complete with pink 'Trilly Lily' cocktails being served at the bar. This wasn't an ordinary gig for a relative newcomer, the way was being paved for a star. There was an air of expectation, and the 200-capacity venue was besieged by over 1,000 punters desperate to get in. The MySpace revolution had ensured that her popularity was multiplying by the day and her early fans were proud to have got there first, proving early that they were seriously loyal, even dressing like her. (Well, the girls, anyway.) The fact that some of them didn't even recognize their heroine in the flesh didn't matter. After some Dutch courage (a Trilly Lily and a shot of Jagermeister) Lily tried to push through the crowd to get to the stage but two girls near the front tried to push her back, protesting, "We were here ages ago, you can't just push to the front." Lily politely informed them she had to sing.

Everything was set, Lily was prepared and the Trilly Lilies were going down a treat. Meanwhile, Seb was busy trying to fend off suits from the label in order to try to squeeze more eager young punters in. "It's heartbreaking when you're in a queue and you see a bunch of cunts in suits walk straight through the door," mused Lily afterwards. "Although saying that, I never queue…"

Once the venue was practically bursting at the proverbial seams, Lily was ready to sing and took to the stage with her band. She looked great, felt nervous but excited until "DISASTER... my earpiece thingy doesn't work and I can't hear myself, I did 'LDN' and everyone sang at me so I don't think anyone noticed how shit I sounded." (It was just as well the crowd enjoyed 'LDN', as they were to hear it twice – as opener and encore – as Lily admitted she'd "only rehearsed five songs".)

However, by the second song, Lily started to feel paranoid; the audience looked nonplussed as she struggled through the number. This was not part of the plan, it was starting to resemble a bad dream. But just as things started to get a bit painful, it suddenly became apparent that someone up there likes her. "As if by magic everything started working, and people danced and cheered," she blogged. Relieved, Lily allowed herself to let go and have a few drinks afterwards, before taking over the decks for a DJ set.

"Woke up on Friday and cried immediately, Lily Week over. Slept all day to recover."

That night was a watershed for her; she had been terrified of performing live but the success of the gig and the warmth of the crowd, most of which had been devoted fans on MySpace, devouring every demo she put up, and snapping up their copies of the limited edition 'LDN' gave her a huge boost. As soon as she'd come off stage, she wanted to do it all over again. Far from being a Barbra Streisand-type, vomiting with fear before every live performance, she found that the gratification and enjoyment of singing live, seeing all those adoring faces singing back at her, was to become the favourite part of her job. But one of the hardest lessons she had to learn was how to deal with her reactions when not everyone was as adoring as she'd like them to be.

Performing your own songs is an incredibly exposed thing to do, and understandably it is a rare performer who can stand by and shrug their shoulders when they themselves or their precious songs are being criticised, especially after experiencing tidal waves of support from the teenage fans who had become rather attached to their idol.

After Lily's euphoric first gig, the queen of blogging suffered a slump in mood. The American *Guardian* music critic Caroline Sullivan had managed to wedge herself in amid a sea of Lily-alikes in prom dresses and trainers to attend her gig the following week. Lily might have been feeling more confident this week but Sullivan unfortunately wasn't buying what she was selling.

The day Sullivan's review came out, two days later on May 13, Lily posted a blog, bearing the current mood of 'depressed', and admitted to being "freaked out, I feel like my live thing isn't living up to what people think it should. People are giving me shit for being a mockney and denying my middle-class roots…"

"Allen had a chirpy way about her that rather undermined her attempt at urban edginess," wrote Sullivan. "There have been comparisons with Mike Skinner, mainly on the basis that her vignettes of fag-end London life share the same glass–half-empty perspective, but on stage she's too sweet to pull it off… In her head, she's probably a cross between Lady Sovereign and ex-Sugababe Mutya, but a girl can only deny her middle-class provenance so much."

Understandably, that didn't go down well with Lily. This wasn't a particularly bad review, but for all Lily's outer toughness, she was affected by every criticism levelled at her. She might have seemed like the type to say, "Fuck you," and keep going, but underneath it all she felt attacked.

Her determination to justify any "mockniness" started to manifest in slightly exaggerated responses to interview questions. She told the US site *Pitchfork*, "My mother came to London when she was 17, no money, no education…" (she'd come to study at the prestigious University College London). "We lived in what you call the projects," (not many people would call even a council flat in Bloomsbury, a stone's throw from the British Museum, the London equivalent of "the projects"…). "My dad left home when I was four. I didn't speak to him really until I was 15."

Again, this is contradictory to what Keith has said – they got together quite a lot throughout her childhood, going away on holiday, going to football matches, going out for meals. But he certainly wasn't around as much as she'd have liked, as she would later outline in the song 'He Wasn't There' on her second album, *It's Not Me, It's You*.

History did seem to be repeating itself in some ways. Keith himself suffered a childhood largely missing his father, Eddie, who was often away with the Navy. And, like Lily, Keith would play up and drive his mother mad. He recalled one typical exchange in his book *Grow Up*:

'You wait till your father gets home.'

'Who?'

'You know, your father. Don't be silly.'

'No I don't.' "I didn't. Apart from the shadowy figure who left a photo on the mantelpiece…"

He was used to his dad being away for years at a time sometimes, and chaos generally would ensue when he was back. Perhaps not quite Keith Allen chaos though. Eddie Allen did witness the detonation of the first H bomb off Christmas Island in 1957 though, which might have set a blueprint for explosiveness within the Allen family. Eddie was a strong handsome sailor, "not blessed with height" according to Keith. Eddie's wife Mary was also little, 5ft 3in, dark skin, black hair, where Lily gets her Romany colouring from.

Keith does admit his daughter can be a "drama queen", and in a way she appeared to be slightly rewriting her past in order to not be so judged for her urban style, and attract sympathy as opposed to inverted snobbery. Not for her the dignified silence. And in a way, that was partly what was so refreshing about her as a persona – where other pop stars kept their lips buttoned and seemingly floated above whatever was written about them, possibly even unaware, and certainly unlikely to interact, Lily was the other extreme, and it wouldn't always be good for her health; the constant focus on what was being said about her, the continual checking and increasing name-googling, poring over posts about herself and fretting over 'fans' who were clearly nutcases and getting abusive, would leave her frazzled and upset. This was something she would have to learn to deal with – she wouldn't be able to control what was being said by others, but she could control how she reacted, and how often she looked at these posts – and she'd eventually have to control how much she shared. Her fans – and soon her critics and the press – would be privy to essentially the contents of her diary. She was inadvertently creating ready-made news stories, especially considering how opinionated most of her postings could be.

Could anyone, even someone as seemingly self-possessed as Lily, be prepared for the roller-coaster ride to come? Maybe not, and while she seemed to deal with it with the kind of shoulder-shrugging dispassionateness we hear in 'LDN', she carefully monitored and sometimes chastised herself as she swung from general amazement at how everything was unfolding so glamorously to slipping into the territory of believing her own press.

In June Lily went out to dine at Nobu to celebrate signing her publishing deal with Universal. The night ended up at Stringfellows, no doubt for some post-ironic chortles at the cheesy Eighties strip Mecca, and they all boozed the night away. Lily could certainly hold her drink, which was just as well – she had to stay relatively fresh for rehearsals at Southwark's Terminal Studios for her appearance on the legendary chart show *Top Of The Pops,* which would sadly be axed that summer. She'd be appearing with her old pals/sparring partners The Kooks, which gave her a boost of confidence. Also, Lady Sovereign was in the next room in the rehearsal studios to Lily ("she really is very small…") and Jamie T caught up with Lily there too. The pair had been talking about recording a track together ('Rawhide'), and Jamie pinned her down (not literally) there and then, whisking her off to Miloco Studios nearby to lay down a vocal track straight after her rehearsals for *Top Of The Pops,* where she'd see her old Bedales schoolmate Luke from The Kooks. They'd both come a long way from singing Green Day songs together in idle moments in the dormitory.

Lily was on the bill for the music-lover's televised summer staple *T4 On The Beach,* a gig Lily didn't feel entirely comfortable with. The thought of singing in front of 30,000 people was, hard as it is to believe now, something Lily baulked at; "So I thought it would be a good idea to get absolutely plastered." She started early, as her slot was at 11.45am. By 10am she was feeling no pain, and by 1pm she was ordered home by the management "for being loud and obnoxious". Lily wasn't arguing. "I could've really, really embarrassed myself if I'd stayed much longer…" The sting in the tail, after she finally got back to Islington, was that she was locked out of the house, and Alison was at a wedding. She sat on her front step, slowly sobering up, still resplendent in gold ball-gown and bright green sparkly eye make-up. By her own admission, she looked "like a mental patient".

Another moment of potential rock-star behaviour occurred after another Channel 4 TV appearance, this time for the music show *Transmission.* As she settled in in the green room at Alexandra Palace, Lily was amused by how her old school friend, Kooks singer Luke, who was also on the show, had become so 'pop-starry': sunglasses indoors, 'bohemian' straw hat, and rolled her eyes at Dirty Pretty Things' Carl Barât for requesting organic sliced bread on his rider and not making eye-contact with anyone. Carl later smirked back in an interview:"Sometimes you meet people you're not interested in. She was one of them. It's like getting slagged off by Jade Goody." (Dirty Pretty Things/Libertines fans were not amused, however, and the threats would subsequently roll in...)

But Lily had to stop herself in her tracks when she realised she was displaying signs of being "just as bad as Luke and Carl. (I) behaved like a knob". Being around certain types of people seemed to give licence for egotistical behaviour, and Lily was aware it was getting under her skin too. But she was not quite at the stage where she could get away with it.

Lily's brand-new handbag, "my favourite new toy", went missing, and Lily was far from calm, not least because it contained, as well as two phones and a wallet, a collection of press clippings about her that she wanted to send to her doting grandparents (her grandmother still occasionally dug out her cassette of Lily singing in the Millfield School Choir, and was always supportive – thankfully she was still unaware of 'Nan, You're A Window Shopper'). Lily had, perhaps unsurprisingly, had a few drinks and, by her own admission, flew off the handle at her TV plugger Helena, who was trying to help.

"For a minute I believed I was more important than I actually am, and took it out on someone who was trying to help," blogged Lily between mouthfuls of humble pie. "My friends Seb and Ben told me to stop being Diana Ross and reminded me of the dick I was being..."

More fame and more adulation was on its way though, as the following month would see Lily well and truly take over the music world with her fresh new sound of summer in the shape of her album *Alright, Still* and the sugar-dusted, flower-strewn hate letter, 'Smile'. (Lily would later become known as the girl who "splits up" with boyfriends for inspiration. Suitors beware...) She'd be designing her own Nike trainer ("in a secret location"), performing at the launch of Jade Jagger's jewellery company, Jezebel – let's face it, Lily was hot property.

Lily set off for some promo in Germany ("a lot of shit food") and Paris, but the UK alone was more than ready for a jolt of acidic pop sunshine to upset the PH, wading as we had been through syrupy sub-jazz smoothness à la Norah Jones and Michael Bublé, the sub-Spector soul of Amy Winehouse (ushering in, for better or worse, a wave of girls with voices like wah-wah-muted bugles), auto-tuned 'singers' and ever more boys with guitars and haircuts they'd spent too much time over. Step up a girl who wasn't too styled, wasn't too tidy, wasn't too thin and was always too outspoken, much to the delight of the press. Never mind 'Lily Week', this was shaping up to be Lily Year.

After returning to the UK, the real excitement was about to start – it was festival season and every performance would feel like a homecoming. After all, festivals were in her bones. Lily and her band would be accompanied on most of their UK dates by Future Cut: their vision and computer wizardry were instrumental in helping create Lily's sound, and now they were proving vital to her live show. They'd even appear in full fancy dress (Elvis Presley and Michael Jackson, to be precise) at the Isle Of Wight's Bestival. That's commitment. "We were asked to help put together the live show," explained Darren Lewis, "and we decided to run the backing track on the PowerBook. It meant we could add or subtract real musicians, depending on the budget or the size of a specific show."

Unfortunately there was no Glastonbury Festival in 2006, but the acclaimed film-maker Julien Temple had made a documentary about it (called, inevitably, *Glastonbury*). Lily watched it to get into the festival mood, although after watching footage of Primal Scream and other rockier acts in the film, she became concerned that her music wasn't anthemic enough to get the crowd jumping. She needn't have worried.

First up was the Scottish festival T In The Park, and after a sunny afternoon spent "mostly drinking and smoking fags" and eating hot-dogs (Lily admitted it was not easy squeezing into her ball-gown when the time came), she performed what she felt was "the most amazing gig ever" – not least because, during the set, her manager, Adrian, walked towards her with a bottle of champagne and the news that her song 'Smile' had topped the charts.

The audience went wild when they heard the news, it was especially exciting that they found out at the same time Lily did, and they all sang 'Smile' together as Lily beamed from the stage. The rest of Lily's night was spent drinking and approaching other artists backstage saying: "Are you in a band? Cool, are you number one?" "In other words I was being a right dick..."

Another run of European dates followed, literally from the next morning – Lily was seriously hungover and emotional, her sunglasses barely leaving her face for the rest of the week. But another triumph would be on the way. After arriving back in England, enjoying a sleep and cuddle with new puppy Maggie May (the offspring of Stella, the dog she shared with Lester Lloyd) it was time to get ready to play the Big Chill. Lily had less time for herself, let alone time to look after a "very bitey" new canine chum, but fortunately Alfie was on hand to toilet train the little pup, which was just as well – Lily had to try out her new sleeper bus in preparation for the next outing.

The beds might have been worryingly coffin-like, but they were still beds, which was a massive improvement. There was even a toilet. On the long drive to the Big Chill festival in Herefordshire, Lily, the band, Lily's brother, Alfie, her best friend–come–assistant Emily Sonnet ("who now travels everywhere with me so I don't lose my mind") and Future Cut's Tunde and Darren would all travel together, playing board games such as Trivial Pursuit and a "CD game of *Name That Tune* which provided approximately ten minutes of entertainment". Shame the drive was four hours long…

Appearing at the Big Chill was a magical experience for Lily, and she felt it was her "Glasto dream" come true – even if it wasn't Glasto.

After playing with her one-month-old half-sister Teddie (Keith Allen and his partner Tamzin didn't live far from Herefordshire, so the clan were in attendance), Lily applied her sparkly make-up, popped on an appropriately sunshine-yellow dress and downed a pint of Magners for Dutch courage. Never mind the thousands of people in the crowd, Lily would be singing to her family too, who were all in the wings – much more nerve-racking. At least Alfie had evidently forgiven Lily for the song of the same name; he would hit the stage himself during 'Alfie', much to everyone's amusement. Keith was "so proud he was almost crying", which gave Lily some much-needed validation. It wouldn't have been the same without his euphoric reaction.

"It's funny how making your parents proud of you has such an effect, but that's another story."

CHAPTER EIGHT

"Oh Jesus, number one, eh? I'm in shock…"

From Lily's blog, July 14, 2006.

July saw the release of *Alright, Still*, which debuted at number two in the UK album chart, selling 523,000 copies in its year of release alone, and 'Smile', which topped the charts from July 9–23, shifting 228,500 copies in 2006. 'Smile' had booted Shakira's 'Hips Don't Lie' off the top spot and was eventually toppled by McFly's cover of Queen's 'Don't Stop Me Now'. Lily was just thrilled to have such success, commercially and, it seemed, critically. The positive reviews flooded in from the music press' great and good – *NME* loved the single's 'Uptown Top Ranking' groove, *Uncut* dubbed the album "a terrific, bolshy eclectic stew of London street pop" and *Pitchfork* gushed that it was a "fantastic success".

Of course, as *Drowned In Sound* admitted, it would divide listeners "like Marmite", and it did – *Slant* magazine simply called it "rubbish" (although most of the critics' complaints were about the inclusion of songs that mocked men for their small penises or unwelcome advances, so who knows, maybe it touched a nerve…). Her conversational style and rough-edged quality naturally drew comparisons to The Streets

– but as *The Guardian*'s Sophie Heawood insisted: "The female Mike Skinner? She's far, far better than that."

Meanwhile, Lily was enjoying her reign of the English fields, which had been transformed temporarily into soundstages, camping sites and giant playpens for indie-loving hedonists. The Secret Garden Party was another festival Lily rocked, and it gave her particular satisfaction to know that Lester Lloyd and his girlfriend were on site, their tent pitched directly opposite the main stage, where Lily would perform. Being able to sing 'Smile' right at Lester, and knowing he'd be squirming, was a memory Lily would cherish.

Lily's guaranteed presence at the VIP bar meant that tabloid journalists at the festivals could walk straight up and attempt to bait her on the subject of fellow 'celebs' she might deem stupid or unworthy, desperate for a pithy, prickly sound-bite. But Lily was wiser to their tricks than she had been. On the weekend of the V Festival that August, reporters tried their best to goad and provoke Lily into starting a fight with Peaches Geldof, the socialite Lily had previously been rather vocal (and, albeit in jest, pretty vicious) about. Such playground silliness did seem an easy way to create havoc and thus a lead story, but despite what was eventually printed, Lily was having none of it.

Whether there was an issue there or not, fans were likely to believe her; after all, she'd never been known to hold back if she had something to say. The fact is Lily must have felt that *she* should be the one in control of how she comes across and what she wants to express – not a mischief-making journalist. If she wanted to say something positive or negative, it would be on her own terms, not because a newspaper just wanted an easy story. The idea of a feud between two 'kids of famous people' is a tabloid's wet dream, however, and Lily had to try hard not to buy into it.

Even the idea of a friendship with a "famous offspring" was something she tried hard to avoid: Rod Stewart's socialite daughter Kimberly approached her, saying she thought the two of them probably had a lot in common. Lily couldn't see it, and still can't: "No offence," she said, "but my dad had his knob sucked by a sheep in *Twin Town* (TV show produced by Keith Allen's brother Kevin)… and your dad's Rod Stewart." And that was the end of that.

After a celebratory cider with her family (and being given some free hand-made frilly pants by the admiring ladies at Flo-Jo, who had a stall there for their vintage-style clothes), Lily had to pack up and get back to London. This year there'd be no time to hang out at the festival, no time to snuggle up around the campfire before bedding down in a tent under the stars. In less than 24 hours Lily and her band would be on a plane to Australia.

A whirlwind stint down under was heightened by a whirlwind romance, or at least a hoped-for romance, when Lily continued her so far unbroken record of falling in love with DJs. This time, after being interviewed by Fox FM's irreverent DJ duo Hamish and Andy, she developed a crush on Andy Lee, a man who was widely known as Australia's most eligible bachelor. "I met this gorgeous DJ…" she swooned on her blog afterwards.

After a gigglesome interview and no doubt much fluttering of eyelashes (hers, and probably his too), she "made sure he came to my gig" at St Jerome's club in Melbourne – an intimate 200-ticket affair that attracted more than 1,500 punters (they opened up a back door so more people could see the gig). Lily went out on a limb and dedicated 'Littlest Things' – the ballad written for Seb Chew – to Andy before blurting out that she was smitten. (She admitted she was "getting ahead of herself" afterwards.)

Lily boasted of kissing him after the show but when Andy, who understandably became quite a figure of interest after this, was questioned on the 'romance' he brushed it off. "Lily has obviously gone back to England," he shrugged. "I'm not sure if she flies in to every city and dedicates a song to a radio host. It was very flattering but I'm not sure how seriously I can take that any more considering she is on the other side of the world." Letting her down gently? Stopping himself from getting his hopes up? And was she just doing it to get a rise out of Seb Chew? Maybe we'll never know…

Lily was increasingly staggered by the level of her own success – she was still scarred by years of feeling like the odd one out at school, the one nobody liked. "I always think of myself as a really naff person," she admitted to George Lamb, when he came back to check how she was doing. "When I was at school I just used to think everyone was talking about me behind my back. I'm so paranoid, and I think when everyone started saying, 'Oh, we really like you', and magazines started writing really good reviews of my album, I was just like, 'Wait a second… but I'm an idiot, everyone hates me!'"

Another memory of school that still loomed large was how instrumental her music teacher, Rachel Santesso, had been in her success, and she ensured there was a mention of her in the sleeve notes of *Alright, Still*. She would also include her estranged siblings Galoushka, Grace and Kevin in the acknowledgements, still yearning for that "big family moment", as Keith put it. By their names, Lily had added: "I wish I saw more of you."

Kevin would later admit that it became harder and harder to get hold of Lily. Indeed, there was a wall being built around her that even her family found hard to permeate, and Lily also kept several mobiles, changing her number frequently, so even her own manager often struggled to track her down at times (which must have been refreshing when she needed a little space, at least).

Yes, their wayward half-sister was a runaway success, recouping her £25k advance within days of the album release, and she was truly thrilled, not least because "The A&R men I've been going into meetings with for the last three years will now be kicking themselves." That competitive, slightly vengeful-but-with-a-twinkle-in-the-eye streak that we would hear in her songwriting (and see in the video to 'Smile') was clearly thriving.

For all her cheekiness, which could sometimes prove an acquired taste, her best pal Miquita Oliver observed that Lily, who had often been difficult over the years, seemed to be in a good place now that she was recognised for her talent. Fame and adulation certainly seemed to suit her. "We have been so up and down over the years. Right now, we are probably the best we've ever been," she admitted. Lily becoming famous, more famous already than Miquita, seemed to help. There had always been a little rivalry between the pair, and Miquita was used to being "the famous one" after becoming a super-hip pop presenter as a teenager. Now there seemed to be more balance in their relationship, even if Miquita might have been a little put out at first that Lily was chasing her tail in the recognition stakes.

Alfie confirmed the belief that fame was proving to be a levelling, healthy influence on Lily. He said: "I think getting what she wants after having worked for so long has made her a happier person. She didn't really have that many friends when she was younger, she was a loner, and she definitely had problems talking to people, she was a bit of a tomboy too. She didn't really get along with (other girls)."

It's true, she admitted once she felt threatened if she saw a pretty girl walk into a bar, dealing with her insecurity by becoming laddish and hanging out with boys instead, taking the piss to hide the fact she feels inadequate: "If a skinny blonde girl comes walking into the pub I'm immediately hating her." This didn't necessarily go away, but she certainly started to feel a little more at home with who she was, as a result of the waves of approval coming at her from all directions.

Ironically, she is a role model, whether she likes it or not, for girls, including perhaps the sort of girls whose confidence and conventional good looks she might have felt threatened by at school or in bars.

But by the end of 2006, there would be Lil-a-likes all over the UK; girls would dress like her and try to act like her, variously bolshy and intermittently girly. There was even a group of fans in the US (known as the Lilettes – presumably they hadn't heard of the tampon brand of the same name) who also spent their time dressing up as Lily and seemingly monitoring her every move. Lily was flattered but wasn't too sure when her mum suggested they should come and stay at their house. "I was like, 'You what?' I'm scared of going home in case my mum meets random fans and brings them home for a cup of tea…"

One can see why girls would look to Lily, and her experience in the music industry quickly led to her becoming something of a feminist. "It's strange," she'd observe. "One of the main markets for buying records is 18-24-year-old girls, so it's really strange there aren't any females trying to appeal to that age group, or trying to talk to that age group on a lyrical level."

Perhaps this was why girls in particular would view Lily as an encouraging force, a symbol that it was OK to be different, honest and intelligent, not subscribing to the usual insidious pressure that was around all the time to be thin, perfect, pretty or nice and unchallenging in a bid to be approved of or noticed – although Lily herself admitted she is far from fallible, having fallen for the promises of magazines herself in her time. But at least she was prepared to face it. "Even I'm guilty of it, 'Ooh look, Jade Goody can tell me how to lose weight in two weeks,' and I spend £3.50 on the stupid magazine..." she mused. "Anyway, because I'm a bit of a fuck-off person, I want to be a bit chubbier than most. If there's going to be little girls listening to Lily, I'd like them to think, 'She writes good songs and she's also not saying we have to be skinny.'

"I'd like to tell all those fashion magazine editors to fuck right off, because I think we're all right as we are, ladies."

The album launch for *Alright, Still* was guaranteed a little more attention than average not least because it was attended by, ironically, the photogenic and rake-thin movie star Keira Knightley, who accompanied her *Atonement* co-star Alfie. Little would Keira realise she'd be on the receiving end of a rather unkind 'impersonation' by Lily a year down the line on her BBC3 show video-log. (The impression, conveyed while Lily was being filmed having her hair and make-up done, was just a jutting underbite followed by peals of wicked laughter. Oh dear.)

The title of the album was inspired by Alfie's slangy lexicon (and is included as part of a line of dialogue from the hapless but eager male featured in the dismissive 'Knock 'Em Out'), and it's been quipped that Lily apparently decided to definitely plump for this as a title because, while in a restaurant, she wanted sparkling water and they didn't have any, so she said, you guessed it, "Alright, still." It's also been said that Lily loved Einstein's concept that 'nothing changes until something moves', everything is alright as long as it's still. Unless you *like* change, of course. (Lily, being a Taurus, probably doesn't, to be fair.)

Bonus tracks would be released on UK iTunes (including covers of The Specials' 'Blank Expression', ELO's 'Mr Blue Sky' and a stripped-back acoustic version of The Kooks' 'Naïve'), but Regal had to put its foot down about which tracks would make it on the album, and that unfortunately included her least favourite track: 'Take What You Take'. This song featured baggy-inspired vocalising over Happy Mondays-esque guitar, self-help mantras galore juxtaposed with lairy, sweary protestations that would give Catherine Tate's character Lauren 'Am I Bovvered?' Cooper a run for her money. ("What the fuck do you know? Just cos you're old you think you're wise/But who the hell are you though? I didn't even ask for your advice… you're doing in my nut, And do you think I care?') "I fucking hate that song more than anything in the world," she later lamented.

Lily would have preferred 'Cheryl Tweedy', her ironic mockery of society's perceived ideas of beauty, and how pressured it makes young girls feel (using samples from drum and bass track 'Valley Of The Shadows' by Origin Unknown) or the moody 'Absolutely Nothing', but the label wanted the dynamic, feel-good 'Take What You Take' to please the "Robbie Williams market".

So 'Cheryl Tweedy', taking its name from the apparently perfect Girls Aloud singer, was consigned to the B-side of 'Smile', but it would get more than its fair share of attention thanks to the line about how she wished she looked like Cheryl Tweedy, but knew she never would.

The lyric was intended as a comment on how teenage girls are fed impossible images of beauty that they try hopelessly to aspire to (often the models and pop princesses they are so desperate to emulate don't even look like that themselves before all the hair extensions/airbrushing/ hours in make-up). It's an illusion, a conceit, but Cheryl herself was asked to comment on it during an interview and got the wrong end of the stick.

Cheryl responded, sweet as aspartame and full of false modesty: "I don't know why she sings about wanting to be as pretty as me, as she looks stunning. I'd like to look like her."

The sweetness soon disappeared when Lily pointed out the song was not meant to be taken so literally, it was about how people think they have to look like an ideal. "I don't want to look like Cheryl Tweedy! It's tongue-in-cheek," she insisted. "It's meant to be ironic. I don't have anything against her as a human being. It was a joke that not many people got." And then, she uttered the line that is now immortal and has been repeated more often in the subsequent 'Cheryl v Lily war' than anyone could have imagined: "Of course nobody really wants to look like Cheryl, they just think they do."

Cheryl took this as a major insult and responded ungraciously when later quizzed about it by Gordon Ramsay of all people. He stoked and prodded the situation like a naughty schoolboy on his TV show *The F Word* until Cheryl sarcastically sniped, "Oh yes, because everyone *really* wants to look like *her!*" (Actually, quite a lot of girls do.) To which Gordon responded, "A chick with a dick?" He then asked her to describe Lily, and she paused before repeating, "Chick with a dick!" Cheryl is perfectly capable of being bitchy without anyone else's assistance but everyone seems to have forgotten it was Ramsay who put those particular words into her mouth, but it is those words that have gone down in history. Ironically Ramsay would later go on to say in interviews how much he loved Lily, mocking Girls Aloud's thinness and vegetarianism. Talk about double standards... Gordon, you really are quite the muckraker.

Lily was never one to mince her words, and the media-fuelled war between Cheryl and Lily (who at this point still hadn't even met) would spiral on, eventually even rivalling the perennial nepotism issue (although as Lily's close friend Pockets has observed, we're now more likely to see Keith being identified in the press as 'Lily Allen's father Keith...'). But no matter how much one would overshadow the other, there certainly weren't any conscious attempts to upstage from Keith. In fact he even turned down an offer for Fat Les to re-release 'Vindaloo' to support the England team at the 2006 World Cup as it would clash with Lily's album release. "He's good like that," admitted Lily, when reminded of this in conversation with Fat Les member Damien Hirst.

As far as Lily was concerned the gloves were off when it came to Cheryl Tweedy, who soon became Cheryl Cole after marrying the randy footballer Ashley Cole. The fact that Cheryl became the classic big-haired, perma-tanned 'footballer's wife' was of even greater amusement to Lily, but she was not the only one to come in for Lily's free-flowing criticism. Allen was a journalist's wet dream thanks to her sharp tongue and bolshy opinions, freely telling interviewers while promoting her album how she felt about her fellow contemporary pop stars.

As well as The Kooks and Carl Barât, already lambasted in her blog ("I was quite annoyed at how much of a bad man [Luke] thinks he is. Get over yourselves,"), obvious targets would also be attacked when she was invited to opine by various publications.

Hotel heiress and perceived airhead (but probable marketing genius) Paris Hilton was told via the media by Lily to "Go away!" when she released her own album. "Paris is hideously untalented. I poured my heart into my album. She just got someone else to do it for her. If she's rude to me I'll punch her. People cheesy enough to buy albums like that should be killed."

And from Jamelia to, in 2010, the ruddy-cheeked Conservative leader David Cameron, she's been railing against accusations that her music is 'unsuitable for their kids' from the word go. "I'm not being funny," responded Lily, "but I never made my album for your child." As a life-long Labour supporter (Green in local elections), losing the Tory vote probably wasn't too bothersome to her.

Mis-teeq singer Alesha Dixon spoke out against Lily's approach: "I don't like hearing her putting down other artists – we should all support each other," while it appeared that Lily's old friend/foe Lady Sovereign was keen to give her a taste of her own medicine – and maybe had observed how much press Lily was getting every time she slagged someone off. Sovereign announced that she, not Lily, was the true queen of MySpace, and that Lily was "the biggest chav going", before reciting the already tired old claim that she is only famous because of her dad. Naturally it didn't take long for Lily to respond. "I've spoken to my dad," she quipped in her blog, "and he says he's happy to adopt you if you think it'll give you a leg up."

While this last jab was funny, and admittedly justified, Lily had to remind herself that sarcasm, the lowest form of wit, "doesn't read very well", but it remains easier said than done for her to keep her trap shut. Even Keith has admitted she has a tendency to go too far.

Madonna was also in the firing line but Lily was at least learning the hard way about how the press worked. "They'll say, 'Who is the most overrated person in pop in your opinion?' And I'll say, 'Well, maybe Madonna,' and all of a sudden it's like 'Lily hates Madonna'. I guess with it all happening so quickly I haven't figured out how it all works yet."

Another hard lesson learned was that you can't be too jokey or ambiguous when talking to a story-hungry journalist. You might think you're not talking to a tabloid hack, but say anything red-top-worthy, and there is no good reason why a supposedly reputable publication wouldn't sell that quote to another paper.

Lily was excited to receive her first interview request from indie bible *NME*, she felt she'd truly made it when they took an interest. The magazine had already heralded her "the perfect modern pop star" and "self-styled Queen of Blogs", while her blog itself was described as "an unbovvered raspberry in the face of celebrity". If anyone was going to 'get' Lily, it was *NME*.

The journalist Tim Jonze was interviewing her and they were having a laugh, Lily seems to respond well to male journalists and was relaxed in his company. He asked, "How are you going to celebrate your number one?" To which she replied, "Oh, gak!" meaning cocaine: they'd been having a tongue-in-cheek conversation about drugs.

Lily went home that day feeling happy and excited about her interview with the respected magazine. Little did she know her 'gak' joke would be taken out of context and offered, for a fee, to a tabloid. Soon it was all over the press, a major blow for Lily. She had to apologise and clarify that this was of course not what she meant, and she would never condone drug use – she was already being cast as a role model for young girls whether she liked it or not, and would have to watch what she said and did from now on. "We've always loved Lily, but that interview was partly what contributed to Lily not speaking to us for two years..." sighed an *NME* insider.

What really concerned Lily was that she'd hoped to be taken more seriously by *NME,* whom she thought would have been "more responsible". She didn't like the chauvinistic whiff of double standards either. "I read articles every week about boys in bands talking about actually consuming drugs themselves and nothing is said. I make a joke about it and they fucking sell it to the tabloids." It would take a long time for Lily to live that 'gak' comment down, and journalists became more and more eager to catch her saying something controversial or insulting to another star – there's little they love more than a 'war' between two celebrities.

But in a way, her media persona was at least not at odds with the image she was conveying through her music. She was not pretending to be an angel, the whole point of her songs was that they were upfront, honest and generally saying things that others didn't have the heart, or the balls, to say. Why would she be any different in real life?

CHAPTER 9

"I feel like I blagged it. Because I'm not very good, am I? I'm not a musician. I don't play an instrument. I write words. I write nursery rhymes."
Lily Allen

Lily's hard/soft, bright/dark qualities were spotlighted perfectly when the highly entertaining video for 'Smile', directed by Sophie Muller (who had also worked her magic on Shakira's promo for 'Hips Don't Lie'), hit our TV screens. It captured the nation's imagination with its dark humour and drew out the vitriol in Lily's lyrics. Lily always insisted she didn't want to think of 'Smile' in too vengeful a way – "It's a period of my life that I would rather not go back to," she'd say. "Things are much happier for me. Discovering I had a talent for making music really turned my life around." But making the video must have been at least a little cathartic for Lily.

The video centres around an ex boyfriend (a DJ funnily enough... just like Lester Lloyd). She starts off comfort-eating in her bedroom after being dumped, before wreaking her revenge. Lily's character has her ex beaten up, his flat broken into and his precious records scratched, and she even personally puts laxatives in his coffee.

Very soon everyone was talking about it – if nothing else here was a female artist who was not trying to be cute and lovable with a carefully constructed, inoffensive debut. Ofcom clamped down on the video because it contained swearing, a violent burglary, a mugging and a drink being spiked. MTV pulled it altogether. And so the video – and Lily – became even more of a talking point. But if anyone was truly offended, it was Lily. Why should she have been banned, when it's supposedly fine that, as she said at the time, "The Pussycat Dolls get away with gyrating with no clothes on and promoting prostitution?" She wasn't impressed that 'bands' such as The Pussycat Dolls were even in favour at all. "Every song on my album is a snapshot of a certain moment; I find it really pathetic when you're watching TV interviews with shit bands like The Pussycat Dolls and someone asks, 'What's this song about?' and they're like, 'Well, you know, it's like that feeling you get when …' I'm like, 'Shut up, you didn't even write it.'"

'Smile' seemed to inspire quite a response from artists as well as fans (and Ofcom). The rapper Example, who would later tour with Lily, responded to the song with his own version, 'Vile', which was sung from the perspective of the ex under attack. Loud-mouthed Radio 1 DJ Chris Moyles also did his own version for listeners to download, entitled 'Piles' (although despite this they became good chums. This might have something to do with the fact that Moyles is resolutely Lily's 'type'. She would later confirm that she likes "big chubby guys with glasses, bald heads and back hair. Someone like David Beckham would be my idea of hell. I would sleep with him for a million quid. But I'd do just about anything for a million quid.")

While promoting 'Smile', ironically Lily was finding it hard to smile herself as she was still struggling to get over her split from Seb Chew. It can't have helped that they were still close friends and saw each other frequently – she hadn't had the chance to get over him even if she'd wanted to. Lily admitted in interviews how she felt "lost and alone, crying uncontrollably", adding that "boys make me mental. I'm really bad and attention-seeking and not a particularly nice person in relationships."

Speaking of which, how did Lester take the fact that he had been exposed in song and a version of him at least had been beaten up in the video, as if the actor playing him was some kind of quasi-voodoo doll? Well, he had heard 'Smile' when it was still a demo. Lily and Lester hooked up briefly the year before, had an amicable meeting, playing with the English bull terrier Stella they had shared together, since taken care of by Lester's family.

Lily had been building up to revealing 'Smile' to him, eager to see whether there was any glimmer of recognition in his eyes. She played the song to him on her car CD player. "This is about us, isn't it?" he'd said. She grinned. He took it on the chin, although he has always contested the "doing the girl next door" line. "I've never cheated on Lily. It's rubbish. I don't even know which friend she means." But he conceded in interviews (naturally the press were quite interested in him after Lily, and 'Smile', became famous) "I know I 'messed up her mental health'." He just hadn't been aware of it at the time. He was certainly aware of it now though.

Mutual friends of Lily and Lester's thought the whole affair was hilarious, by all accounts, and despite how it might have appeared, artistic licence aside, Lily had got most of her anger out of her system and could think fondly of Lester again – at least, until he sold his story to the *Sunday Mirror*. It seemed Lily wasn't the only one with a big mouth and a taste for revenge.

It seems everyone has their price, and Lester's was £20,000. He obligingly went into explicit details about their sex life during their time together, their drug use (pills and marijuana), having sex outside after going clubbing, even describing the pattern on her knickers. "We made love for hours," he boasted, taking the opportunity to talk up his sexual prowess.

Lily was furious but had to let it go, fearing that a counter-attack would result in him getting nasty and spreading lies about her. "He sold his story for an hour and a half of talking. He got about as much as I signed a record deal for, and it took me three and a half years to make that album," she complained. "I put in all that work and he broke my heart and fucked me over, and now he and his girlfriend are living in New York through me. I didn't love reading about it in the papers – my grandparents didn't either..."

But she slightly derailed her own moral stance by being unable to resist the snipe, "I slept with all his friends actually."

Lily would receive another jolt, albeit professional as opposed to personal, when the UK music industry's annual Mercury Music Prize swung around. *Alright, Still* hadn't made the shortlist. Lily had maybe become so quickly accustomed to being adored and lavished with praise and attention, not to mention success, that it was even harder to accept that she was not in with a chance for this prestigious award, but fellow MySpace success story Arctic Monkeys were (they'd been around a little longer to be fair). Other nominees shortlisted were Editors, jazz pianist Zoë Rahman, Isobel Campbell and Mark Lanegan, Guillemots, Hot Chip, Richard Hawley... The prize went to Arctic Monkeys.

Lily was gutted, but as far as the Mercury panel was concerned, her material was not up to scratch — some felt "she doesn't really mean it" and questioned her commitment as a performer, which of course, Lily had to respond to: "I think that's a pretty stupid comment assuming the Mercury Music Prize is not about live performances. But I suppose the prize is there to help people and I've sold a lot of albums already..."

At least the press shared Lily's outrage at how she was passed over, and as a result she would rake in more valuable coverage than ever, maybe even more than the winners. Lily, none too sportingly, shrugged: "It's nice to be nominated but where are the past winners now?"

Lily's next single, 'LDN', was being readied for a September release. The original low-budget promo of Lily wheeling around the city in her yellow coat was fine for the initial limited release but for the re-release, something extra was needed to visually bring out the darker side of the song. The first video was too one-dimensional. It was still very Lily, and for a contemporary female pop artist, still very different — it didn't show her gyrating in a skimpy outfit for a start, which was quite unusual. But if you listened to the words of 'LDN', there was a sinister element that needed highlighting.

A new promo was prepared, this time directed by Nima Nourizadeh, who had created videos for Hot Chip and Lily's friend and one-time collaborator Jamie T (Lily sang on Jamie's track 'Rawhide', the B-side to his 2007 release 'Sheila').

Nourizadeh also would end up directing videos for Bat For Lashes and spoof band Flight Of The Conchords, which proved he had the perfect mix of subversive humour and visual quirkiness. Just right for Lily, who wanted to make people think, not just smile.

The new video for 'LDN' remains set in Lily's heartland of Ladbroke Grove and Kensal Green as opposed to roaming all over the metropolis, and filming took place just before Notting Hill Carnival (where Lily would play a set at YoYo for the first time since her debut gig in May). The 'LDN' promo seems very personal to Lily, we feel we know her, and her West London, a little better after seeing it. It also displays the sharp contrast between the two realities of Ladbroke Grove – 'Heaven W11', colourful and fun (and immortalised, perhaps bowdlerised, in the movie *Notting Hill*), and the gritty, sometimes hopeless 'Notting Hell'. Both are very real, and characteristic of London's contrasting streets – one road could be tree-lined and perfect, the next could be a ghetto. As Lily sang, "That's city life..."

Our heroine, clad in full-length red ball-gown, Nikes and cartoony eye-make-up, starts off in her favourite record shop, Rough Trade off Portobello, the sound of her own reggaefied track 'Friend Of Mine' playing liltingly in the background. (Rough Trade is transformed into 'Tough Grade' in the video – introducing the concept that everything 'nice' has a harder, darker edge if you choose to look twice.) Lily, with blank-eyed cockiness, asks the shop assistants if they have any examples of a kind of music that seems to defy genre: "punky electronica, kind of grime, kind of like new wave grime, but kind of like maybe more like broken beats... like dubby broken beats, but a little bit kind of soulful... not kinda drum-and-bass-y, but kinda more broken drum and bass, like broken beats, like break-beat kind of broken drum and bass..." Tough Grade's assistants simply stare back at her. (These were all descriptions that had been used to try to define Lily's own music by the press. Lily was making a point...)

As Lily ambles out of the shop, London, depicted as a Technicolor fairyland, swiftly turns into something rather more scuzzy wherever Lily turns. The slightly dodgy, dark sights, to Lily, are "priceless", and she describes the petty crime that is around her all the time with a sly grin as she skips and twirls lazily down the street. (At one point, she drifts past a smiling young man who holds out a bouquet of flowers. That man, pop-pickers, is the sometime jailbird Blake Fielder-Civil, the fellow who would soon otherwise be known as Mr Amy Winehouse. Not exactly a paragon of society, and an ironic, accidentally very appropriate choice of extra for this particular video.)

The video ends with Lily calling her friend (boyfriend?) as she approaches West London's imposing Trellick Tower, but she realises her date is letting her down. The scene changes from a summery, cosmopolitan setting to the reality: grey concrete, abandoned shops, tramps. She stomps off disconsolately, kicking a bin bag as she goes.

After the shoot, an exhausted but happy Lily would sleep for a marathon 18 hours before getting up again, As festival season drew to a close, hangovers faded and Lily's hard-working, muddied ball-gowns were sent to the dry-cleaners. Lily opened up her laptop and read her messages – more and more were from increasingly angry fans, chastising her for not updating her blog or responding to their comments and messages soon enough. It seemed that her dependence on her fans was matched by their dependence on her updates and personal interaction with them. To be fair, life had been busier than ever before, but also her blogs were attracting the attention of the press, who, according to her, would take her comments out of context or twist the meaning of what was meant to just be a space for her personal musings. This was starting to put her off. "I know I've been well slack with blogs recently and I'm sorry," she wrote. "It's mainly cos I'm lazy but also cos I end up seeing bits of it in the papers and it's boring…"

She didn't mind attracting the press when she was on a night out, however: her relationship with the paparazzi remains complex to this day – one minute being matey and cooperative, the next minute kicking at them and swearing – but one former showbiz columnist remembers very well how Lily would be quite tactical in her attempts to have her picture taken for the newspapers.

"Early on, when she was starting to become famous, she announced to paparazzi that she gave the 'best blow job' in London," recalls the columnist. "She's like a child/adult. Very mature in some ways, very intelligent verbally, but also has horrible temper tantrums, she can lash out or get very upset. She flirts with the paps, but sometimes she attacks.

"One night, I remember she was outside a club and she decided to buy all the roses from a rose-seller, and she started throwing them around, giving them to people, just for attention. She was heard saying, "This'll get me in the papers tomorrow.'"

This kind of behaviour isn't unusual, of course, and most celebrities and newspapers have a mutual understanding and a kind of trust.

Cooperation with paparazzi and feeding stories tends to increase, naturally, when something – a film or a record – is about to be released. The days of newspapers relying largely on members of the public phoning in with 'scoops' are dwindling. Stories are often buried, editors can be surprisingly discreet: the relationship between the paper and the star is worth so much more.

Whether or not this was what was happening with Lily (she says she has little time for tabloids and refuses to do interviews with them), she certainly has an innate understanding of how the media works. Unfortunately, she opened the floodgates early with her approachable persona, and as a result paparazzi would overstep the mark frequently until she started to rage and cry. The result, of course, was that the pictures would be sent to tabloids and the captions would claim that she was "crying over lost love" when generally hers were tears of frustration at being hounded and shouted at.

"I remember when I was at the *Sun*, at the showbiz column *Bizarre*," said a former reporter, "and some photos came into the office of her crying. *Bizarre* editor Gordon Smart found out, and he was like, 'We're not going to use these pictures, she's crying, photographers are shouting abuse at her.' That happened all the time. At *OK!* they'll get the photos in and they might print them. But that was a good moral stance, Gordon's." Lily might not believe it, but there are some people within the big, bad press who are looking out for her.

As September edged to a close, Lily prepared for two more months of UK tour dates as her single 'LDN' was released, like a final rush of summer warmth before the nights drew in; the CD single bearing 'Nan, You're A Window Shopper' as a B-side, and the vinyl single boasting 'Knock 'Em Out' on the flip-side. The single entered the UK chart at number 27, peaking at number six. Another hit for Lily. Simon Cowell's *X-Factor* 'stars' such as Chico, Shayne Ward and Leona Lewis (of whom Lily was a fan) might have maintained an iron grip on popular culture but there were enough slits being made in that seemingly impermeable curtain for something truly interesting to shine through, something that didn't involve Mariah Carey-style ululating and sob stories, though when the moment was right Lily was still a great one for reminding us of her childhood adversity.

The rise of the internet was, as Lily had anticipated, causing a seismic shift in how the music industry worked, and this was the year many of the effects could be seen. For a start, artists such as Lily herself and fellow MySpace networker Sandi Thom (of 'I Wish I Was A Punk Rocker With Flowers In My Hair' fame. No, the title didn't make sense to me either) rocketed to fame, and the top of the charts, largely thanks to the web, and downloads had officially taken over – why go to the record shop and trawl through discs when you could access whatever tracks you wanted from your home computer? It was a digital revolution, and artists such as Lily were at the forefront. But while the winds of change ushered in exciting new times and possibilities for artists, it also swept away some valuable pop treasures – the much-loved magazine *Smash Hits*, famous for its irreverent humour but which had admittedly turned in recent years into a magazine aimed at teeny-boppers, ended its 25-year reign in 2006, and we also said farewell to *Top Of The Pops*, a pop-lover's staple since 1964.

Pop music was embracing progress – the future was faster, constantly accessible and online. Magazines like *NME,* the only weekly music paper still standing, stepped up their online content and accepted that print sales were slowly petering out. Being on the cover of *NME* was still a major coup for a new artist, however, and when Lily was told she was not only number three in *NME's* annual 'Cool List', but that a selection of women from the list would be on the front cover in November, just after her final UK gigs of the year at London's Astoria, she was more than a little bit excited, even deciding to put the 'gak' debacle behind her despite having vowed never to work with the weekly again. In her opinion, flagging up a "strong female presence in music" was important enough for her to want to get involved. And, differences aside, she probably quite liked the idea of being on the cover of *NME.*

Alongside fellow 'Cool List' inductees Lovefoxx (from Brazilian group CSS), Yeah Yeah Yeah's Karen O, beret-sporting Long Blondes singer Kate Jackson and list-topper Beth Ditto from Gossip, Lily agreed to pose for a cover-shoot. Nevertheless, why the women had to be separated from the list to be photographed reeked of yet another slightly patronising dimension to this rather sorry tale. Good intentions aside, the message can often appear to be: 'Aren't we subversive supporting, you know, women artists?' Especially when, once the 'women artists' box has been ticked, they are quietly shelved away until another 'female-specific' issue comes around.

When the issue came out, the 'cover shot' was miniaturised and consigned to a small section in the top left-hand corner, to make room for "another fucking Muse cover", as Lily put it. Needless to say, she wasn't happy. And, added to the 'gak' gaffe, this was the *other* reason why Lily refused to speak to the magazine for two years. Lily was beside herself with frustration, and needless to say, an angry blog was not far away.

"I don't like the Cool List and I said this to them in the interview," fumed Lily. "I don't really think the *NME* are in any position to tell us who is cool and who isn't. Personally I don't think a bunch of people sitting in an office drinking tea, inventing musical genres and watching *Nathan Barley* DVDs are leading any kind of cool brigade."

The tagline to the article did not go down well either: "From Beth to Lily to Karen, they've brought new energy to a scene dominated by men. They're also living proof that you can still rock a crowd wearing stilettos."

"How fucking patronising," she raged indirectly at *NME*'s then editor Conor McNicholas. "Is that all we are? Stiletto-wearing people? Don't make me sick, we've always been here, you arrogant prick." That was it, as far as Lily was concerned. Hell would have to freeze over, she insisted, before she worked with *NME* again.

When Lily's heated views made the newsstands, Beth Ditto waded in, keeping her head but agreeing that the move was "another weird, backhanded gesture towards women in the music industry".

As *NME* presumably rubbed its slapped cheek and wondered what it had done wrong, Lily rolled her eyes and carried on working. Almost as soon as her run of UK tour dates had come to a close, she could barely turn around before she was on her sleeper bus once more, on the way to Paris. Lily needed all the energy she could muster but clearly there was someone trying to tell her something about the possibility of 'burn-out': the tour bus actually caught fire while driving through Maidstone in Kent.

It was a full-on fire, not just the sort that can be put out by chucking a damp tea-towel over it, and a fire engine hurtled up to sort it out.

No one was hurt, just a bit shocked and cold, after having to wait for a replacement bus on the hard shoulder of the motorway. The glamour of life on the road…

After a gig in Paris, Amsterdam (plus a bit of obligatory coffee house-sampling) and Switzerland ("well boring" was the summary according to Lily), Tokyo beckoned, and Lily had to endure an unnecessary altercation with a jobsworth airport security guard, who deliberately held her back in the security queue just because she was famous, to "take her down a peg or two" at Heathrow. It drove her to tears of frustration and embarrassment, an occurrence that was becoming less unusual the more famous she became.

At least, when she arrived in Japan, she was welcomed by the sight of her own video playing on billboards in the streets of Tokyo. If that doesn't make you feel at home – being greeted by yourself – it's hard to say what will.

Around the time of her brief Japanese jaunt (during which she could fully indulge her love of dressing up in funny costumes – Elmo, dinosaurs, they had them all) back in the UK her first appearance on TV music quiz *Never Mind The Buzzcocks* was aired.

Lily, sporting geek-chic glasses and a strapless prom dress, sat next to show staple Phill Jupitus (who might have inadvertently influenced her decision to wear glasses: "We look like the Two Ronnies!" she chirruped). She impressed contestants and audience alike with her sharp bratty wit. (When asked, during a clip of Catherine Zeta Jones singing in what looked like, according to Jupitus, the set of the *Antiques Roadshow*, she ventured that Jones might have met her considerably older husband Michael Douglas there.) Lily might have guffawed at her own jokes a fair bit but she was amusing enough to be forgiven.

Only two weeks beforehand, Lily's perceived rival Amy Winehouse had also appeared on the show, beehive wig a-towering, playing up to her role, demanding "another drink" and provoking titters with her proclamation that she'd rather have "cat Aids" than do a duet with her fellow Brit School graduate Katie Melua. Maybe the fact Lily and Amy had plenty in common – an outspoken nature, a gift for writing songs, a snubbing of the mainstream and a certain strength of character and 'no angel' reputation – was what made Lily and Amy's relationship so tricky, like siblings who are too similar. They are distinct enough not to have to see each other as rivals, but there would be occasions when Lily would give reason to believe that she felt insecure on the subject of 'Winehouse', as she would often refer to her.

When she was nice (about Amy), she was very, very nice. She'd often speak out in support of her, even if occasionally it did have a ring of the 'official statement' about it. She made a point of saying she had sent flowers when she heard Amy was going through drug problems. It made sense for them to stand up for each other.

But Lily couldn't resist giving her typically honest slant on Amy, particularly in response to the admittedly somewhat OTT Amy-mania of 2006/7. When asked about her in an interview with *New York* magazine, she responded: "I think she has a cool voice," before adding to this faint praise, "I don't think it's her real voice, though. I'd like to hear her real voice." Lily Allen's own voice might not have been deemed as strident or characterful as Amy's, but it wasn't really like anyone else's.

There was another figure in Lily's life that sparked that sense of competition – her dad, Keith, although she dealt with it with a twinkle in her eye. Most of the time. At least, unlike Amy, he wasn't directly on her patch, but there had been almost relentless mentions of him in all of her press so far. After such a successful year, Lily was already starting to be seen in her own right. But while Keith had shelved his music career to keep out of Lily's way, he was apparently doing a fine job as the evil Sheriff of Nottingham in a new BBC TV series of *Robin Hood* that winter. "Great!" Lily grumpily squeaked while in make-up for yet another shoot. "Now I'll just be 'Keith Allen's daughter' again…"

CHAPTER 10

"My mum, my sister, and my brother all have blonde hair and blue eyes. I'm the only one like this. My sister's tall and beautiful. But I'm talented and rich."

Lily Allen, *New York* magazine.

In the last week of November 2006, after recovering from jet-lag, sleeping off any accumulated hangovers and settling back into London life, Lily was preparing to give a charity performance for Mencap as part of the Little Noise Sessions at the church her parents were married in, for better or worse (but not 'til death do they part). On the 27th, she headed over from her mum's house nearby to the candlelit Union Chapel in Islington – better known as a magical, atmospheric gig venue rather than a place of worship now – and soundchecked, before settling in and getting ready to sing. James Morrison was also performing that night, as were the Automatic (whom Radio 1 DJ Jo Whiley had popped by to watch, even bringing them some extra goodies for their rider, rumour has it. Bit of favouritism there…) and the audience was filling up nicely as the evening wore on.

Whatever Lily did, wherever Lily went, she was almost always guaranteed to grab headlines, but talk of her gig was all over the press the next day for not quite the reasons she'd have hoped.

After a summer of high-profile gigs, Lily was feeling pretty relaxed about performing live, it had become one of her favourite things about her job. As we know, it was not uncommon for her to have a quick drink before the show, and often during. But you don't want to get so relaxed that you find that the words you were about to sing have completely gone out of your mind. Which is what happened to Lily that night when she started to sing her second number, 'Everything's Just Wonderful'.

Confident as Lily perpetually appears it would be easy to assume that she was getting a little complacent, but an audience member admitted she looked dazed, as if the intimacy of the venue and the knowledge of who was in the audience watching (not to mention the fact her parents were there too) had distracted her and made her more nervous than she would normally be.

"Sorry," she shrugged, "I can't remember it. I'll have another go later." An onlooker said she looked "mildly embarrassed but quite jovial", probably the best way to handle every performer's nightmare. Before moving on to the next song in her set, she sent a member of her crew to Google the lyrics. By the time she'd finished her song, a print-out of the words to 'Everything's Just Wonderful' was ready and handed to Lily, who sang the song while clutching the lyrics. Thank God for Google. If that had happened to a pre-Google star, they'd have just had to abandon the song. Not internet queen Lily.

The festive season was fast approaching, and Lily's final single of the year, the plaintive, romantic 'Littlest Things' was scheduled for release soon after her appearance at the Union Chapel. It was the perfect song for a sentimental winter spent snuggling up by the fire. That was something Lily was still quite keen on doing with Seb Chew – nine months after their split and she was no closer to getting over him.

The video to 'Littlest Things', again directed by Nima Nourizadeh, depicts Lily as an Audrey Hepburn-style character (no Nikes in this promo) on a movie set, watching her former self with her ex, her sophisticated retro image juxtaposing with the teenage street-speak and slangy language of the song. The monochrome video was bursting with lonesome metaphor, a piano that plays itself, Lily staring glumly into a mirror as she gets ready for bed, a building that collapses around the lead character, watching herself dancing with an actor who plays her lost love interest in full Forties romantic hero garb.

'Littlest Things' remains one of Lily's favourite videos, even if her handsome dancing partner did apparently loom in for a cheeky snog when he tipped her backwards during the dance. She later admitted that it was "disgusting. And actually he was a bit disgusting". Oh dear.

Fortunately, the song worked like a magic charm on Seb. Lily was back in his arms before the song's release on December 11 because, Lily says, he'd heard 'Littlest Things' and understood it was about him. Who could hear the words, "Dreams, dreams of when we had just started things, dreams of me and you," and not melt? Particularly if the listener knew those words were written for them. It was an incredibly personal song, a direct open love letter to Seb, "I was just so happy in your boxers and your T-shirt… drinking tea in bed, watching DVDs…"

"He must have heard it and realised how special I am," Lily beamingly told an interviewer. "He welcomed me back with open arms." They still had a fiery relationship, but the enforced absences caused by her packed touring schedule at least meant they were arguing less.

'Littlest Things' hit the chart, debuting at number 53 and peaking at 21, her only single that year to miss out on entering the top 20. 'U Killed It' was the CD B-side, and fans who still wanted to buy vinyl were treated to Lily's cover of Keane's 'Everybody's Changing'.

But by the time the single was released, Lily was travelling again, this time to the US, kicking off what would be a characteristically incident-packed December. There'd be tears, there'd be father-figure guitar techs, there'd be madness and missing dogs and Christmas on the beach, but most importantly, after a lonely year despite having "the most friends in Great Britain", there'd be Seb.

After waving her family, Seb and her dog Maggie May goodbye, Lily jetted to the US for gigs in San Francisco, LA and Seattle in the first week of December to promote *Alright, Still,* which would see its US release in the New Year of 2007.

Guitar tech Del 'Strangefish' Greening, who, when not providing succour to Lily, plays with gurning Oi! band Peter & The Test Tube Babies (a founding member no less), was now a mainstay of the Lily Allen tours, and he didn't give her a chance to feel homesick, whisking her to the

Guitar and Amp Center on Sunset Boulevard to choose a guitar for her (she picked a 1972 Fender Telecaster for $6,000). "She is chuffed to bits," reported Del proudly after teaching her a few chords, "(She) has already learned 'Hey Jude'." Always good to start with The Beatles.

No matter what Lily says, she does seem to have a bit of a penchant for impressing and surprising people with her fame and means, particularly when they have already assumed otherwise about her – and this was one of those occasions. "When I came to buy the guitar there was this businessman playing 'Stairway To Heaven'," she later told her friend George Lamb. "He (the manager) was so disinterested in us, I'd come in my tracksuit, and then I just went, 'Excuse me, can I buy this?'" Cue peals of laughter. She loved prodding people's preconceptions and forcing them to reconsider them.

Between the whirl of promotion, not to mention trying to learn more chords and harden up her fingertips, Lily and her crew still found time to do what any self-respecting Los Angeleno would find time for – lazing about in the roof-top pool of their hotel. At least this time Lily managed to extricate herself from her room (and huge TV set) and brave the pool-side – last time she was in LA she couldn't bear the idea of being judged by skinny LA posers – but rather than sit back and relax, she spent half of the time running about like a big kid, and Del, quickly becoming the father figure, got the brunt of her naughtiness. "Went for a relaxing swim…" he blogged. "But got hassled to death by Lily trying to pull my trunks down and pouring lemonade over my head." Touring with Peter & The Test Tube Babies must have seemed like a breeze after putting up with Lily's antics. (Although Del would later admit that Lily was like a punk herself, just born too late – or not as the case may be. We need a few latter-day punks to shake things up a bit.)

Lily clearly had a soft spot for Del. He certainly proved a levelling influence whenever tensions rose or the super-close Lily and Emily, family friend-turned-assistant, had a barney. Lily often liked to share a room with Emily, she wasn't fond of feeling like she was on her own in strange places, but sometimes lack of space and frazzled, tired nerves could take over.

At least she wasn't feverishly trying to write new material for the next album while she promoted *Alright, Still*, as some bands do, possibly as a result of pressure from the record label to "not let the ball drop" after the success of the first release. But Lily consciously was trying to concentrate on one thing at a time, determined to have a break between the promotion of *Alright, Still* and writing her sophomore album. After all, what was so charming and easy to relate to about her first album was how it took the everyday and looked at it close-up, she wanted to write about what was around her and what was happening to her. Not many of Lily's fans would relate so easily to an album written about hotel rooms, tour buses and backstage bars, which was largely what her life was revolving around at that point.

"Because my lyrics are so observational," she explained to Australian site *Musichead*, "I don't think people will be very interested in hearing me singing about the speck on the TV in my hotel room... 'This TV's not big enough!' I'd have to experience real life again. This isn't real life, it's all fake."

Christmas was looming (fortunately Lily had managed to get all of her Christmas shopping done at Macy's in Seattle) and no December would be complete (for some at least) without Jools Holland's *Hootananny* to ring in the New Year with eclectic, contemporary music and the inevitable accompaniment of Jools' boogie-woogie piano. The 2006 *Hootananny*, filmed several weeks in advance of New Year (drunken interjections from well-oiled guests presumably making it too risky to air live), would feature the delights of Lily herself, jetting back for three days of rehearsal and the show itself, performing 'LDN', 'Smile' and 'Friday Night.'

Other artists on the show included close-to-home contemporaries such as Amy Winehouse, singing the reggae classic 'Monkey Man', and The Kooks, as well as Paul Weller, Sam Moore, The Zutons and Madeleine Peyroux.

Lily's sarky wit was as sharp as ever, and despite being a relative newcomer there was no way she was going to be sycophantic or pretend to be "impressed" just to be liked. When Jools sat down for a chat with her in front of the cameras and asked: "So have you seen anything that has inspired you tonight?" Lily retorted: "Not yet!"

After packing a fresh lot of clothes and essentials (and some not so essentials) and placing Maggie May into the care of her dog-walker

Jeremy Goodman, Lily was back at the airport waiting for another plane. But this time she didn't have a band in tow, she didn't have a pang of homesickness in her stomach and she wasn't feeling stressed. This time it was just her and Seb, reunited and on their way to Jamaica for a Christmas of sunshine, sleep, jerk chicken and TLC. The break was just what they needed after so much time apart and they were just starting to fully relax before looking to the year ahead.

Just three days after Christmas Day, Lily received a call from a friend to tell her that Maggie May, her canine companion, had been stolen the day before. Goodman, the dog-walker, had put her in his van in order to take her over to a friend of Lily's, but when he was about to make the journey, he realised that Maggie May was missing, but other, more expensive dogs had been left behind. Maybe she had been taken not by an opportunist, but possibly by someone who knew she was Lily's dog, and knew the value of that.

Lily was torn apart at the news, and felt terrible that she was so far away. Lily was rarely able to walk her dog because of the attention she attracted every time she emerged from her house, but she was devoted to her. Goodman, meanwhile, was beside himself, putting up posters and admitting he felt like he'd "lost a child". Lily blogged about her loss and put up Emily's number in case anyone had any information, before packing immediately, cutting her holiday short to return to London and help look for her. Lily's fans were very moved and supportive, and many vowed to help where they could.

Lily endured a painful New Year, desperate for news about Maggie May, but just after New Year's Day, Emily's mobile phone rang, an unknown number showing up on the screen. Filled with anticipation, Emily answered the phone to hear a woman claiming to have 'found' the dog in Leytonstone, East London, not far from Goodman's home.

Lily and her friends rushed straight over to the address she was given, and it was indeed Maggie, skinny, flea-ridden and "sad", according to Lily. Suspicions were understandably high, especially when the woman who had 'found' Maggie May then tried to sell Lily's friends more puppies, but Lily, simply glad to have her dog back and get out of this strange flat, paid the reward and left the matter in the hands of the police and RSPCA.

"I can't tell you how overjoyed I am to have her back," Lily told her fans on MySpace. Even the fact Maggie May had started chewing on her precious Christian Louboutin heels wasn't a problem. Lily might have preferred it if Maggie May had had a gnaw on her presumably slightly less expensive trainers, but the pooch clearly had more sophisticated taste. Either way, she could chew what she wanted after her ordeal. Lily concentrated on getting her beloved dog healthy again. She also toyed with changing Maggie May's name after hearing that Kerry Katona was thinking of calling her first child the same name. Any association with the one-time Atomic Kitten with a (then) cocaine problem subsidised by appearing on Iceland supermarket commercials was a bit of a no-no for Lily. 'Kerry Katona' had become a byword in Lily's lexicon for cheap, unlovely catering from cut-price supermarkets (such as Iceland) at gigs or shoots.

Lily enjoyed a precious week with Maggie May and her family before preparing to set off to Tokyo once more, then heading to New Zealand and Australia for what would be a very eventful Big Day Out festival. She would also squeeze in another video shoot for her next single – 'Alfie'.

Alfie himself would be played by a puppet, which was a nice touch, but also necessary as Alfie had refused to play himself in the video. The director, Sarah Chatfield, was keen to create a 'Tom & Jerry' feel – the colours were heightened, there was a Disney-esque vibe and initially Sarah wanted Lily's character to be just a pair of legs, like in the vintage cartoons. But Lily was far too photogenic to not feature properly in the promo, and she would be seen bouncing about, having her hair pulled by her malevolent little puppet brother, and wagging her finger at him like a Fifties housewife.

Out of the studio and in the big wide world, Lily was becoming more and more recognizable, and it was around this time that she made the discovery she was finally too famous to step on the London Underground, a seminal moment for any British celebrity.

"I'm a bit haunted by it," shuddered Lily to the *New York Times*. "People started shouting and singing 'Smile' at me and I was in tears: 'Just leave me alone!' People were like, 'What the fuck are you doing on the Tube?' I thought, 'You know what? I'm not going to get on the Tube for a while...'" That's when you know you've made it.

CHAPTER 11

"I bought a key ring shaped like an edamame (soy bean) and a small remote control helicopter, which I now have to carry all around the world, because it won't fit in my suitcase (this place makes you do weird things)…"
Lily Allen on shopping in Tokyo.

Lily prepared for her long trip, unaware even of exactly when she'd be back in London. She and Emily, her Girl Friday – essential in the male world of touring – packed up their favourite TV box-sets and raided the newsagent for magazines to stave off boredom during any downtime on planes and trains, after soundchecks or (preferably) by the pool…

But stocking up on reading material and having a relaxing browse was never just an exercise in switching the Allen brain off – it was actually a slightly sado-masochistic thing to do. After all, she was in most of the publications, and when she wasn't having her music picked over, she was generally having her looks and image scrutinised. And this occasion was no exception.

"As usual I feature in the 'circle of shame' section in *Heat* magazine this week," she wrote in her blog. Appearances in 'hot or not' style features were now the norm for Lily, having her own unique sense of style had made her all the more visible and of interest. But this time she chose to pick up on it, not because she was upset that *Heat* didn't like her dress, but because it was being implied that she was doing something she wasn't. This was something that had become a bit of a craze amid gossip mags, and something that would plague the likes of slightly less than clean-cut celebs such as Kate Moss and Amy Winehouse. Yes, forget up-skirt shots, paps had suddenly become extremely interested in zooming in on certain people's nostrils...

"A lovely paparazzi got down on the floor and took a picture directly up my nose," she fumed. "The caption reads something along the lines of "glow in the dark bogeys". Like everybody else in the world, the inside of my nose consists of some moist matter that might shine when a huge fuck-off camera flash is pointed at it... I wouldn't like to speculate what the magazine in question were trying to insinuate but they were wrong." *Heat* magazine adored Lily Allen as much as the next pop culture publication did; former editor Mark Frith proclaimed her the "best pop star in Britain" no less, but they still weren't above those up-schnoz shots.

After boarding the flight to Tokyo, with Emily in tow, Lily decided to leave her magazines safely in her bag where they couldn't trouble her and sleep the whole way. She'd need to top up on her rest as she'd be performing a gig the day she arrived, but, as she admitted to her fans, it "wasn't great, due to my awful rendition of 'Littlest Things' and jet-lag, but the crowed seemed to enjoy it". She could sleep off her jet-lag the next day though, as she had the day free to relax, but the lure of the exotic shops and sights was too great for anyone to languish in bed.

She snapped up a North Face camouflage jacket for her jaunts to Glastonbury (OK, so maybe not that exotic) and a colourful hoodie. Lily's purchase was almost in protest to the 'fashion blogosphere's' concern about hoodies, presumably because hoodies are now increasingly associated with disaffected kids hanging around the London suburbs with nothing to do. The downside, for a Labour supporter such as Lily, is the prospect of Tory leader David Cameron carrying out his 'Hug-A-Hoodie' campaign... But the possibility of those two sharing an embrace is pretty slim.

After snuggling up at the hotel and relaxing in front of a few episodes *of The West Wing*, Lily set off to soundcheck at the hip Tokyo venue The

Liquid Room in readiness for a typically enthusiastic Japanese audience of Lily fans.

Lily returned to her hotel room after the gig, switched on the TV and fell into bed, still slightly out of sorts from the time difference. She drifted into a jet-lagged sleep but her eyes pinged open at 3am. When she realised she would not be dropping off again any time soon, Lily sat up in bed and turned to that old friend who was always there whatever the hour: her laptop. It had been a while since she'd looked at her official website or checked in on the forum to say hello to the fans, and as a result there was some brewing unrest on there. Her fans were feeling neglected.

Such are the demands made of a thoroughly modern pop star in the age of digital interactivity. Once upon a time the idea of having any contact at all with a favourite pop star was enough to make a fan faint – now, if a celebrity such as Lily, who had set a precedent with her open nature and accessibility, found herself too busy to respond for a while, fans were quick to complain about it...

The following day Lily would head to the shops again and bumped, randomly, into fellow British funsters/pop-challengers Basement Jaxx (with whom she had worked the year before, singing on their track 'Lights Go Down') in the Tokyo version of Woolworths before scurrying back to her *West Wing* box-set. Sound like something's missing? No mention of getting drunk or having a hangover? You'd better believe it. Lily announced to her fans she had "given up booze for 2007", and instead of going out to the pub with her crew, she stayed in and watched Steve Jobs give a presentation on the iPhone. (Yes, a world before iPhones – it seems like such a long time ago.)

Back in Britain, Lily's old acquaintance and admirer Kate Nash was starting to make waves, helped along by the fact that Lily herself had put Kate Nash's MySpace profile in her top friends – something that gave Nash's fan base an inevitable boost and also made the press sit up and notice: if Lily was giving what amounted to a hearty digital thumbs-up to Nash's music – which was an admittedly familiar blend of honest, observational lyrics in an unabashed London accent with quirky tunes (albeit altogether more English and pared back) – then perhaps they should get in there quick and herald her as the next big thing?

After her initial, jagged debut, 'Caroline Is A Victim', Kate Nash did indeed seem to be the perfect successor to Lily Allen; music aside, her bright-eyed, bushy-tailed image was not dissimilar to Lily's at the time (although in latter years she became altogether sleeker and more chic). Vintage-style dresses, an apparent snubbing of mainstream trends, a refreshingly curvaceous figure and very much a style of her own. Kate, like Lily, also loved and respected punk and all that went with it, and was unafraid to swear in her songs. Lily had opened the door for female artists such as Kate − and later Adele − to walk through and plough their own individual furrows, writing their own songs and refusing to do or be what the industry expected of them.

However, predictably, the advent of a star such as Kate meant that, lazily but understandably, she became the "new Lily Allen", which was as reductive to Kate as it was alarming to Lily. Lily herself had only just really started, was she being shoved aside already? Obviously not, but it wasn't a message that either artist would appreciate, even if Kate initially took it as quite a compliment.

"Can everyone please stop calling Kate Nash the new Lily Allen?" Lily blogged testily from Japan. "Kate is a very talented songwriter and her music sounds nothing like mine, she exists in her own right and it must be really annoying for her to be compared to me the whole time."

This might have been Lily also insisting that she wanted to exist in her own right too. She'd spent enough time trying to be appreciated as a separate entity after all the 'dad' references, and she probably didn't want to be shoved into another category − out of the 'famous person's daughter' box and straight into another pigeonhole that lumped her in with other similar artists. If Lily was going to be in a box, it should be her own − there wasn't room for anyone else. And in standing up for Nash, she was also, subliminally or nay, underlining her own stance too. Who could blame her? If the press were going to pick over everything Lily did, and more crucially, everything she wrote in her blog, she might as well use it to assert her own position − she knew she'd be listened to there, she knew they'd be reading.

By January 21, Lily was still booze-free and had reached Australia for the touring Big Day Out festival. Even "boring" sobriety couldn't mar her experience of the festival, which was, she assured fans, "FUCKING AMAZING!!!" The first day of Big Day Out was in idyllic New Zealand, where Lily was treated to some serious hospitality, courtesy of EMI. Glamorous yacht parties, a private beach house… the lot. There was just one thing that was annoying Lily Allen now – the fact that her band and crew were lazing on the beach and chatting up bikini-clad babes. For once, Lily was not Queen Bee – and she had to do something about it. "We hid their clothes in the trees while they were in the water." Didn't they realise that part of the deal for being in Lily Allen's band or crew was that they had to worship her over any other woman? At least some of them did – one journalist observed that there was at least one roadie that would literally bow and scrape with mock-worshipful deference whenever he addressed his mistress, even getting down on one knee. It may have been in jest, but she still loved it and went into peals of girly giggles. And a happy Lily made for a much smoother tour.

Lily was having the time of her life on the festival stages – festivals seemed to be her natural home, and she was enjoying checking out acts such as Muse, Kasabian, Hot Chip and Lupe Fiasco (although offstage the latter was apparently a bit preoccupied with playing Pacman). She also watched the legendary Mancunian punk poet John Cooper Clarke: "He was incredible and I'm trying to convince him to come and support me on my UK tour…"

They certainly had plenty in common – Cooper Clarke took to the BDO stage with a cup of neat Bourbon, raven hair sticking up and gold teeth glinting, chanting his stark but often funny street poetry to a transfixed Antipodean audience. Australian publication *The Age* hailed him as the "spiritual godfather" of The Streets and Lily Allen, and while Cooper Clarke retorted that The Streets' Mike Skinner had probably never heard of him, Lily chipped in to say that not only had she heard of him, she "did a gig with him. I would have been about 13. I was singing backing vocals with Joe Strummer from The Clash, and John Cooper Clarke warmed up doing a poetry thing." But as for a tour together, either she went off the idea or he didn't agree – it didn't happen.

As much as she was enjoying herself, Lily was feeling the strain watching everyone else get drunk while she continued abstaining and took to her bed.

Apparently her self-imposed booze ban wasn't to last much longer, and as if by magic this clean-living, clear-eyed little princess transformed into a lairy ladette. At one of the Big Day Out after-parties, she spotted Chris Cester, the hirsute drummer from the Australian band Jet. Lily remembered the last time she'd seen him – it was in Japan the year before, and he had, in her memory, "snubbed" her. And no one snubs Lily Allen and gets away with it.

Lily brought up the issue with him, addressing him as "arsehole" and making him realise in no uncertain terms the nature of her beef. She also reminded him, as she was often wont to do, that she was far more successful than Jet: "I was like, 'You've had one song on iTunes (advert), let's not get too excited.'"

Cester, in true dismissive rock-star style, disdainfully tossed his cigarette at her. This was, in Lily's eyes, a declaration of war. The red mist descended and Lily drunkenly hurled a bottle at his head (someone caught it) and, as she recalled, "all hell broke loose".

It turned into what one can only imagine was like a *Beano*-style fight, a whirl of arms, fists and legs, only belonging not to Dennis the Menace or the Bash Street Kids but huffy rock stars. Leicester indie kings Kasabian had to wade in and gruffly told Lily to "stop being an idiot". Kasabian were starting to get used to breaking up fights between Lily Allen and other hapless pop stars – on another occasion they had to step in when she launched herself at Mike Skinner: "I can't even remember what it was about. The boys were dragging me off him, saying, 'Stop it, Lily!' They're such a good influence on me," she cooed.

A contrite and no doubt slightly embarrassed Lily later blogged about the Cester debacle, insisting she had no memory of it, and this is simply why she should be kept away from booze.

Unfortunately, the festival organisers' memory of the bust-up was as clear as day, but unlike *T4 On The Beach*, who ordered her home after being "obnoxious" the previous year (admittedly she was a bigger star by now), they were obliged to indulge the situation, prudently moving Jet and Lily Allen's festival trailers away from each other to prevent any further upset. The cooling period seemed to be effective though at least – Cester and Lily made up by the end of the festival, and the rest of Jet, when questioned on this (as they would be, frequently) always insisted it was just between Cester and Lily, not the rest of the band. "It was like a two-day beef," insisted Chris.

Any issue with Jet, resolved or otherwise, would be momentarily forgotten on the 16-hour flight over to Los Angeles, where Lily and her crew would change for another flight (a mere six hours this time) to New York, to record her appearance on *Saturday Night Live*. Half an hour from LAX, however, there was, Del Greening recalled, "a deafening bang". Lily smelt burning and burst into tears, not a fan of flying at the best of times. The plane had been struck by a bolt of lightning.

"It hit one wing, travelled across the plane and left via the other," blogged Del. "A massive wobble and a sudden drop in altitude immediately followed this..."

Del concluded his blog post with the words: "High Point: Narrowly Avoiding Death..." Lily meanwhile "cried all the way to Baggage Claim".

Unfortunately for Lily, the air-travel heart/brain-ache was not over yet. Thanks to the price of fame, Lily found her name was on a security list, which meant she had to undergo a "humiliating security search" courtesy of the less than charming airport security officials every time she flew in the US – which was quite a lot.

Having got used to the harsh unfriendliness of US airports, Lily also struggled to get used to the climate; going from the intense heat of Australia to freezing cold New York, Lily's "body went into shock. I spent the next couple of days sick, and in bed vomiting." As she convalesced in the comfort of her luxurious hotel room at the Soho Grand (her 'neighbours' included fellow *Saturday Night Live* guests Cameron Diaz and Drew Barrymore), preparing to sing on the hugely popular TV show, it also hit home how far she had come, and how fast her ascent had been. "Things started to feel a little Hollywood," she admitted. "It was only last May that I was playing in London at the Notting Hill Arts club to 250 people. Talk about mind fuck..." At least she wasn't having to deal with these staggering transitions by herself – alongside Emily and Del, Seb and Lily's mum, Alison, flew over to New York to proudly watch Lily's appearance, much to her delight. Lily's godmother, Angela McCluskey, was also in New York, and was, by the way, quite stunned by how Lily had already changed from a down-to-earth little girl to, well, a pop star. Lily might like to think she hadn't changed, but how could she not have done after such a stratospheric rise to success and all that comes with it? "Lil's terribly glamorous," McCluskey told *Interview* magazine. "It's hard for me to come to terms with the fact this is our Lil!"

Lily and her band, presented on the show by none other than Drew Barrymore herself, performed a pitch-perfect 'Smile' on a set reminiscent of a train station (and why not?), Lily with a Sixties-style beehive-esque hairdo (don't mention the Winehouse – there are beehives and there are beehives) and a pretty black dress and heels, while her band dressed down in jeans and green t-shirts.

And, as Lily's record label surely anticipated, America well and truly fell for Lily Allen, sending *Alright, Still* rocketing up the iTunes chart to second place, and ensuring that the next day, while perusing the shops, more than a few people stopped her in the street, which was a new experience for her in America at least. Being a celebrity in America was, for Lily, especially enjoyable because she was never judged because of her parentage – no one knew or cared who Keith Allen was.

But before long she'd have to be packing up her bags again, preparing for another gruelling flight back to LA for a show in San Francisco and another string of interviews. Worst of all, this meant saying goodbye to Seb and Alison again after an all too brief encounter.

Lily loved being famous, it was what she had wanted ever since she'd seen how well her dad was treated on shoots when she was a little girl, and since she realised it was the best way to be noticed, listened to, taken seriously. But missing her loved ones was one thing that she could never get used to.

Still, she'd be back soon – temporarily: "I'm coming back for 18 hours next week for the Brit awards," she chirped on her blog, even though she'd seriously considered not bothering turning up for them at all. (Keith talked her into going, and would accompany his daughter up the red carpet on the big night.)

Lily was leading the nominations but since she'd had her fingers burnt after losing out on a Mercury she felt convinced she deserved, she knew not to be too complacent this time. In fact she would claim she "already knew" she would win nothing, and wasn't about to play the game by pretending to be in the dark. Lily remarked to a reporter that the Brits panel are "all industry insiders" connected to Universal; she was on EMI. But Lily would still be the talk of the Brits whether she took a gong away or not.

CHAPTER 12

'She has a public persona that doesn't do her justice.'

George Lamb

'Love and hate' was the theme of the 2007 Brit Awards, and this was nothing short of appropriate as far as Lily was concerned. Her 'love/hate' relationship with Amy Winehouse would be dragged into the spotlight, for one. As she hit the red carpet, looking cute in a green dress with yellow ribbons in her trailing black hair, she dutifully spoke to the reporters outside, attempting to put paid to the supposed 'Amy versus Lily' feud by saying that she hoped Amy would win. (She was up against Amy in both British Female and Best Album categories – and Amy would indeed pick up the Best Female gong. You have to be careful what you wish for.) Amy meanwhile returned the compliment by insisting that she believed that Lily would win. The mutual appreciation society wouldn't last long.

Indeed, Lily had saved any barbs for her label-mate Corinne Bailey Rae, whom she branded "boring", and admitted blankly that The Kooks would almost certainly beat her in the British Breakthrough Act category, which was voted for by the public (or rather, legions of young girls who fancied Luke Pritchard in this case).

"I think they'll walk it," she shrugged. "I hate being in competitions because I never win. When you get nominated it's really nice, but at the same time I'm going to have to put on my, 'Ooh, I'm really happy Corinne won,' face, I know I am.'" Neither Corinne nor Kooks would win (The Fratellis bagged the Breakthrough gong), but crucially, neither would Lily. Not winning competitions or awards was a big thing for her, she'd talk about it frequently in subsequent interviews and made no attempt to hide her disappointment. While these were all things other artists might have felt but tried to hide beneath a gleaming celebrity smile, Lily was nothing if not honest, heart very much pinned to sleeve.

Lily's fellow caners Oasis performed on the Hate stage that night, and they whisked Lily off on a bender afterwards – Liam and Lily doing their best cartoon snarls to the cameras on their way to the Cuckoo Club in Mayfair to celebrate Oasis' win of the Outstanding Achievement Award (they're an excellent Beatles tribute band, it has to be said). The party was a very exclusive one: Noel Gallagher personally vetted everyone who wanted to get in – James Morrison, Badly Drawn Boy and even national treasure Suggs were turned away.

There were so many photographers surrounding the club that, when Lily emerged into the flash-bulb-pricked darkness, she couldn't find her own car for ages. Police were called because of an impending crush, cars were getting scratched, Liam drew on a pap's lens with a marker and Lily allegedly threatened a snapper with her stiletto. So, Brit or no Brit, guess who took up plenty of column inches the next day?

Amy Winehouse might have been crowned Best British Female, but Lily certainly had the last laugh: for the rest of the week the newspapers were ablaze with speculation on why she had been so royally snubbed. Winehouse was becoming increasingly irked because every time she was interviewed she was asked about her thoughts on Lily. At one point, she finally snapped, reportedly shouting at a journalist: "I don't want to talk about that little prick. I laughed when I saw how fat she'd got." Lily more subtly showed concern for Amy's "need to be famous". In a way, Lily had won after all when it came to attention and public/media support.

"'Outrage!!!'" screamed the American showbiz blogger Perez Hilton (when he still liked her). "The only way to take that is as personal snub or some vendetta. Better than any Brit award though, Lily is 'making it' in America, achieving that rare crossover success that many UK artists unsuccessfully strive for." This is an honour Perez has since rescinded, lavishing it upon Winehouse, somewhat strategically, instead.

Ever since Lily had played a small, star-studded gig at LA's Troubadour in October 2006 (to an audience that included Gwen Stefani, Orlando Bloom and Sean Lennon), America had been desperate to get their hands on *Alright, Still*, which was released there in January 2007. Out of all the critics, Perez Hilton was the most gushing. And yet, as we know, there is a thin line between love and hate, and like many figures in Lily's life that had admired her, he would become a sometime enemy, "an irritating wasp in the beautiful rose garden that is my life", said Lily, rather amusingly, to *Billboard*.

Lily didn't want to change for America, and that may be partly why Perez has since turned against her. Her penchant for booze has prompted him to label her a 'trainwreck', 'Silly Allen' etc, but Lily wants to be free to say that she 'drinks, smokes, gives her boyfriend blow jobs occasionally'...

Back in Blighty, the press attention surrounding Lily's 'Brits snub' was starting to pall. Lily was having to put up with constant claims that there was supposed to have been a 'slagging match' between herself and Amy, particularly when paparazzi shots of Lily sobbing outside her flat the day after the Brits were printed in the red-tops. Lily hotly denied it... (although she would insinuate later that they *did* have a beef).

Lily had to fly straight out to Washington the morning after the Brits, followed all the way to Heathrow by the paparazzi, and it was only when she reached her hotel and settled in that she opened an email from her record company about the post-awards debacle, 'crying' pictures and reported brawl with Winehouse.

She later clarified: "The pictures of me crying in the papers were taken when I was saying goodbye to my boyfriend who I haven't seen much of recently. I've been working really hard and travelling a lot and I only got to see him at the Brits, so the tears were just because I was leaving to get on yet another plane."

But Amy and Lily were too similar in their sensibilities to really get on, and it didn't help when they were pitted against each other by the press. It must have been truly irritating when journalists and uninformed bloggers accused Lily of 'doing a Winehouse' when she tumbled out of the Groucho – they should have known that having a drink or five was in her DNA, it didn't have anything to do with trying to "compete" with Amy Winehouse. But the crux of it was that there simply didn't seem to be room in the media's opinion for more than one woman who behaved like that.

Although, according to Lily, her own booziness was dwindling. She'd reached a peak and now was starting to think about her health, supposedly. "I have had my days of going out and getting trashed but I really don't any more," she told *Entertainment Weekly*, somewhat unconvincingly. Famous last words.

Understandably, thanks to her unique style and natural love of playing around with fashion and colour, Lily would frequently grace 'best-dressed lists' (and, implausibly, she would 'win' an *NME* Worst Dressed award this year too, probably as a two-fingers in response to Lily's anger towards them). To many people's surprise, she would even become the darling of Chanel's Karl Lagerfeld no less... a man famous for being rather snooty about women-shaped women (in 2009 he would say that "no one wants to see curvy models". Nice!). Funnily enough, at this point it was Lagerfeld who had to convert Lily, not the other way around, as she admitted she'd previously thought Chanel was a bit of an old ladies' label.

After being wooed by Lagerfeld and taken around Madame Chanel's shrine-like apartment, it soon became her "favourite label in the world". She'd soon be seen wearing Chanel at her own shows, and she'd increasingly be seen on the front row at catwalk shows sitting between the likes of Kanye West, Katie Holmes, Victoria Beckham... "I still sort of see myself as this kind of naff person no one like them would want to get involved with. A kind of Kerry Katona type," she'd say, unable to believe her own luck. But increasingly, Lily would get used to being part of the jet set that she previously snubbed, albeit keeping at least one foot firmly on the ground.

But no more would we see those 'Argos-chic' earrings (a nod to her Romany ancestry on her paternal grandmother's side), even the trainers would eventually be phased out and a new, lady-like Lily – generally in vertiginous heels – would totter to the fore.

Knowing that Lily was invited to the best parties, all the awards shows and was appearing frequently on TV, designers galore would send her bagfuls of clothes for free in a bid to have their togs seen on everyone's favourite fashion icon (a title she always refused to accept) but, gorgeous as they were, Lily would have to donate the clothes or (look away now, fashionistas) throw them away because everything they sent was "tiny".

No surprise then that the next step would be a fashion range with Lily's name on it that would cater for women who were bigger than size 10.

Lily signed a £250,000 deal to design a collection called 'Lily Loves' for the UK high-street chain New Look: six dresses, some jewellery and trainers. The collection would be launched in stores across the UK as well as in France, Dubai and Belgium in May. "I did them for a reason," she said. "I was a bit larger than some people, I suppose, and I found it difficult to go into shops and find things that would fit me properly, so I wanted to make clothes that suited every kind of body shape, that was the idea."

It was a good time for celebrity high-street collections – Madonna launched her 'M' collection for H&M and Allen family friend Kate 'the Mossette' Moss at Topshop. Again, Lily took a somewhat competitive stance, forgetting what she had often said previously about not being a role model: "I like what New Look are doing and I like what they are about... they have responsible role models like me and Drew Barrymore and they're very conscious of having positive body images and promoting positive women. Unlike Kate Moss and that fucking billionaire (Sir Philip Green) who's thrown a load of money at her so we get to see what her wardrobe is like. It's madness."

Lily had previously said she "only has nice things to say" about Kate Moss, because she had once saved her from being beaten up at Glastonbury Festival some years before. "These girls were beating me up and she was the only person who stood in and said, 'Leave her alone, you're being bullies,'" she said during an interview with *This Morning*. "They stabbed me in the ear with a beer can," (rather reminiscent of a jokey jibe she had made about Peaches Geldof), "and cut my ear open, I also had two black eyes – it was a bit of a nightmare! It was just girls being girls. I think one of them thought that I was sleeping with her boyfriend, which I wasn't..."

But despite her friendship with Moss as a result, there was always a bit of tongue-in-cheek rivalry and teasing – high-street collections aside, she branded her one-time saviour a "fucking clotheshorse" in an interview with *Marie Claire,* and chastised the paparazzi outside the Groucho one night, after learning they were waiting for Kate to emerge: "Come on, who gives a fuck about The Mossette, anyway, seriously? Please promise me when Kate comes out you won't take pictures of her. It would really piss her off and be really funny. I'll pay you all £1,000..."

While Lily might have been occasionally dismissive, she did love fashion and enjoyed being wooed by the world of couture – she was a sartorial inspiration to many anyway. She already had one *Vogue* cover-shoot under her belt and by March would be in Paris for a photo-shoot with Stella McCartney during Fashion Week. But she'd soon be kicking herself that she wasn't at home – while in Paris, it would be her family, not her, who would make the news. Namely Alfie and Alison.

Alfie's behaviour had been spiralling, he could lapse into violence, and this time a row with his mother had escalated at home in Islington, resulting in Alison reportedly sustaining a minor head wound. Alison had called the police in a moment of panic.

Lily was devastated when she heard about the ruck, and was quick to defuse the situation in the press, so that the Allens could be allowed the space they needed without further intrusion. "I love my family and I wish I had been there to help calm this situation down," she said in a statement. "I have spoken to my mum and everything is fine now."

After this upsetting news, Lily, relieved to hear her family were getting back on track, had some bridge-building of her own to complete. After her Paris jaunt, she flew to Austin, Texas, for the new music-lovers' staple festival, South By South West, where she was part of a killer line-up that included fellow West Londoners The Good, The Bad and The Queen (Damon Albarn's supergroup with The Clash's Paul Simonon and the legendary Afro-beat drummer Tony Allen), Gossip, MIA collaborator Diplo, Lethal Bizzle and a raft of exciting new talent from around the world. There was more seasoned talent too – The

Who's iconic guitarist Pete Townshend even made an appearance. It was a dream line-up, and one that held plenty of interest for Lily. And it was fair to say, Lily herself was a hit. SXSW Creative Director Brent Gulke was impressed not just by her music but what she symbolised: "Young women view her as powerful and as someone in control of her destiny." This was certainly reflected by the seemingly endless queues leading to Lily's appearances.

Another British artist gracing the bill was Amy Winehouse, and it seemed right after the Brits debacle that they should try to bury their grievances. They were bound together – in reviews at least: both female, both British, both feisty, they were destined, or doomed, to be lumped in together, so they may as well stick together. Or at least try. Lily titillated her fans – and the press – by declaring on her blog: "Me and the Winehouse have made up, we're now lesbian lovers." At least that might mean the media would stop pitting them against each other for a while.

No, the media would be far too busy making a meal out of a rather unfortunate remark Lily made at the festival, which she made, she insists, under the influence of booze.

"It's all very weird here," she blurted while talking to a reporter. "They're all backward in Texas but not as much as they are in Arkansas or Wyoming, where I'm going soon. I can't really speak for the American population, I'm so far away from anything they are and stand for." The good people of Arkansas and Wyoming must have been looking forward to her visit… Needless to say, news of her American slur spread like wildfire. The internet helped to make her, but the internet would so often bite her in the backside too.

"The blogosphere is going crazy right now," she later said in her own blog. "Apparently I said that all Americans are backwards… I don't actually remember saying these things… I must have been very drunk and showing off…"

SXSW was also where Lily chose to reaffirm her hatred of *NME* after feeling so let down by them (unfortunately they were also the co-promoters of the show). "Everyone at *NME* can fuck off!" she proclaimed on stage, before claiming that one reporter had 'the smallest penis' she had ever seen. (She obviously didn't care what people thought of the idea that she had supposedly slept with journalists.) Before leaving the stage she added: "I just want to say once again how much I hate *NME*." Things would eventually change, not least because *NME* now has a female editor in Krissi Murison, who would ensure no such snubs would ever occur again. But back in 2007, Lily was still smarting.

It was difficult for Lily to throw things off, understandably; she had worked hard to get where she was, and often felt alone no matter how many people surrounded her – they couldn't create a barrier between her and the media or 'blogosphere', and she admitted that there were times she would pore over online entries and posts about her on the internet, and defend herself (incognito, of course), pretending to be someone else and hitting back: "Have you ever stopped to think how hard her life must be?..."

The other difficulty was the more she put into her online interactivity, the more she got out – and that could be negative as well as positive, particularly as her fame was growing. Writing her blogs used to be one of her favourite things to do, the perfect way to unwind and empty her head, with the added bonus of adoring fans writing back. But things had changed. "It can be so quick and so vicious," she said in an interview. "There's so much information, I've got to stop Googling myself because as far as I'm concerned everyone in the world hates me now. With blogs it's not as easy to sue as it is a multi-national corporation.... There are lies and rumours that can be started in the blogs, and the papers pick up on them."

Part of the problem lay with her lifestyle, and that old favourite theme, her family. What the media, and sniping fans, couldn't seem to grasp was that her upbringing was simply very different from that of most other people. She wasn't trying to be something she wasn't, but many people took exception to the mere fact that her life was naturally quite glamorous.

"I get slagged off for going to premieres and showbiz parties," she told *Word*'s Rob Fitzpatrick, "but my mum's a film producer and my dad's an actor! Those parties are where my family are. It would be more weird if I didn't go, wouldn't it? I know I've been dealt very strange cards. But this is me. This is what I was born into."

At least she wasn't holding back on her cheeky humour. During a radio appearance on the 'Love Line' show with Dr Drew and Stryker, Lily was typically outrageous, asking if men could give themselves a blow job, would they? The presenters said that they would. Lily responded by musing that she'd be too lazy to risk hurting her neck by giving herself oral sex, before changing the subject and deadpanning that she'd only agreed to appear on the show because she thought she'd be meeting Dr Dre, as opposed to Dr Drew…

After the whirlwind of SXSW had calmed and Lily was able to take stock, she wrote a blog post, but it was not what they, or she, would have hoped for. She seemed to be steeped in ennui, questioning the intensity of her lifestyle and whether there was a point in all the hard work she was doing.

"I haven't really had much to say, I still don't," she wrote listlessly. "I've started to feel it's my duty to write blogs, I didn't feel that before."

Lily was starting to ponder on whether she really cared about "cracking America" – did she really have to go through the motions for months on end? Could she not have just stayed in England and spent more time with her boyfriend? It was clear which choice she would have taken, if it was up to her. Lily wasn't trying to snub her fans, and she was careful to point that out – if there was one thing Lily had learned, it was that she had to be super-clear what she meant to minimise any misunderstandings or backlash.

"It's the songs," she admitted. "I'm bored. Since January I've toured Japan, New Zealand and Australia, I've done a European tour, gone to Paris Fashion Week, done a UK tour, spent one night at home, apparently I beat up some paparazzi (after the Brits), and now I'm on a US tour. It goes till May. I dunno what to do."

For most people, it would be hard to see how such a lifestyle could be "boring", but this was clearly too much of a good thing. Lily was missing home, missing Seb, missing the opportunity to do what now seemed like the ultimate luxury – nothing. It had come to the point that even reading texts or posts by friends who were doing no more than hanging out in the park eating a pie would bring Lily to tears.

But there was no time to feel sorry for herself. Lily had a run of American dates to honour, and her touring 'family' would have to fill the gap while she pined for London and Alison's roast dinners, Seb's cuddles and little Maggie May's friendly biting. Lily would be thinking of them all the time, and she proved that by buying mountains of presents for her family as she made her way around the States. Maggie May, for example, would soon be the proud owner of a canine wedding dress, bought by Lily at a 'gay pet store' in Miami...

CHAPTER 13

"So much is written about you, and you look at it all with these photographs, and you think: 'Everyone must think I'm a total twat.' Suddenly I'm this cartoon of a party girl. If I didn't know me I'd think I was a twat, too."

Lily Allen

For all Lily's momentary lamentations and homesickness, she and her entourage certainly knew how to have fun on the road, and it wasn't all going out and getting drunk, although there was plenty of that too. Most of the time they were like a bunch of big kids, buying toys and trainers, dressing up as animals, going bowling, having Easter egg hunts and, while in Mexico at the end of March 2007, getting kitted out in wrestling gear, even wearing their colourful masks in departure lounges.

Mexico was a trip – the first night they were there, Lily generously took everyone out for a meal, and they all knocked back frozen margaritas as if they were going out of fashion. (They'd regret this – the ice was bad and everyone spent the night clutching their stomachs in pain.)

Tummy troubles aside, the show went well, 2,000 good-natured Mexican fans packed the venue and Lily was lifted up by their good vibes. The following day, complete with a monster hangover, Lily was up at the crack of dawn, as she was scheduled to appear on MTV

Latin America programme *Turismo*. It was worth the somewhat painful early start. MTV Latin America treated them well, drove them around to show them the sights, and tried to persuade them to sample some local delicacies, such as ants' eggs and grasshoppers. Lily wasn't too impressed.

That night at the hotel, just as everyone was ready to hit the sack, Lily spotted a bunch of pro-wrestlers "on their way back from *Friday Night Smackdown* in the elevator", according to the ever-watchful Del. "Lily invited them back to her room for a party but they didn't show. Thank God! I didn't fancy throwing them out at 5 in the morning…" Undoubtedly they would have been intimidated by the pictures of Lily and her mates in *their* wrestling masks that she had posted up on her blog…

Onstage, Lily was her usual outspoken self – it wasn't unusual for her to muse, beer in hand, on the unfortunate reality of men with small penises (generally as a lead-in to her song 'Not Big'), or make a spiky, topical retort on something that had been bothering her, but America was still feeling sensitive after the "backwards" comment she had made at SXSW, and wasn't ready for her to air her views on its then president, George W Bush.

Headlines were inevitably grabbed by Lily after she branded Bush an "arsehole and a cunt". To balance out her attack, she did at least call the then UK Prime Minister Tony Blair a "cunt's bitch". Nobody was safe.

As if that wasn't enough to ensure she was in the newspapers, bringing hoity-toity US housewives and moralistic types out in hives across the Bible Belt, she declared herself "probably bisexual" and praised San Diego's "crack-whores". (San Diego was, of course, where Lily found herself enjoying some sapphic attention. "I did once snog these identical twins in San Diego," she told *Diva*. "I was on the sofa and I had them both. I was dancing and shoving my arse on one of them and one on my front bottom. My assistant has got the picture." Quite a busy trip then.)

A fan at the concert told *The Sun* that the audience "went a bit quiet"… They were also nonplussed when she admitted she was bored of her usual setlist, and treated them to Keane and Blondie covers instead.

Montreal and Toronto beckoned (Toronto being her "first sober gig since January"), before another run of shows on America's East Coast and a gig in LA before band and crew – and Lily – took a well-earned holiday before things kicked off again in May.

Unfortunately, despite Lily's insistence that Amy Winehouse and she were friends, many of her interviews were spent fielding questions about her prickly relationship with the *Back To Black* singer. She kept her dignity with regard to the subject, which was not her favourite, but tried once again to set things straight in her blog. "Why do people always try and play women off against each other the whole time?... Why don't they try and create a feud between me and James Morrison or Amy and Paulo Nutini? Or why not create a rivalry between the boys?" While we've come a long way, this inherently chauvinistic bear-baiting still seems to be boringly rife.

Whether with the Amy issue or preconceptions about her family, Lily knew how to handle the media, and generally used humour to dissipate any silliness. Lily was getting exhausted, the constant travelling and drinking was starting to take its toll on her immune system – and her performances – and she decided to pull out of many of her American dates in May and June. She didn't want her fans to pay good money to see a below-par Lily.

Lily was also careful to blast apart any false reports before they had even been printed: "I am not falling apart at the seams, I am not suffering with exhaustion, I am not pregnant, and I am not going to rehab..."

Being in LA had given Lily the opportunity to hook up with the producer Greg Kurstin again, who had worked on several tracks on *Alright, Still*. Greg and Lily worked well together, and despite speculation that Lily would team up with Mark Ronson for her next album, there was only really one man Lily wanted for the job. It was still early days, but Lily had Kurstin earmarked for what would be a very different album from her first opus. Not that there was much time to talk about it yet. Lily had to jet back to London because it was finally time to launch her 'Lily Loves' clothing range for New Look on Oxford Street.

Everyone was there from her tour, from her Man Friday Del, to Darren and Tunde, the management, the crew, people from the record label and of course, Keith Allen would accompany his little girl on her big night. Allen's pal Lisa Moorish and the TV presenter Fearne Cotton were also in attendance, and the paparazzi were out in slightly alarming force but that was the idea – all the more exposure for New Look.

It was a full-on evening and Lily was almost too busy to speak to the 'family' who were on tour with her, not least because a real member of her family, namely Keith, nearly didn't make it to the evening at all. Keith made his way to the wrong branch of New Look – one that had been destroyed by fire. He simply thought it was a nifty, subversive look and hung around, waiting for everyone else to turn up.

"When he got there he thought it was a publicity stunt. He thought it looked amazing because they'd burnt it all out!" laughed Lily. "I had to phone him and tell him he was at the wrong place…"

Lily looked a picture as she posed in a floral prom-dress from her collection alongside Keith (after he finally arrived), and, after her earlier comments on Madonna and Kate Moss, the press were keen for a typically acid quote from her on her older 'rivals'' high-street collections. But Lily was having none of it. "I don't see any point in comparing these things," she said. "I did not go into music to compare myself to other artists… it's a bit boring really. We are just women and trying to get on with our lives. They are both totally different women and have totally different fan bases to me. Kate Moss is a model for God's sake.

"Of course they are going to sell more than I do – they are massive international names. I do not see it as a competition." Which was probably the wisest thing to say – tabloids and tabloid readers tend to make their own minds up regardless of what the celebrity says, but she may as well present a gracious front. And tonight was her night, she wanted to celebrate, not simmer in pointless resentments.

After performing a brief set at the launch, Lily slunk off and changed into another dress from her collection – 'the graffiti dress' – straightened her black-lace fascinator that was positioned prettily in her hair and prepared for a night at the Groucho. She'd been away too long, and the Groucho was a home from home. She'd be back on a plane before she could turn around, so she might as well make the most of a big night in London before heading back to the States.

Lily was now so used to flying back and forth to the US that she could almost do it in her sleep, and probably occasionally felt as if she *was* doing it in her sleep. She was also unfortunately used to being stopped by security every time she wanted to fly in the US. But she wasn't prepared for what was around the corner. Safe to say, it sounded as if certain authorities had been reading a few too many sensationalised reports on Lily Allen, and were basing their prejudice of her on those. Despite Lily insisting she had not even been charged or arrested in conjunction with the accusations that would be levelled against her, US passport control were only too happy to haul her aside.

After landing in Seattle three days after the 'Lily Loves' launch, Lily logged on to MySpace and fumed: "Today I was at passport control where I was sent to an interrogation room for questioning... A few weeks ago I allegedly hit a photographer. According to the newspapers, I have been sent a letter by the police asking me to report to the police station to face questions in relation to this incident.

"I have not received any letter and I have not had any contact with the police, so it seemed odd to me that the United States Citizenship & Immigration services should have access to such information before even I have been notified of these charges or enquiries... I doubt that a United States Government agency would use unreliable sources such as Wikipedia or Google news quoting tabloid gossip and lies as factual evidence, would they?"

Who could say, but this unwelcome jolt at customs would not be her last, and she was already feeling fragile. That night in her hotel room in Seattle, on May 13, Lily wrote a blog that few of her fans could forget, and it exposed her true feelings of insecurity next to her contemporaries – one in particular – and even sadder, showed that despite her strength and individuality, she had been worn down by the media's obsession with image and had started to wallow in self-pity, taking her blues to her fans, whom she could always rely on for support. Having had a chance to take stock, hearing insults across the media about her, particularly Cheryl Tweedy's "chick with a dick" remark, had genuinely hurt Lily. And to make matters worse, seeing pictures of herself launching 'Lily Loves' in the paper, especially as many papers had positioned a picture of Lily next to Kate Moss, made Lily feel "grotesque".

For some unknown reason, someone had also sent Lily a link to a blog on which there were images of her, under which were reams of comments by kids with nothing better to do, insulting Lily and saying how much better they thought Amy Winehouse was. They do say there is a special place in hell reserved for 'friends' who pass on the mean things others might have said about you. Lily was already feeling raw and tired, she's emotional at the best of times, and finally she caved in to feeling truly low.

"Fat, ugly and shitter than Winehouse," was the title of this post. "I used to pride myself on being strong-minded and not being some stupid girl obsessed with the way I look... I'm afraid I am not strong and have fallen victim to the evil machine... I have spent the past hour researching gastric bypass surgery, and laser liposuction."

Of course, plenty of fans wrote straight back, some duly dishing out the compliments, some telling her to pull herself together and cut out the self-pity. Either way, it caused a stir, and even had the world press concerned (they all picked up on it as a handy story, anyway).

Self-pitying or not, it's tragic when a seemingly immune, refreshingly confident woman falls prey to this. Once any blithe happiness in her own skin has been destabilised, it is very difficult to set things back on track. (It would always be different for men, but in support, Lily's loyal pal Del put up his own humorous blog post, proclaiming himself: "Fat, Ugly, but Fitter than Vegas and Jupitus.")

Fortunately, and only by the following day, Lily had the fight back in her. Maybe it was the wave of immediate support, maybe it was how harsh those words looked on the page, or perhaps just that, in the cold light of day, some things were just clearly more important, and the fact many people loved Lily was because she gave two fingers to body fascism. Whatever it was, the old Lily was thankfully back and feeling strong, not least because her mum had jumped on a plane to be with her daughter after learning about how unhappy she was feeling.

So what about the liposuction, the gastric bypasses? All but forgotten. "Instead I will be eating lots of bread and pasta and thinking about what to write about for the next album."

She must have been feeling better, because instead of feeling cowed by Cheryl's bitchiness in return for misunderstanding Lily's lyrics to 'Cheryl Tweedy', she added: "Cheryl, if you're reading this, I may not be as pretty as you but at least I write and SING my own songs without the aid of auto-tune. I must say taking your clothes off, doing sexy dancing and marrying a rich footballer must be very gratifying. Your mother must be so proud, stupid bitch."

Yes, Lily was definitely, defiantly back. And this was war. Even if Cheryl hadn't read Lily's blog herself, the press would waste no time in letting the Girls Aloud singer know about it and push her for a response. And a response she gave.

"She should keep her mouth shut instead of feeling sorry for herself," she said. "I left school a long time ago and I have no time for this."

And about the 'auto-tune' slight? "I'm currently on a big arena tour with the girls, singing live each night," Cheryl countered. "Lily, I could find you a ticket if you'd like to experience a live arena tour, as it's the closest you'll get." For two people who had, up to this point, never met, there certainly was plenty of bad blood. But whether or not it affected her, Lily did her best impression of someone who didn't give a toss.

"Cheryl-gate was fun," she shrugged, like an imperious cat that had become bored of playing with a ball of string. "But we have moved on..."

Was that the royal 'we'? Maybe, and she had the right to use it. Because when it came to British pop, Lily *was* Queen, after all.

CHAPTER 14

George Lamb: "Mark Ronson said: 'There are three Lilys. The first one is the sweet, cool friend, second Lily is the genius in the studio, third Lily the outspoken starlet."

Lily Allen: *"There's definitely more Lilys…"*

Not only was Lily queen of British pop, she was also, in many people's eyes, the queen of summer – that sunshine sound of 'Smile' and 'LDN' from the year before was etched firmly on everyone's memories, associating Lily forever with the sunniest time of year. You didn't have to call yourself a Lily Allen fan to somehow feel, once the sun shone down on the city pavements, as if you wanted to inexplicably start slow-skipping through the urban sprawl in a ballroom gown and Nikes (easier for women to fulfil this fantasy than men, admittedly) and maybe, in a reference to the original 'LDN' promo, hug a few policemen. OK, maybe that's going too far.

But whatever that Lily Allen summer sound made you feel like doing, it was here again, May was turning into June and 'Smile' was back in force on the radio playlists, booming out of car windows in bank holiday traffic jams, beaming out tinnily from other people's iPod earphones on trains, tubes, buses… and if that wasn't enough, thousands of girls all over the UK were freshly made-over Lily-style in dresses and jewellery from New Look's 'Lily Loves' collection.

Yes, British summertime, Lily-style, was back. There was just one thing missing: Lily Allen herself, who was still in America – away from her family, but also away from those boring, constant references to her dad from media and fans alike.

Every day for Lily was packed with memorable incident, she played a show at the Wiltern in LA, joined by The Specials' guitarist Lynval Golding, which thrilled both audience and Lily alike, and then she, Emily and the DJ Aaron La Crate, who had been accompanying Lily on her shows in support slots, went to a Chanel catwalk show.

After the show, Lily, Emily and Aaron headed down to a glamorous club called Les Deux, where they would get another taste of Hollywood hierarchy: "It was really fun until Lindsay Lohan arrived and had us thrown off our table…"

It's amusing to think that fairly soon Lily and Lindsay would be the best of friends, even getting matching tattoos. The fickle finger of fame/friendship…

Lily and co then jetted across to the East Coast for an interview with heavyweight US music magazine *Rolling Stone*, before, according to the lady herself, getting a manicure. Yes, Lily Allen getting a manicure. Seems a bit unlikely, but the 'fuck you' image was having its rough edges sanded off slowly but surely. Nikes were often replaced by heels, hair extensions would be fixed into her existing barnet, yes, Lily was becoming a bit more of a lady all the time. Her language might not reflect that, but she was starting to enjoy the trappings of being a groomed, gorgeous pop star.

After getting her nails done, Lily headed off to meet the new wave queen herself, Debbie Harry, and the rest of Blondie (who probably didn't mind what state Lily's nails would have been in anyway). The pair were preparing to sing a rendition of Blondie's hit 'Heart Of Glass' on the *Today Show* early the next morning.

Lily was terrified of meeting the group she had long admired, and convinced herself they were probably only agreeing to work with Lily because their record label had pressured them into it. But they did their best to make Lily feel welcome and the experience was an unforgettable one.

Lily loved keeping her fans informed of her progress and what she was up to – and it helped her to remember the details of all of the exciting things she was doing; life was moving at such a rapid-fire pace, she didn't want to forget any of it. But her every move was also being charted by the media, and the fact she kept offering information up in her blog, which was in the public domain, meant it was of constant fascination to them. This was useful if she wanted to get a message across, but it wasn't good news if they simply ended up twisting everything she wrote. On June 14, she glumly wrote that she would not be posting so many updates onto her blog.

"The tabloid fucks have ruined it," she wrote. "Everything I write here gets twisted and rewritten by a bunch of lazy fucks who haven't got anything better to write about.

"The world is MELTING, we are KILLING innocent people so we can steal their oil," she continued. "But then again Lindsay did work out at the gym this afternoon and that's what really counts." She had a point, even if she was fighting a losing battle.

But this was all part of Lily's contradictory nature. She might have insisted she didn't want to be a star on one day, but then she would goad the paparazzi and go to Nobu, the Groucho, chat with snappers, some might say encouraging them. She would dismiss award ceremonies as back-slapping industry nonsense one minute, and then would lapse into protracted sulks when she didn't win a prize. Lily might be seen to be fighting for her privacy on one hand, but then she would appear on the TV comedy quiz show *The Friday Night Project* and display her 'third nipple'. Then, when subsequent questions in future interviews arose about this curious asset of hers, she would often sigh and become huffy. But what did she expect? Had she been acting on impulse or was it strategic? It was confusing for all concerned to say the least.

While her blogging might have subsided slightly, a chance to glimpse the "real" Lily was granted to fans when her old manager and friend George Lamb, at this stage an eye-candy presenter on T4, made a documentary series for the weekend pop show entitled *Still Alright?*

George had flown out to LA to be with Lily and make the show, and it was intriguing and poignant to see how this big brother figure to Lily responded to the new, starrier version of his former charge. The hook of the programme was that he would be seeing if she had "changed", and to be honest, seeing how he looked at Lily with tender fascination and a tinge of sadness, almost, showed that in some ways she almost certainly had. Who wouldn't have done in such strange circumstances? One thing hasn't changed though – she still has an old head on young shoulders.

The show is revealing and Lily, to her credit, put on no airs and graces. We see her swing from stroppy and exhausted as her dressing room was being shaken during a booming soundcheck, up at the crack of dawn, busy and preoccupied at a photo-shoot for *Elle* at the Chelsea Hotel, then playful and girlish with her crew, outspoken, emotional, even chilly… there was no PR front.

By this stage, Lily had been on tour for a year, having flown back for just one night for the Brits before flying back out again. Lamb observed carefully after a prickly interchange: "She's exhausted and not overly enamoured of life on the road."

"I came back for one night, didn't win anything and then went back on tour," Lily told him, still sore and not afraid to show it, and also displaying the side of her that did indeed want to be a celebrity with all the trimmings, no matter what she'd said in her blog. "I went into this industry because I wanted to be a bit of a pop star, what's the point of being a pop star if you can't walk down the red carpet? I'd never walked down a red carpet and I was nominated for four Brit awards, I knew when I turned up all those cameras were going to flash and I was quite excited about it."

Lily then tells George that Seb has come over to be with her for a while. Lamb offers her a lift, but she replies, surely with her tongue in her cheek, "Er, I think I'd rather have a driver…" Know your place, Lamb!

Lily would later tell Lamb that she "isn't in it for the money", before getting the car to stop at Prada as she has to pick up a dress "real quick". Again, either this contradictory behaviour is just part of her multifaceted character or the joke is on us. If we are unable to work out what is real and what is not when it comes to Lily, maybe she hopes we'll just give up and leave her alone. But that in itself is hard to believe too.

At least Lily would counter any possible suspicions of diva-ness by turning her nose up at the celebrity set in LA. "I went to the most up its own arse restaurants," she sniffed to Lamb while traversing the city in the back of a car. "There was Kate Hudson, Russell Simmons, Elvis Costello, Cyndi Lauper, and I felt like a part of the club because I got the 'famous nod', when they walk in they walk past and give you a famous nod, or the famous wink to break the ice."

Ironically, the following evening Lamb admits he has "lost Lily as she was whisked to a celebrity party", which he, presumably is not allowed to attend. The next day, as she drives with him through LA, describing the party, she pauses to take in the sight of a huge billboard with her face on it. "That must make you happy?" he asks. She just stares ahead, gives a serene smile and nods regally. (Later, when she sees a huge billboard with a picture of Keith on it, for the TV series of *Robin Hood*, she seems laid-back and a touch dismissive, 'Oh yeah, hello dad...' as if that old spectre is coming back to haunt her in the very place she thought she was safe.)

However, she later admits that her own ubiquity is somewhat unsettling – the 'leave 'em wanting more' adage is far from being adhered to when it comes to the amount of promotion she was expected to do. Proud as she was of her achievement, it still didn't sit entirely comfortably with her. "[Cracking America] was not important at all," she shrugged. "I didn't even know I was going to crack England. The deal that I've got now, I could have sold 120,000 albums and got away with it. I've now sold two million, it's like yes it's nice to make a go of things, but there's making a go of it and shoving it down people's necks."

Lamb is, of course, obliged for the sake of the T4 audience to cover certain subjects in his grabbed chats with the star, and one of them is her reputation for "bitching", and the resultant, often embroidered, press coverage. Any regrets?

"I don't wish that I hadn't said anything," she insists. "I like to think there are people out there that are clever enough to know that what they're reading is bollocks. I have to sit in interviews all day, I don't want to sit here and say nothing. I've got to play the game but I want to play it my way."

However, the sometimes brutal honesty and humour in her lyrics, she admits, is often her way of skirting around subjects she finds difficult to broach. Over milkshakes in a classic American diner, George praises her inspiring sense of 'girl power', only to be told, wistfully, that it is all "a bit pretend".

One thing George ascertains is that Lily is never really on her own. She responds by admitting she doesn't really like being on her own. "Emily my assistant sleeps in my own room, I don't like being alone, you close the door and you're like 'I can't deal with this.'"

George has a chat with Del Greening, who praises Lily to the hilt of course, compares her to the late Ian Dury and talks about how far she has come and how rapidly she has learnt – from being "frozen on the mic" to being super-confident on stage and knowing exactly how to work a crowd.

Another similarity with Ian Dury, creativity and lyrical honesty aside, is of course her attitude and ability to push people's buttons. Del admits to George and the cameras that "we've always got on well, you just have to learn when to step back in the queue a bit; when she's in a bad mood, she just likes to see how far she can push people sometimes…"

Lily repays Del's remark by telling George: "Del doesn't do any work at all, but I'm cool with that. I need his company." Backhanded compliments at dawn…

So would we say she was 'Still Alright?' after watching this? Moments of slight indulgence aside, she was probably more 'alright' than ever. As Alfie had observed, and Miquita, she was easier to get along with, happier, since she'd become famous.

By the time *Still Alright?* was screened that summer on T4, Lily would be on her way down under for an exhausting run of dates before she dashed back to LA, Las Vegas and then back to London. All the touring, changes in climate and strange food were also taking their toll on Lily's stomach, and while often the adrenaline of being on stage can magically seem to override any symptoms of illness, diarrhoea is one condition that is hard to ignore.

Lily recalled in an interview that she had managed to get through one particular show without anything terrible happening, although as soon as it was over she had to rush straight to the loo. But disaster struck just as she was supposed to strut back out to perform an encore. "I got stuck on the toilet, and I could hear people going, 'Lily, Lily!' And I was like, 'This has got to end! I've got to get back on there.' It ended eventually. I had my band members outside going, 'Lily come on!' and I was like, 'I can't move!'" The glamorous life of a pop princess…

Touring was as always a constant rollercoaster of ups and downs and strange experiences. Lily also had been working with some session musicians who were, she claimed, "a bit gospelly", and she had to extricate herself after they tried to persuade her to "pray" with them every day. "I was like, 'Hmm, maybe not...'"

Her time in Australia was less than enjoyable thanks to "arsehole photographers at every airport" according to Del, one snapper even claiming he had been "assaulted" because Lily refused to be photographed by him. Lily and her crew got the last laugh on the photographers, stipulating that they could only take her pictures at her gig if they wore cute green Shrek ears. Which they did. The lengths these snappers will go to...

This at least would give Lily a smile when she looked down from the stage, but she was starting to get tired and weak, and she still had to fly to LA again to shoot her next music video before she'd be able to go home, despite, as the newspapers wasted no time in informing us, "not being allowed to work there".

The "alleged violent clash" with a photographer in March after the Brit awards was still haunting Lily, and after flying in from Australia she'd be detained for five hours at LAX before having her working visa revoked. Lily had, "insiders" insisted, been given special permission to make her video but the newspapers still had a field day.

Having already recorded guest vocals on the track 'Drivin' Me Wild' by US rapper and actor Common during her previous stint in America, Lily was also due to appear in the video to accompany the release of the song, which would be on October 1, 2007. Lily had been introduced to Common by Kanye West, whom she had met earlier in the year and hit it off with, and as Kanye was producing the song, he was keen to involve Lily, and Common agreed, appreciating her free, uninhibited style in the studio. However, when it came to the shoot, after her ordeal at the airport and increasing fatigue, facing the dusty, desert heat of Las Vegas was not an attractive prospect. She wasn't feeling well at all, but, she insists, she wasn't treated particularly well, and would put the shoot down as one of her least favourite experiences.

"I was really ill and nobody seemed to care, 'Who is this British chick anyway?'" she said in an interview. "Everyone was a bit mean and ungentlemanly. I had to run after this truck with a camera on it in Doc Martens and a prom dress and a wig in the blistering heat, and at the end of the scene they didn't offer me a lift in the truck back to the starting point, I had to walk. I was so ill I had to have a Vitamin B12 shot in my arse, which really hurt."

By the time she did return to London she had gone down with painful sinusitis and strep throat. She was advised to take two weeks off and had no choice but to cancel a handful of European dates with the hope she would be well enough to perform at the V Festival in Chelmsford and Staffordshire. As always, as soon as the artist has a chance to stop and have a break, their body suddenly gives in to illness and Lily was no exception. (Lily was careful to post up a picture of her doctor's note onto her blog, just to allay any angry accusations that she might be lying.)

Fortunately Lily was well enough to attend Notting Hill Carnival that August Bank Holiday, prompting tabloids to sneeringly point out how she had "suddenly perked up" in time for her favourite event despite blowing out her gigs. But Lily had been recuperating, and a bit of rest and relaxation and fun with her friends and family was exactly what she needed.

If there had been any danger of Lily having forgotten the voraciousness of the British press in her absence, she'd soon be reminded of it. The newspapers were rubbing their hands together when they received reports, and video footage, of a drunken Lily Allen smoking an "unusual roll-up" and then "storming the stage" during a set by her friend, the white Lover's Rock revivalist Bobby Kray. At one point it appeared that she was trying to "push him off" the stage, and in retaliation, Bobby poured a glass of Guinness over her. Welcome home, Lily…

This humiliation and subsequent tabloid bear-baiting convinced Lily not to take any chances again, although whenever she tried to hide from the press, she simply ended up drawing more attention to herself: a few weeks later paparazzi pictures appeared in newspapers and gossip magazines of some girls, including Miquita Oliver, struggling up Oxford Street in the small hours, seemingly carrying a heavy load in a Habitat shopping bag. Yes, the precious cargo was Lily Allen.

Lily and her friends had just left the Soho nightclub Punk before realising, clearly too late, that Lily should be incognito, particularly as the newspapers were constantly insinuating she had been exaggerating her illness in order to "bunk off". The friends slunk off to a nearby building site, bundled Lily into the bag and dragged her up the road before getting into a car and speeding off. It only served to attract more attention of course. Whatever she did, whatever she didn't do, Lily was in the papers daily, and it didn't feel quite as friendly as it did a year ago.

At least there was something around the corner that would take her mind off the feeling of being trapped by the press. It had been part of her life since she was a baby, and finally a special dream was about to come true: Lily Allen was going to sing at Glastonbury Festival.

"On the first night I got here I got drunk with my friends, and at 5am we thought it would be a good idea to just go and sit at the front of the stage when there was no one there and it was all empty. I just looked at it, and I was like, 'Phew, OK...'"

The festival had been such a huge part of her life since her first few weeks on earth – the fact she was on the line-up for this year's event meant the world to her after years of pitching up with her family and hanging out around the campfire watching her dad cause trouble. They'd be doing that too, but this time Lily would also be looking out on that huge crowd of face-painted, flag-waving, pear-cider-quaffing revellers from the stage.

CHAPTER 15

"The only reason I got into singing was from coming here every year and thinking, 'I've got to do this."

Lily Allen on Glastonbury Festival.

Resplendent in a fuchsia pink party dress, matching lipstick, swingy black pony-tail and a hoodie, Lily, used to rocking out at Glastonbury as a punter, not a performer, took the Park Stage with her family and friends in the wings. She had taken MIA's slot, who had cancelled, and Lily was nervous, "big shoes to fill", but it didn't show; only her folks had any idea how jittery she felt. As usual, it was good old Jagermeister that gave her the Dutch courage to throw off her nerves and give a fine festival performance, which featured a special guest appearance from Specials Terry Hall and Lynval Golding. They sang 'Gangsters' and 'Blank Expression' together, Hall stock still and characteristically glum, eyes cast to the floor, Allen, in contrast, bouncing about as if on springs, and some festival stalwarts – including Billy Bragg – skanking in the wings. This moment Lily would hail as one of the happiest in her career so far.

Lily's sister Sarah was over-awed by her little half-sibling's performance: "I don't know how she does it. She was nervous before Glastonbury, headlining there was a really big deal for her. We've gone every year of our lives, so it was the ultimate I've–made–it gig. I was nervous just being in the wings."

After falling into the arms of her family and having a well–deserved drink, Lily headed up to be interviewed by Lauren Laverne and Phill Jupitus for the BBC TV coverage of the festival. They were charmed by Lily's fresh cheek and precocity – not to mention her enthusiasm. "It was the most amazing experience of my life ever," she told them. "I feel like my whole life has been working towards this point."

She also boasted that this was the first time Hall and Golding had been on stage together since 1973… Seeing as The Specials only formed in 1977, it's fair to say there might have been a bit of festival fever setting in there. (Two-Tone expert Jupitus gallantly refrained from contradicting her.)

Blame it on all the pear cider, the euphoria and the fact she'd been up all night; early that morning she'd watched the sunrise with Alex Turner from Arctic Monkeys and James Righton from Klaxons: James dressed as a swan, Lily as a mushroom and Alex as a dinosaur. "We looked like something out of Super Mario Park," Lily chortled. "It was quite amazing."

Once the festival season ebbed away and the summer leaves began to turn brown, Lily had an opportunity to take stock and realised there were things in her life that needed to change. She was understandably feeling bruised and unhappy about certain elements of her career – particularly as, at the time, she felt she should be continuing her conquering of America. She was now effectively banned from working there, scuppering a string of sold-out September tour dates on the West Coast, and leaving her bereft as she watched her contemporaries, one of whom was Amy Winehouse, zoom past her and grab all the glory. This was to have been her opportunity to try again in the US after scrapping so many dates earlier in the year due to homesickness. She was also missing out on the MTV Awards.

So Lily decided to try and go it alone and sacked Empire Management, disappointed that they hadn't been able to untangle the visa mess for her. (She always insisted she had never signed a contract with her management, so she could "walk away whenever I fancied".) She remained close friends with her original manager, Adrian Jolly, and the pair decided to continue working together.

Meanwhile, her relationship with Seb Chew had also become strained, not least because of the constant travelling and absence they endured, and they finally made the painful decision to split up again. Who knows whether Lily was on the rebound or not, but she would soon be getting very cosy with Chemical Brothers' Ed Simons, another older man, this time 15 years her senior.

Lily looked better than ever, despite the recent upheaval. She dropped two dress sizes, she claimed, as a result of the split from Seb, but the real reason for her impressive weight loss would be revealed as something less than happenstance: she'd been working out at the gym and had cut out all junk food.

There were a few motivations for Lily's sudden body-consciousness: one of which was that she was fed up of having her physique scrutinised in magazines, but also, more seriously, she had discovered, after a visit to her doctor, that she had a heart murmur.

"I found out about three months ago. I have been asthmatic all my life but this was really quite scary," she said in an interview. "When they asked me how much exercise I did, I had to be honest and say hardly any. Now I make sure I work out three times a week.

"I used to love nothing more than sitting in front of the telly with two packets of Ginger Nuts and two bags of milk bottle sweets. I'd devour the lot.

"But this heart thing has made me cut back on that kind of crap. I haven't done this because I want to be some skinny minnie. I just like being more toned. It has made me really happy. I should give up smoking but haven't quite managed that yet."

Her new management were already pulling their weight, no pun intended, as they recommended the perfect person to motivate Lily and drag her out of inertia and into a life of fitness and better health: the 'Body Doctor', David Marshall, who was famous for toning up Russell Brand, Frank Lampard and Rio Ferdinand and transforming the once Rubenesque size 18 Sophie Dahl into a slender gazelle (thus arguably taking away her most noticeable USP). Even Ant and Dec (do they ever go anywhere separately?) attended Marshall's six-week transformational course in London's chichi Primrose Hill.

So, for Lily, those prettily forgiving prom outfits would make way for hot pants and shorter, tighter dresses. She could wear what she wanted, and despite having turned her nose up at the uber-sexy stylings of the likes of Girls Aloud, she'd discover that she really did enjoy dressing to kill from time to time. No one said it would be easy though…

As well as cutting out sugar and wheat, Lily had to drink cocktails of vegetable juice every day and put up with Marshall's hard-line approach, often yelling: "Fuck off, you bastard!" in response to his constant boot-camp-style encouragements.

A hot new physique aside, Lily was soon firing on all cylinders again, enjoying London life and thinking about her new album. With the exception of a collaboration with her mate, Bow-based rapper Dizzee Rascal ('Wanna Be', sampling the hook from the *Bugsy Malone* song 'Boxer' and swapping the key word for 'gangster'), she was starting to focus on what she needed to do next.

Not only was she becoming leaner, she wanted the production on her next record to be leaner too. Lily loved the sound of her first album (even if the lyrics now made her cringe – too adolescent, too bolshy, in her opinion), but she was concerned that, should the production be as slick and fulsome the next time around, critics might suggest that it was merely to create a smokescreen to hide the fact that she didn't really have what it took. Maybe that's what stopped her bagging those awards, maybe she had to strip her sound back and expose herself (metaphorically speaking of course, although she was frequently pictured in the tabloids accidentally flashing a bra-less boob now and again) in order to be taken more seriously.

She was also aware she had to get on with it, more than aware that EMI were concerned that someone might take her place if she didn't knuckle down and rush out a new release to sate the fickle pop audience. But, as Lily was keen to point out, she'd had her whole life to come up with the material that ended up on *Alright, Still*. And she'd had just over a year so far to produce a follow-up. Did they want it quick or did they want it good?

Lily might have had some ideas swirling around in her head, but as was her method, she didn't want to commit to anything until the time was right. And this time, it would have to be with just one producer to create a cohesive sound and vibe. "I wanted to work with one person from start to finish, to make it one body of work. I wanted it to feel like it had some sort of integrity," she said. The reggae sound would be shelved, and another idea she'd had a while ago – to go down the retro Phil Spector 'Wall of Sound' route – had to be ditched thanks to the fact that 'Winehouse' and Duffy had already locked onto it and were making it their stock-in-trade.

Lily knew who she wanted: Greg Kurstin. She'd already talked to him about it a few months earlier, discussing her hopes – that the record would reflect her new-found maturity – and playing him records for inspiration, from The Smiths to Coldplay to Keane to New Order. He in turn had tinkered on the piano and came up with some ideas that Lily loved. The tinkering turned into writing, and the pair grabbed the opportunity to work together when he was over from the US, hiring a cottage in Morten-in-Marsh in the Cotswolds, close to Lily's dad. They came up with five songs in Kurstin's makeshift "laptop studio". Things were going well.

So, the news that he suddenly had to go off on tour with his own group, The Bird and The Bee (with Inara George, the singer daughter of the late Little Feat singer and guitarist Lowell George), who had previously toured with Lily on her own tours, was not particularly welcome as far as Lily was concerned. She didn't want to be coerced into trying out other producers just for the sake of getting on with it, but EMI were keen to see results. They tried to team her up with Gonzales, who had struck gold producing Feist, with Bjorn from the Swedish group Peter Bjorn and John, and even her fellow West Londoner Damon Albarn. Famously, this pairing was not a success.

Damon: "The record label thought it would be a good idea. She came down to my studio and she said normally she would just sit around and listen to a musician and come up with some ideas. I jumped on the piano and played some mad stuff and she just looked at me – it didn't exactly go well. She's a really talented kid but it was a bad idea."

Lily later gave her side of the story to Radio 1 DJ Sara Cox: "I love Damon but he's really annoying when it comes to music: 'Oh I'm such a muso... The way I work is sometimes I like to make a piano loop and loop it around so I can listen to it,' and he was like, 'I don't work with computers' and I was like, 'Er, you're in Gorillaz, I think you might do!' He was just doing it to annoy me, I knew he was.

"I was sitting on the sofa and he was playing the same thing on the piano over and over again and every so often going, 'Have you got anything yet?'"

To make matters worse, and even more tense, as the day ground to a halt, she accidentally flashed her boobs at him when her blouse popped open: "All three of my buttons came undone at the same time and my boobs were hanging out. I was like, 'Well this has been a really brilliant day…'"

A week with Mark Ronson also came to nothing, and apparently contributed to a period of silence between the pair. They holed up at a studio in Henley-on-Thames but the usual 'sit around and come up with stuff' technique just turned into, well, sitting around. The fact he was her ex-boyfriend Seb's close friend can't have helped, but there was another reason she didn't feel comfortable at the studio. She happily provided backing vocals alongside New Young Pony Club for Kaiser Chiefs' album *Off With Their Heads*, which Ronson was producing, but it wasn't proving quite as easy for this combination to come up with the goods for her own record this time around.

"Literally I sat on the sofa for a week and didn't do anything," she sighed. "It felt really tainted as well because we were in the studio that he'd been working with Amy Winehouse in, and I was kind of in her bed, and it was all very weird." She joked that she'd found all sorts of "strange things" there, presumably connected to 'Winehouse'. After this, Ronson admitted in an interview that she hadn't been returning his calls, so he doubted he'd be on the new album. It sounds as if the combination of Winehouse vibes and connections with her ex made it impossible for Lily to really focus on herself and what she wanted. She'd just have to wait for Greg to come back. She knew it would be worth it.

Before the end of turbulent 2007, Lily and Greg would shake the pretty Cotswolds area of Gloucestershire again, working from Keith's house for some of the time, and even hiring a space in a castle to work in – if that didn't project a message of regal maturity through the music, it's hard to say what would.

"That room was kind of challenging," admitted Greg in an interview with *MixOnline*, "because the sound was so echo-y with the stone everywhere, the vocals had so much natural reverb and it picked up every little foot noise."

The writing process was simple, a continuation of how they had worked before: "I break out little piano riffs or simple guitar riffs and she'll like some and reject others. I have to pull out whatever will inspire the best songs, so if she's not feeling it right off the bat, it's usually not going to happen. If she likes an idea, maybe I'll put it on a loop for her and then, literally, like half-an-hour later, she'll say, 'OK, I have something.'

"The lyrics will often give me ideas where to take the track. Usually, by the end of the day I'll have a finished demo of a song. We work pretty quickly together. Production-wise, I'll try out all sorts of things, trial and error, and sometimes it takes me forever.

"I might try 100 things in a chorus until I can figure out how to make it work. Sometimes it comes together easily, like 'Everyone's at It' and 'The Fear' came together quickly."

EMI had to trust Lily's judgement – good decision – and were happy to know that finally something was happening, and happening fast. Everyone was champing at the bit to find out what all-grown-up Lily Allen was going to come up with next.

Music wasn't the only thing on Lily's mind, however. Her romance with Ed Simons had been going well, and, while she had been in the studio, she knew that she was keeping a beautiful secret – she was expecting his child.

Lily Allen had always been a defiantly family-oriented young woman, almost in reaction to her own fragmented family life, and it was no secret that she longed to be a mother, couldn't wait for the opportunity to retire early, move to the country and have children. And now, it seemed, she was closer to her dream than ever.

Lily and Ed made the happy announcement that she was pregnant in December 2007. She dropped her party lifestyle, cut back on the booze and changed her outlook. Messages of support poured in on MySpace from excited fans and her family rallied round. As Christmas drew near, she felt happier than ever.

More good news was around the corner too, not that it could have topped the feeling of being an expectant mother. The Orange Prize panel was announced that December, with Lily being named as one of the judges for the female literary award. She was honoured to be asked, and thrilled to accept, but the decision to have on the panel a celebrity who wasn't even a writer, song-writing aside, sparked criticism. Lily would be judging alongside seasoned journalists Lisa Allardice and Bel Mooney, the fiction writer and playwright Philippa Gregory and broadcaster Kirsty Lang.

Royal Society of Literature chairman Maggie Gee complained: "Where is the seriousness here? Lily would be fine as the light relief, her songs are great. But the chair herself (Lang) is not an author. There is a shortage of serious writers on this panel. It seems to be another consequence of this obsession with celebrity. We seem to have to have them on panels like this whether they know anything about books or not." Lily simply saw this as an opportunity to prove her critics wrong, and set to work reading.

Another burst of good news broke before Christmas, when Lily announced to her fans that "the BBC have been silly enough to fund my very own TV show". Lily had been in talks about the celebrity chat show with youth channel BBC3 for a while, and it was decided that it should major on her online following and internet rise to fame. *Lily Allen And Friends* was the title, a reference to her many MySpace 'friends', some of whom would be able to watch the filming of the shows, the first of which would be aired the following spring.

Lily also had the opportunity to indulge her A&R aspirations and sought out new bands to publicise on the show. Viewers and fans could write in to the website and suggest artists they thought were worthy of some Lily-style exposure – it was all very interactive and fresh, just what the Beeb needed.

It had been a tough year but Lily was feeling contented at last, and excited for the future. So much so that, shock horror, "as I am happier and happier I can't bring myself to bitch any more".

Maybe it was all those motherly hormones coursing through her system, but she was amazed to find herself even "jumping to people's defence", particularly those she had chosen to single out and pick on in the past. "I saw Paris Hilton on the *David Letterman Show* and I was like, 'Why is he being so horrible to her?' And I can't think what

'Cherylgate' was about? What a waste of time. Cheryl Cole? Who is she? Just someone from a manufactured band, whereas I write and perform my own music." OK, so she still couldn't resist a little bit of a snipe, but this was definitely progress.

This new-found joy for Lily would cause her to look back at this particular Christmas with bittersweet fondness. She told Rob Fitzpatrick for *Word*: "That Christmas I was at home with my family and Ed, and I wasn't drinking, and I just sat there knowing I was having a baby and I was in absolute bliss.

"Sitting round eating turkey, playing games, watching everybody getting drunk, and being really excited knowing this time next year I was going to have a baby. And I haven't."

CHAPTER 16

"Then something much bigger than all of it happens. At some stage the axe is going to fall."

Lily Allen in *Love Magazine*

New Year 2008 would be far from happy for Lily. Numb with shock after her tragic miscarriage, unable to really take in what had happened, she was thrown straight into a whirl of dealing with it publicly, going through the motions while slipping back into bad habits. "I didn't even know what I was going through, and I'm there and I have to put out a press release to say I was losing my baby. I didn't deal with any of that at all. I just went out.

"I didn't actually start dealing with it until the baby's due date," she explained in an interview with *Love Magazine*. "Then it all hits you and you can't escape and you have to just do something. You have to start dealing with reality."

The situation seemed unreal, she was so sure she knew how 2008 would pan out: complete the album, release it in the spring, tour, have the baby and then take a few months off before another tour and then step away from the limelight as she and Ed brought up their little one. But not only did she lose the baby, Lily and Ed would split up the following month after less than six months together. They had taken some time out in the Maldives for some sun and space, but by the time they returned to London, it was clear that their relationship had foundered.

"You can kind of say, what if?" mused Lily in her frank interview with *Word*. "Maybe if I'd stayed pregnant and had the baby then things would have worked out between me and Ed. I don't know. You could drive yourself insane thinking about it."

Poor Lily almost did lose her way, she had become depressed and "lost the plot for a bit. It was quite a nasty time." She bravely admitted later that she went to a "nut-house" and stayed for three weeks, a vital chance for her to have some peace away from the questions, the snappers desperate for a picture of "devastated" Lily, the reminders of her loss. "Actually, it was quite nice being in there," she said. "No one could get to me; no one knew I was there."

Despite her two-pronged heartbreak, Lily, with some help from her "rock" Emily, managed to eventually emerge from her dark state to join her family in supporting Alfie in his debut stage performance in the lead role in Peter Shaffer's play *Equus* at the Chichester Festival Theatre. Alfie was taking over the role from *Harry Potter*'s already seasoned lead actor Daniel Radcliffe as Alan Strang, a teenage boy with an obsession with horses.

Everyone would have let Lily off for not making it, hers were extenuating circumstances, but there was no way she was going to miss her little brother's big night, even if she did make it there a little late. (Again, this is an impressive gig for a 21-year-old's first theatre job – why Alfie didn't get the same flak as Lily did with the old 'nepotism' card, seeing as this is more directly linked to father Keith's own career, is a mystery.) The newspapers, in particular Lily's sometime nemesis *The Daily Mail* (Lily even had a badge proclaiming she was 'hated by the *Daily Mail*', which she wore with no small measure of pride), made a meal of the fact that Alfie would be "stripping naked" in front of the audience, as the script dictated. A brave role for any actor, but it was nothing Lily hadn't already seen. The Allens were far from prim and proper about these things. "Alfie is fantastic on stage," Lily enthused. "I was so proud I cried."

Lily was still not 100 per cent healthwise, but had used her downtime to read the nigh on 40 books for the Orange Prize. The youngest judge on the panel in the prize's history, she was determined to prove herself. However, it appeared that her best was not enough: she was, she says, "sacked" from the panel because she couldn't attend meetings, due to being in the clinic. She had missed a longlist meeting, phoning in instead. But when she missed a debate about the shortlist, it was taken out of her hands. Lily was "infuriated", she told reporters afterwards, particularly as the party line was that *she* had "stepped down" as a result of ill health.

A spokesman said: "Lily had read extensively for the first stage of the judging process but recently found that she was unable to commit 100 per cent to the role due to ill health. Rather than do a disservice to what she sees as an incredible array of female literary talent, it has been agreed that she will withdraw before the final judging takes place.

"Lily hopes that her withdrawal will not detract from the huge importance of the Orange Prize and sends her sincere apologies to her fellow judges and to the individual authors." Of course, any perceived snubbing of Lily Allen ensures a sting in the tail. She proclaimed the winning book, Rose Tremain's *The Road Home*, "boring".

She and Tremain might have had more in common than she first thought though, seemingly sharing similar sentiments when it came to winning prizes. "In this country, prizes are like bumps in the road, sleeping policemen," Tremain said after scooping the £30,000 prize. "You can't pretend they are not there, and anyone who says they don't care about them is being disingenuous. So to have won one of the major prizes feels great." Lily wished she could say the same about herself – there was still a disconcerting amount of space on that mantelpiece.

A prize of another sort had been won, however: just weeks after Lily's split with Simons, her musician friend Robertson Furze, frontman for public school indie band The Big Pink (named after legendary Americana pioneers The Band's first album and home studio), beloved of *NME*, jumped in to mop up her tears, and it wasn't long before friendship turned into something more. It wouldn't last, but it gave her some much-needed support and lighter times after her darkest hour. Even after their split she remained deeply fond of him, ribbing him in interviews: "He thinks he looks like Barnes from *Platoon* but actually he looks like the disabled guy out of *Forrest Gump*," Lily would later surmise. Robertson, an ex-Harrovian who also looked slightly James Dean-esque at the right angle, took her out, made her laugh and took her mind off everything. She needed to keep her spirits up in order to take on her next challenge – working on her new TV show at Pinewood Studios.

Her first guests would be the *Peep Show* actor and writer David Mitchell and American star Cuba Gooding Jr, and Lily admitted that she was "shitting it". The recording went well, and she was impressed by how well-behaved her audience of 'friends' were, standing for several hours in a stuffy studio.

The first show was aired on February 12, 2008, and the audience certainly approved of the guests – Cuba Gooding Jr presented Lily with flowers before mounting her bed-shaped sofa (very Paula Yates) for their interview. He cheekily said that usually he's naked when he gets on a bed. Lily responded by telling him to "feel free" to strip. The shirt duly came off, much to the near hysteria of the audience.

Cuba flattered Lily after he talked about winning an Oscar, saying that she might win something for her TV show. "I'd like to win something for music, to be fucking fair." Lily had not been nominated for a 2008 Brit, and watched as her closest contemporaries cleaned up: Kate Nash walked away with Best British Female and Adele, also a guest on Lily's show, won Critic's Choice. (Ironically, when Lily finally won a Brit award in 2010, she would later say in an interview "it meant absolutely nothing" to her.)

She teased Mark Ronson on the show about his own Brit win – "That award is a little bit mine…" – and displayed that the old feelings of competition with Amy Winehouse were still flourishing when the video to his track with Lily – the cover of Kaiser Chiefs' 'Oh My God' – was screened: "Thanks for turning up to the video, by the way," he quipped. (The video for 'Oh My God' is an animation.) "What, like Amy Winehouse?" Lily screeched back. "Fuck off! At least I turned up for the cartoon drawing session, she didn't fucking turn up at all. Anyway…" (the Amy Winehouse video is just lots of women dressed and made-up as Winehouse).

There was plenty of outrageousness on the show, which was, of course, why Lily was approached as a presenter for BBC3 in the first place. She displayed how she could fit her fist inside her mouth, she exposed her breast to her guest comedian and *Phoenix Nights* actor Paddy McGuinness, she revealed she had been "blacklisted" from the Spice Girls' reunion at the O2… it was never a dull moment.

Another highlight of the show, which centred around the online world, YouTube, MySpace and blogging, was her video diary, in which viewers could watch Lily playing in the park, her dad Keith telling her to "fuck off", and on one occasion, inviting the cameras in to what would be her first flat, in the throes of refurbishment.

Lily was putting on a brave front for her show, which was proving a success with the niche audience it was targeted at, but as she neared what would have been the due date for her lost child, she faltered at the thought of performing live. She pulled out of her scheduled appearance at the Isle Of Wight festival, citing professional reasons, but organiser John Giddings openly said he thought that the party line was probably a "lie". "They said she hasn't delivered her record, and I said I haven't booked a record, I've booked an artist," he said. "I think the poor girl has got a few problems. It's a good job she pulled out now and not the day before. I wish her the best and hope she sorts herself out."

After the difficult start to 2008 she had endured, Lily decided she could do with a treat. She'd already snapped up a MacBook Air, and now she had bought herself a spanking new BMW. Who could begrudge her treating herself?

But it seemed that maybe she would have been better off not advertising the fact she had splashed out on the motor: just weeks later, Lily emerged from the Groucho with her pals to find that the car had been vandalised by, according to Lily herself, a vindictive paparazzo. The press reported that a window of the car had been "smashed by vandals", but Lily wanted her fans to know the truth – revealing in her blog that the "vandals" were in fact paparazzi.

It couldn't have happened at a more unfortunate time, as Lily struggled to come to terms with how 2008 was panning out, trying to keep her chin up and keep socialising, but having to face the increasing aggression of the paparazzi. At least her music was one thing she could rely on to help her lose herself and forget about the outside world, even if her lyrics very much dealt with topical issues. The next album would be quite political in comparison to her previous, more personal release, but there would still be plenty of observations from her own everyday life in there too.

Lily was going in a new direction (even marking this new era by going movie-star blonde) and toyed with what to call her next album. She'd considered *Stuck On The Naughty Step*. She'd joked to George Lamb the previous year that she might call it *Making Friends Wherever She Goes*. But after the year she'd had, and the amount of therapy she'd undergone to move on from feelings of guilt, anger and confusion sparked not only by the tragic recent circumstances, but also by her treatment in the media, there was only one title that would do: *It's Not Me, It's You.*

It was perfect for Lily in defiant mode, and she admitted it popped into her head when she was taking a male friend out for brunch. He was considering splitting up with his girlfriend, and had no idea how to go about it or what to say. Lily rolled her eyes and blurted, "Why don't you just say, 'Look, it's not me, it's you...'" And then, a eureka moment occurred... Who knows whether he used the line on his hapless soon-to-be ex, the main thing was that this was the ideal witty album title. It also summed up how she'd had to throw off the barrage of online judgment and abuse. It wasn't about her really, whatever was being said. It said much more about the 'haters' that were posting up insults about her online. It was never about her, it was them, really. Lily couldn't control what was being said, but she could control how she allowed herself to feel.

It's Not Me, It's You was scheduled for release a year later, in February 2009, and its inception came at a tricky time for EMI. The label was undergoing significant "restructuring", laying off staff left, right and centre as the music industry was finally showing signs of strain, not only because of the download revolution and the prevalence of illegal file-sharing and downloading, but because more and more artists were doing it themselves, passing over labels in favour of distributing their own music and marketing on their own terms. This had never happened before in this way, and the major labels were, to use a Lily phrase, "shitting it".

"Everyone is terrified of losing their jobs, so no one wants to make decisions in case it comes back on them," stated Lily. "As an artist, that really is terrifying." Lily agreed to have the album release pushed back to the following year, and continued to refine it, posting up demos on her page as before.

One of those demos we now know as the song 'Fuck You' was Lily's strident march into political territory. It was originally an anti-BNP rant, but lent itself equally to her feelings about George W Bush. It morphed from being titled 'Guess Who, Batman?' (check out the initials) and 'Get With The Brogram' before settling on 'Fuck You Very Much', which captured fans' imaginations immediately and became something of an anti-bigotry anthem.

Lily's MySpace fans loved it, and were all the more devoted to her after being given the chance to join in on her show. They felt close to Lily and protective of her, particularly as many of them had avidly read her blogs, and thus observed her highs and lows since the beginning of her career. They were fond of her, and wanted to see her happy. And it looked as if there might be a chance of happiness on the horizon when a certain young man who was just Lily's type came on the show.

"This is the first time we've been in bed together," Lily said flirtily to James Corden, the cuddly, charming heart-throb of *Gavin And Stacey*. It was clear that the pair got on well, and that Lily already had a bit of a crush on him: they had first met a year earlier at the premiere of Alan Bennett's *History Boys,* in which Corden starred. He was there with his girlfriend, *Two Pints Of Lager And A Packet Of Crisps* actress Sheridan Smith, but Lily, who was "twatted" according to Corden (told you he was a charmer), was swooning over him, gushing: "You're sooo funny, can I have your number? Come on, just give me your number."

Corden took *her* number, but, as he recalled, "it was so awkward". He kept her number though, much to Lily's delight.

Corden gazed at Lily on the bed-shaped sofa, telling her her dress is "a triumph, and the shoes". The princess is slowly being coaxed from her ivory tower...

"Stop being mean to me!" she squirmed. "You're trying to flirt with me with your dazzling eyes." Witnessing this potential blossoming romance, the audience was almost as enraptured as Lily. She added in a little self-pity when she wailed, "I'm not used to people being nice to me..." James fell for it hook, line and sinker, and what followed would become TV history.

"I think that's true," he said. "You want to know the truth? I don't think you know how lovely you are. Let me tell you this, it won't be very interesting to anyone else other than you, on my life, without irony or agenda, truly, I don't think you know how lovely you are and I think you could do with someone to tell you. Ignore everyone just there…"

No one, not even James, could have anticipated what Lily would say back. Suffice to say, it didn't match James' eulogy for romance. "Just fuck me!" she blurted, before giggling coyly, her fans reeling at her directness. "Thank you very much. That is how you get into a girl's pants. Well done, James. Are you single at the moment?"

"It's complicated," he replied, before adding. "Yeah, I am", as if he'd just decided it on the spot. During the rest of their interview, they even joked about sexual positions, and imagined sitting in front of *Strictly Come Dancing* with a takeaway together.

The story goes that, in fact, Corden was still with Sheridan Smith, but needless to say, he wasn't for much longer after this little love story was splashed over the newspapers that April.

A sleeker, more sophisticated Lily Allen emerged to promote her album *It's Not Me, It's You*, Sydney, Australia, March 2009. (*Carlos Furtado / Newspix / Rex Features*)

CHANEL

Who'd have thought it? Lily Allen during her stint as
a face of Chanel. Paris Fashion Week March 10, 2009.

(*Pascal Rossignol/Reuters/Corbis*)

Lily Allen and Jaime Winstone, her pal and the
then-girlfriend of Alfie, watch the Luella LFW Autumn
Winter 2008 show from front row at Claridges Hotel
on February 14, 2008 in London. (*Rosie Greenway/Getty Images*)

Lily Allen performs during the presentation of the Chanel Ready-to-Wear
Spring/Summer 2010 collection during the Paris Fashion Week (*Lucas Dolega/epa/Corbis*)

Back in 2007 with her "darling ex boyfriend",
the DJ Seb Chew, the inspiration for 'Littlest Things'.
(Richard Young/Rex Features)

Big brother… former manager George Lamb and
Lily cosy up at a swanky party. *(Richard Young/Rex Features)*

…y Allen and her former boyfriend, Chemical Brothers'
…d Simons, at his home in Notting Hill. The pair sadly
…t up in 2008 after Lily suffered a miscarriage. *(Rex Features)*

A penchant for the older man. Art dealer – and Keith
Allen cohort - Jay Jopling and Lily Allen had a brief fling.
(Richard Young/Rex Features)

Lily Allen performs on the Pyramid Stage at her home-from-home: Glastonbury Festival, 2009. (*Jim Dyson/Getty Images*)

orget trainers and prom-dresses – Lily goes space-age.
(Marcos Brindicci / Reuters / Corbis)

Wigging out – Lily Allen on-stage. *(Brian Rasic / Rex Features)*

What a trouper - Lily Allen in pain after falling and
urting her back, struggling on in concert at The Flow
tival, Helsinki, Finland, August 2009. *(Ilpo Musto / Rex Features)*

Lily Allen attends the 2010 Brits at Earl's Court.
And this time, she'd actually win one. *(Rune Hellestad / Corbis)*

Lily Allen in the dress that had everyone talking, holding her Editors Special award during the Glamour Women Of The Year Awards. (*Jon Furniss / WireImage*)

Another gong, Lily Allen rides high at the 2009 *Q* Awa held at the Grosvenor House Hotel on October 26, 20 in London, England. (*Dave Hogan / Getty Images*)

Demure (but don't be fooled) Lily Allen at the 2010 Brit Awards at Earl's Court. (*Rune Hellestad / Corbis*)

Quite a 'retirement' gift: Lily Allen with her three Ivc Novello awards, May 20, 2010. (*Dave Hogan / Getty Images*)

Lily Allen gives Bjork a run for her money at Bestival, 2009 on the Isle of Wight. *(Samir Hussein/Getty Images)*

Lily Allen at the Big Day Out music festival, 2010 in Sydney, Australia. *(Brendon Thorne/Getty Images)*

Sweetness and light. Lily Allen on a MuchMusic Channel TV programme in Toronto, Canada – February 9, 2009.

(Canadian Press / Rex Features

CHAPTER 17

Damien Hirst: "What are some of the obstacles you've confronted as a woman?" Lily Allen: "Putting on a bra is quite complicated…"

Interview magazine.

Naturally everyone was gagging for a glimpse of Lily and James Corden together, convinced that they'd make the perfect couple. Fans at least were relieved that they'd seen for themselves someone who evidently looked as if they were dead-set on taking care of Lily.

Corden and Allen, sadly, despite sounding rather like quite a nifty old-time music-hall partnership, were not to be partners of the romantic kind, but the media were desperate to catch them making overtures to each other. That ever-reliable source of information *The Daily Star* even wrote that Lily had displayed her affection for James by writing him a special song called 'From Barry To Billericay', the title a homage to the sitcom *Gavin And Stacey,* which he wrote and starred in. She apparently sent the lyrics sealed in an envelope to Corden at the Baftas ceremony in April, where Corden was picking up two awards (Best Comedy and the Audience Award).

As May swung around, the paparazzi had a special date in their diary – Lily Allen's birthday on the second, and they knew exactly where she'd be. One thing they weren't sure of was whether she'd have a certain cuddly knight in shining armour by her side at the Groucho Club or not, but that was the shot they were after.

To sweeten up the birthday girl, and in a rare gesture of paparazzi-humanity, the photographers had clubbed together to buy a birthday cake, and they waited for Lily to come out of the club for one of her inevitable cigarettes.

Lily, blonde and wearing an angelic white feathered hair-clip, emerged with Madness singer Suggs and, lo and behold, James Corden, and the two men festively broke into a rendition of 'Happy Birthday' on seeing the cake. Lily on the other hand, like a spoilt little girl at a party, grabbed the cake from the photographers and hurled it back at them. Understandable in a way though, considering. "There's nothing professional about them," Lily later grumbled. "Most of them look like they wouldn't be out of place at a BNP meeting."

After her birthday celebration, which also saw Robertson Furze and Gail Porter joining in the fun, Lily decided to escape London for a few weeks and take a holiday. She needed a change of scenery and headed down to stay at a friend's house in the South of France, enjoying some R&R and topping up her tan before joining Keith in Cannes. Keith had been busy too, mostly filming *Robin Hood* in Hungary, but he was in Cannes to herald the screening of his documentary *There Are Dark Forces*. The film, which looked into the inquest of the late Princess Diana's death in 1997, was described as a "damning indictment of the establishment and the media's reporting methods" – something Lily too was quite familiar with. And like Diana, while Lily would play the media, courting and flirting at times, the force of the press was not to be reckoned with. "This is the inquest of the inquest," Keith told reporters at Cannes.

For once, Lily wasn't working, and she made the most of it, swimming, sunbathing, getting into her glad-rags for parties. But as usual, there were plenty of photographers snapping away, taking pictures of her topless on the beach (cue lots of captions along the lines of 'Thrilly Allen' etc), hanging out with socialites on a yacht – and apparently "being thrown off it". Lily denied it, but also was quick to remind the judgmental tabloids that swimming topless and drinking wine was not actually a crime.

Lily was still fuming that she was being lambasted for having a good time – she was perfectly in control. Or so she thought. Her next blog would tell a different story, and to Lily's credit, she wasn't going to try to defend herself this time. (Although she would later claim she'd had her drink spiked.)

On June 4, 2008, Lily's blog subscribers found a post entitled: 'Oh Dear'... "Last time I wrote here I was defending my honour and dignity, explaining my innocence and also outrage at the press for insinuating my behaviour was embarrassing. This time I'm putting my hands up, I got very drunk last night, too drunk...."

The afternoon of June 4 saw Lily getting ready for the Glamour Women Of The Year Awards – "celebrating the most beautiful and powerful women around the globe" – to pick up the Editor's Choice award. She had laid out the perfect outfit: a pink satin dress with pictures of decapitated deer all over it, and was dying her hair pink at home to match. "In my own bathroom," she proudly told reporters.

It was a big night, and Lily was among friends – Beth Ditto was there to pick up a gong for International Musician, Mark Ronson won Man Of The Year, Jo Whiley won the Radio Personality Award and Leona Lewis, the *X-Factor* winner Lily so admired, bagged the UK Solo Artist prize.

But after the awards party, Lily was seen "too drunk to walk" according to eager tabloids, and was carried into her car, seemingly comatose. Extreme as it may have seemed, many people were wondering why the press were acting so surprised. However, at an exhibition at the Royal Academy later that week with the actress Jaime Winstone – Alfie's girlfriend – by her side, Lily was heard telling the broadcaster and journalist Janet Street-Porter that she believed someone had put something in her drink... Who knows what happened, but as usual, Lily was all over the newspapers and magazines. She'd be glad to escape to LA again, having an album to fine-tune. She planned to stay on track diet-wise by eating only sushi while in America (with the exception of one In N' Out Burger on the way over). That is if they let her in. They did: immigration only kept her for an hour – things were looking up.

The summer marked what would have been the due date of Lily's baby, and she made sure she had plenty going on in her life to distract herself. Her flat, which she had bought the previous autumn and, as we saw on her TV show earlier in 2008, was in the process of a complete overhaul, would finally be ready for her once she arrived back from America.

"I've got a bath in my bedroom, yikes, and a remote control fire," Lily gushed. "I've been collecting art for years, but I've never had my own place to put it all up in so, I can't wait."

But in the meantime, Lily just had to put up with staying in another rather luxurious room in LA's infamous Chateau Marmont, a hotel where all manner of decadent and dark Hollywood shenanigans had famously occurred over the decades. Lily was morbidly fascinated, as most people would be, to discover that the actor John Belushi had died in the room in which she stayed.

Perhaps unsurprisingly given the circumstances, EMI had not chosen the Chateau Marmont for Lily to stay in while she finished her album; they were pulling in their purse strings wherever they could and, according to Lily, opted to book her into a "horrific apartment." There was nothing else for it – she threw all of her luggage back into the car and whizzed off to the Chateau Marmont. "I'm no diva but I am here for three weeks..." she protested.

"The guy on the desk told me there was just one vacancy, which was (a bungalow) in the garden," she continued in her excited blog entry (entitled: 'John Belushi Died In My Room', naturally). "It was the place John Belushi died in. He asked me if that was a problem. As if..."

One of Lily's all-time favourite movies was *The Blues Brothers*, and she joked that she wanted to tune in to his "Blues Brothers Don-ness", and maybe write a song about his final hours.

After settling in, she drove back out to Santa Monica, where her Aunt Kai was living, and whisked her back to the Chateau Marmont poolside where Kai, "progressively loud and drunk", kept Lily and Emily thoroughly entertained with anecdotes galore. Lily's fellow residents, however, were less than enamoured of the rather vocal visitor. "Everyone hated us," chuckled Lily.

Just because Lily was away from home – and the Body Doctor – didn't mean she was shirking her routine. The following morning, before heading to the studio, Lily was up with the lark working out with a personal trainer for over an hour. She also had to move out of the Belushi bungalow and into a room in the Chateau itself – the bungalow was cripplingly expensive, but it had been fun for a night. "Sadly John Belushi's spirit is no longer with me," Lily blogged, tongue firmly in cheek, "and I have to actually walk up stairs to get to my room." It's a tough life.

From the relative peace (at least, after Auntie Kai had left) of the Chateau Marmont, Lily was plunged into the most intense paparazzi experience she could imagine on the way to the studio. She admitted she had never been followed by photographers to such an extent, although they were at least surprisingly polite.

But as is always the way with a life of relative extremes, the highs that most of us might never dream of experiencing are balanced by lows that average people would never consider. Lily was never going to be one of those stars who could refuse to see press coverage of her, even if it was just from a sniping blogger, and her former number one fan Perez Hilton had turned into exactly that, on a grand scale. Lily suspected his sudden u-turn might have had something to do with him having a crush on her former manager, whom she had sacked. Whatever had happened, it certainly seemed personal.

Lily had endured his sneering at the fact that she likes to go out and get drunk and let off steam, this seemed to be the main criticism of her (he rubbed his hands together gleefully when images of Lily 'dead drunk' after the Glamour awards came to light) and he would frequently put up images of Lily on stage or out and about with insulting names written across her head, sometimes even a picture of a penis attached to her head. Infantile was not the word, and often even his own fans would pick him up on this insidious, strange and almost obsessive behaviour.

But while Lily was in LA, Perez crossed the line with his bitchy blogging, insinuating that Lily had smoked during her pregnancy – she hadn't – and that there was "something suspicious" about her miscarriage. To say it was a low blow is an understatement.

Perez Hilton had also gleefully proclaimed that: "She's known these days more for being a tragic train wreck than a musician," before announcing that she had been "replaced" by the singer Katy Perry. Perez then wrote that the only thing that could "save" her was "if she makes a good sophomore album, but, from what we're hearing, Lily's new material s-u-c-k-s."

Lily responded by admitting that it did pain her that she received more attention for her lifestyle than her music, but she insisted it was about time bloggers stopped suggesting she was having feuds with "rival" singers, emphatically stating that her life was not about "jealousy".

Lily must have known that that last sentence might have prompted many people to think, "So what about all that tension with Amy Winehouse?" She wisely had that covered too, and did herself credit in being honest, confessing she was "a little jealous" when Amy came steaming into the charts with her powerful voice and persona, but her feelings were never "unhealthy".

Once it had been a relief to go to America, where she never came up against accusations of nepotism, but Perez was getting poisonous and it would be hard not to associate Hollywood with him. Fortunately there was plenty going on in Lily's life not to have to think of him too much, although it would be hard not to fight back whenever he posted up one of his ridiculous attacks.

At least Lily's favourite landmark of the year was swinging around – Glastonbury Festival. With her pink hair messily tied up, Lily would celebrate by hanging out backstage with her friends the Radio 1 DJ Annie Mac, Mark Ronson and even her ex Ed Simons (prompting a flurry of reports that the pair were rekindling their romance – they weren't). This was also the perfect opportunity for Lily to try out her beloved dinosaur costume that she had picked up in Japan – it was pure Glasto. She might have performed that year in a swingy blue denim summer dress but offstage you'd have to look out for a little pink-haired Lil-asaurus if you wanted to find the hottest performer at Glastonbury.

This particular Glastonbury was historic, not least because it was Lily's twentieth (or that she'd had to take her lyrics onstage with her as she hadn't played a gig in such a long time), but organiser Michael Eavis had chosen a groundbreaking headline act – the hip-hop star Jay-Z, a choice that had divided the music press and festival-goers.

But Lily, who watched Jay-Z's set with Eavis and his daughter, co-organiser Emily, knew he would be a smash. "We were like, 'Haha! You're all wrong, it's brilliant,'" she said shortly afterwards in an interview. Interestingly, when asked (inevitably) what she thought of Amy Winehouse's set, she said it was "funny", before skipping off to sing 'Oh My God' with Mark Ronson on the Other Stage, relying on the audience's singing skills for support. Lily was, as usual, not particularly sober during this festival performance, but something else was hanging over her: it was while she was at the festival that she heard the sad news that her grandmother on her father, Keith's, side had passed away.

She dedicated the bittersweet 'Littlest Things' to her beloved grandmother, whom she had been especially close to, telling the crowd, "My nanny Allen died last night, so this one's for you. I love you."

The price of fame meant that, even when she attended the funeral in Llanelli in the Allens' native Wales, sang a farewell ballad at the service and comforted her grieving family, Lily, and therefore the funeral, was surrounded by paparazzi.

For all of Lily's rebelliousness, her family and how they would feel came first, and for this reason Lily decided to say a solemn goodbye to her punky pink hair and go "back to black, bitch" (a play on a certain nemesis' hit album title). "My nan would have killed me if I went to her funeral with pink hair."

CHAPTER 18

"I've been in my new flat for a week. Don't get too excited, burglars: I've got metal roller blinds that go down at night and a panic button by my bed. No panic room though..."

Lily's blog, July 7, 2008.

L ily wasn't used to being alone – she'd been staying with friends or in hotels for the best part of the past 18 months and thrilled as she was with her swanky new three-bedroom pad in North-West London (a stone's throw from her mother's, but also just a walk away from vibrant Ladbroke Grove), she admitted she felt "weird".

A new mongrel, Honey, reclaimed from Battersea Dogs Home, helped to ease her solitude and provide a pal for her other dog, Mabel (formerly known as Maggie May), and before long Lily would be putting up her grandfather Eddie, because he was having to get used to being on his own too. Lily would take the care of her new nest very seriously, not least because of the presence of Eddie. "I don't want people crashed out here all hours of the morning," she insisted. "I don't want any drugs in this flat." Lily was more than happy having Eddie around, and it wasn't unusual to see her turning up to BBC Radio 1 for a session with her grandpa in tow.

When she wasn't taking care of the interiors – light floorboards, dark walls providing a backdrop to her extensive art collection (including prints and originals by Clash bassist Paul Simonon, Keith Haring, and also a framed copy of her 2007 police caution after she clashed with a paparazzo: 'offence: common assault. method used: punched/slapped') – she was primping the garden, which had been landscaped with pretty pebbles, verdant herb bushes and an olive tree, and taking care of Eddie and the dogs Lily would, as always, stay abreast of what was happening in the news. She didn't like what she was reading, and for once, it wasn't about her. There had been an increasing flurry of teenage knife crime in Britain, particularly in urban areas, and Lily knew she could wisely use her fame to make a stand and speak out against it. Her turn of phrase might have seemed slightly flippant at first glance, but the effect was ultimately positive.

"Please can everyone stop stabbing each other in the UK," she wrote in her blog. "It's really sad, my thoughts are with all the families affected by these heinous crimes…" And then she appealed to the mayor of London, Boris Johnson: "Boris, if you're listening, call me, man…" Lily knew this was a battle Johnson was trying to fight, and even though he was a Tory, Labour-loving Lily was prepared to put this aside and team up with him for the greater good. This blog post understandably sped around the blogosphere and into the papers, and before long, Boris Johnson was indeed getting in touch with Lily, with the pop star becoming something of an advisor to him on 'youth' matters.

The pair met up just two weeks after Lily's post, with Boris telling the radio station BBC6Music: "I welcome any constructive suggestions on combatting knife crime and Lily Allen has already proved her commitment to help address this problem. There is nothing romantic or glamorous about knife crime and I'm delighted Lily will be using her considerable profile and fan base to spread that message."

It certainly made Boris' job easier to have a popular star like Lily fighting his corner. And Lily caused those ruddy Johnson cheeks to blush a little harder when she admitted to "quite fancying Boris. Even though he's a Tory."

Lily did take politics seriously though, and knew the difference it would make having a high profile artist putting the pressure on, and environmental issues were no exception – she was praised by eco-warriors when she wrote to MPs urging them to back an amendment to an energy bill, helping to cause a parliamentary rebellion against the Labour PM Gordon Brown. You don't get nominated as 'The Greenest Star In Europe' for nothing, which Lily was, for Disney Playhouse's 'Playing For The Planet' Awards.

After playing her political part and making a stand for a more peaceful, greener, knife-free Britain, Lily booked herself a break away in Ibiza in August. It was something of a trip down memory lane, particularly as she hadn't been in Ibiza since her lost few months of decadence and danger when she was 15, just before she met George Lamb and her life changed. "It was nice to experience the island in a different way..."

At least she could relax in the knowledge that she had crossed every 'I' and dotted every 'T' as far as the album was concerned. It was now in the hands of EMI but, of course, this was the first of several turbulent years for all large record labels, and Lily's was no exception. As usual though, Lily laid down the facts for fans who were desperately awaiting her next album in her blog. "Lots of people have been fired or have taken redundancy recently as the company was taken over by a private equity firm called Terra Firma," Lily explained. "Many of these people were people assigned to my projects and now I don't quite know what's going on." She assured her subscribers that there would probably be a release sooner rather than later and, if nothing else, they could look forward to some sneak previews as always on the player on her MySpace page. After coming back from Ibiza, she almost considered going on another holiday again, "nothing else to do".

Since Terra Firma had taken over EMI, Lily had become displeased at the way she was being treated, and "wished she could get dropped". She told *Word* magazine that she adored the people she worked with at EMI, it was just Terra Firma that were "arseholes", and she complained at how, back in the day, she'd have been treated far better than she was now.

"I know that 20 years ago I'd have been booked in at the Ritz with five grams of cocaine on my table and ten bunches of flowers. Some new clothes. A chauffeur on 24-hour call. Now I'm lucky to get an Oyster card. I make no money from selling records – obviously – but they're still arsey about hair and make-up. They don't understand anything."

At least she had a new project to take her mind off things – Lily had, as you do, bought herself a three-mile strip of private beach in Jamaica after falling in love with the island on her Christmas holiday there 18 months before. Lily was savvy, and for the same reason that she invested in art, she was putting her money into land in her bid to beat the recession and have a gorgeous holiday retreat into the bargain.

"I went there and it was so beautiful and all the people were so friendly," she told Radio 1 DJ Sara Cox, "and with the credit crunch all the prices have gone down, so I just thought, get it out of my bank account, where it's probably all about to fall through… and buy property." Cox found it amusing that Lily talked about snapping up land as the prices had gone down in the same tone that many of us would talk about maybe buying that pair of jeans that was finally affordable because of the recession.

Yes, Lily might be richer than most but she was perfectly aware of the financial climate – and how it might be remedied: "I think I might start to make my own cereal called Credit Crunch," she joked to Damien Hirst in *Interview* magazine. "It would just be a cereal laced with speed so you don't need to buy food for the rest of the day."

It was during her trip over to Jamaica that she dropped a bit of a clanger and raised Simon Cowell's temperature somewhat. Lily had been sharing a jokey text conversation with her godmother, the singer Angela McCluskey, and "we'd been talking about Simon Cowell, and I was like, 'Maybe I should make him my next conquest', and you know when you're talking about someone and then their name is in your head, and then you text them by accident… I texted him that maybe I should make him my next conquest. Simon Cowell texted me back and said, 'What are you talking about?' and I was like, 'Nothing!'" So now we know why Lily is so devoted to *X-Factor*…

Finally it was announced that *It's Not Me, It's You* was scheduled for release the following February, with first single 'The Fear' in the shops on January 26, 2009, and the digital release on December 9, 2008. It was a little festive treat complete with a video that saw Lily, long black hair swinging as she pranced and strutted through a hall filled with dancing men, balloons and giant presents, "I had such a laugh doing it," she said. The biggest present, of course, would be that, after its official release, 'The Fear' would hit number one and stay there for four weeks.

'The Fear' was a telling slice of observation, satire and wry self-contemplation (subliminal or otherwise) by Lily. It was airier, dancier and lighter, musically, than her previous work, and a chance for Lily to give her incisive take on her situation – being so famous and scrutinised, and partly enjoying it, that she no longer knew what was "right or real" any more. In subsequent interviews Lily would claim she was singing in character, as it were, as someone who had totally bought into consumerism and the materialism of the modern age, blunting any spirituality or old-fashioned basic values. "It could be adopted as an anthem for a generation of London-based microcelebrities whose lives revolve around appearances in free-sheet newspapers," mused *Popjustice* in its review of the single. "A celebration of defiant self-belief followed by crushing doubt and worthlessness."

Many who listened to the words immediately assumed she was singing as herself, at least, herself as seen through the filter others view her through. "I look in *The Sun* and I look in *The Mirror*..." she crooned softly, "I'm on the right track, yeah, we're onto a winner." Lyrics such as "Everything's cool as long as I'm getting thinner" were particularly pertinent as Lily was already keenly aware how much more accepted by the fashion world she was since she'd lost weight, not just thanks to the Body Doctor but also the Harley Street hypnotherapist Susan Hepburn, who had treated Lily by reprogramming her to choose healthy food over junk, and, crucially, try not to use alcohol as a crutch.

And talking of haute couture, it was time, once September rolled around, for Lily to select the perfect frock for a big night alongside the grand dame himself, Sir Elton John. Elton was fond and protective of Lily – he was apparently one of the few people who checked in with Lily after her miscarriage to see how she was – and he had invited her to co-host the *GQ* Awards with him.

Both stars were outspoken and prone to unpredictability, which was no doubt part of the charm of their onstage partnership, but no one could have known quite how memorable – and uncomfortable – their appearance would be. Lily would insist that their spiky exchanges were in fun, but the audience weren't sure whether to laugh or cover their mouths in shock.

Up on the podium, Elton looked on as Lily, every inch the lady in a stunning Dolce & Gabbana gown and Chopard jewellery, introduced

Carol Vorderman for an award, managing to get at least five 'f-words' into her greeting. Afterwards things went further downhill…

"And now the most important part of the night," slurred a considerably refreshed Lily, to which Elton, leaning on the lectern and looking grumpy, retorted: "What? Are you going to have another drink?'"

Lily responded predictably: "Fuck off, Elton," before sniping, "I am 40 years younger than you and have my whole life ahead of me…" Elton pushed the bitching even further by replying, "I could still snort you under the table." Lily piously said, "I don't know what you're talking about."

Later she thrust her brother, Alfie, and his then girlfriend, Jaime Winstone, into the limelight, drunkenly declaring that Winstone was her "soon-to-be sister-in-law Jaime", before shouting, "Show off your rock, show off your diamond!" Jaime and Alfie were nonplussed, not least because they apparently weren't even engaged anyway.

The much-loved jazz singer Tony Bennett was collecting the Inspiration Award, but he nearly got more than he bargained for. Lily also displayed her famous lust for older men when Sir Elton made reference to the singer's age (then 82). "I'll still fuck him," blurted Lily. Bluntness aside, admittedly this wasn't an unusual response for Lily – she also once proclaimed that she "wanted to shag" the artist Lucian Freud, 86 at the time, when she met him: "It would be funny, he's four times my age." Not sure her father, or indeed grandfather, would find it funny. Lily often protests that her grandparents were often upset by scandalous reports of her in the newspapers, but to be fair, they'd probably have been quite shocked by her own undoctored remarks too.

At least it seemed that Eddie Allen, Lily's grandfather, was trying to get used to Lily's fruity language. "Lily's had her moments, but she's still a sweet kid," he'd said in an interview. "Of course, her gran and I are proud of her. Neither of us are very keen on some of the swearing or things she might do or say. But you have to accept it. That's the way things are today. If you don't accept it you'll lose her." He was used to waywardness from bringing up his son Keith, so this was nothing new, it was just on a larger scale.

Maybe you had to know Lily to realise that her bolshy upstart 'rant' at Elton John was really nowhere near as dramatic or damaging as it seemed but, needless to say, no one was sure how to react, and the papers went wild with the story the following day.

Again, Lily took refuge in her blog, rubbishing the newspaper claims that there was any kind of feud between herself and Elton, before adding: "This isn't meant to be a place for me to respond to journalists, but I am very grateful I have this page, if I didn't then I would have absolutely no voice when it comes to this stuff."

Lily also added that her brother and Jaime "had never been engaged" and that she was just trying to wind Alfie up. (Keith admits in his book *Grow Up* that this was how he proposed to his second wife Nira Park – because Lily wound him up and pushed and prodded, in front of Nira by the way, until Keith had no choice but to propose, and Lily realised her dream of being a bridesmaid. Unfortunately, if she was trying to repeat history here, it didn't work – Alfie and Jaime split in 2010.)

Despite Lily's strong front on MySpace, it was a different story, apparently, on her Facebook page. She first alarmed friends by posting up the words "dying inside" on her status update, after writing allegedly that she "has had enough" and felt "like killing" herself, before taking it back down, presumably after being taken to task by concerned friends. Lily had holed up in her flat, having stocked up on food and cigarettes and was making sure she had no need to go out for as long as possible in a bid to let the press furore die down and avoid the photographers outside. She avoided even going to Mark Ronson's birthday party.

Later Lily led the media to believe she was talking about her feelings about the GQ Awards debacle when she then posted up: "Was he upset? I'm worried now. Was I mean?" to which a friend responded: "It was priceless. Hope you got rid of the hangover in the end." The tough, ballsy Lily, so confident in her own actions, still needed the reassurance of friends and fans because, underneath it all, she'd either felt destabilised by the constant scrutiny over this situation, or she knew, underneath it all, that she had in fact crossed a line with Elton. It seems no coincidence that, the following year, the video that accompanied the single 'Who'd Have Known?' featured Lily gazing up at large pictures of Elton, an "obsessed" fan who eventually kidnaps him. Maybe this was her way of reconciling with Elton, whom she deep down feared she had indeed offended, saying, "I love you," in a cheeky, witty way.

She later told *Word* journalist Rob Fitzpatrick: "I told him to fuck off, but I tell everyone to fuck off all day long. Todd, my manager, works for his company, so it would be quite awkward if we fell out. I'd hate to fall out with him and still have to give him 15 per cent of everything I earn."

Fortunately for Lily, she had another chance to throw herself into work after a period of relative down time. Once the release date of the album was confirmed, she had plenty to do in the run-up, preparing tracks for "some websites who won't put an album on their front page unless you give them exclusive tracks…" Lily knew what she had to do to maximise her chances of another hit.

One of those extra tracks that Lily was working hard on was a cover of Britney Spears' 'Womaniser', which surprised some of her fans when word got round. Lily had sent the song to Mark Ronson as he had asked her for something he could play on his radio show that no one else had heard yet. She had her cover of 'Womaniser' as an attachment on her BlackBerry, and as she hadn't had time to get home and send him another track, that was the song she sent, on the understanding that he talked all over it "so it wouldn't get ripped". He didn't, and as a result the song was all over the internet before you could say, "Britney"…

The day before the digital release of 'The Fear', a 'fan playback' was organised at Slim Jim's Liquor Stores in Upper Street, Islington, near Lily's old home. For Lily, the fans always came first and it was important to her to show them that. A crowd of Lily-lovers flocked to Highbury that evening and revelled in the opportunity to be the first to hear Lily's new material. It had been a long time coming, and Lily was more nervous about how it would be received than she had been about her debut.

"The first album is like: 'I'm right and you're wrong,' this one is questioning things rather than making statements."

CHAPTER 19

"The lyrical themes range from the sublime to the ridiculous, but nobody says this sort of stuff quite like Lily Allen. Most people never even say it at all."

Popjustice's take on *It's Not Me, It's You*.

'The Fear' was released on January 26 in the UK, and after the madness of the festive season faded into a memory, Lily decided to try and calm down her social schedule and knuckle down to prepare for its release. She also joined the micro-blogging site Twitter to vent her spleen and plug her work in a slightly more measured way than on MySpace. With a limit of only 140 characters per tweet, Lily would have to choose her words carefully and be more considered with what she chose to share anyway. It seemed perfect for the impulsive, outspoken Lily Allen. Not that that would save her from causing a stir with her cheeky humour and strong opinions… she'd always find a way to throw the cat among the pigeons.

Lily had already raised eyebrows when she was interviewed on T4 by her childhood pal Miquita Oliver. Miquita, known for her special brand of sarcasm designed to dispel any 'starriness' in her interviewees, was not going to make an exception with Lily, and soon the old friends were bantering away, any trace of the 'pop superstar' eradicated, for the moment. Naturally she chose to take the opportunity to respond to a less than flattering comment made by the then pop newcomer Katy Perry. "[She said] 'I'm like a skinnier version of Lily Allen and a fatter Amy Winehouse.' The thing about me and Amy is that we're both British and we write our own songs," said Lily. "It doesn't matter if you're skinnier or fatter. There's no comparison I'm afraid…"

Lily also revealed her best Geordie Cheryl Cole (in *X-Factor* judge mode) impression after a little encouragement from Miquita: "A dowen't think we've sin the best of yuz yet…" Watching Miquita and Lily giggling wildly and taking the piss out of her rivals was just like seeing two naughty schoolgirls sitting on the sofa after school, screaming with wicked laughter about someone they didn't like in class. Miquita admitted they'd been having a hoot at Lily's Cheryl impersonation for months. So no sign of a reconciliation on the cards just yet…

During the whirlwind of promotion, there was, however, the jokey suggestion of a coming together of the Allen and the Winehouse during an interview with Absolute Radio DJ Geoff Lloyd. Lily teased that she wanted to unleash an alternative Spice Girls on the Brit Awards ceremony that year and sing 'Wannabe'. "I would be Posh, Adele would be Ginger, Amy would be Scary and Duffy would be Baby and Sporty Spice would be Lady Sovereign." (Geoff Lloyd left quite an impression on Lily, it seemed. After their interview Lily wrote 'Geoff Lloyd is cool' repeatedly on her blog, and even brought him a packet of 'posh' Jammy Dodgers the next time she went into the studio, remembering a conversation they'd had about the biscuits the previous time. It must be love…)

Lily certainly knew how to pepper an interview with shocks and cheeky surprises – no beige media-trained trotting out of the same old responses here. She admitted live on air to Radio 1 DJ Chris Moyles that she'd sent a picture of her breasts to Kaiser Chiefs singer Ricky Wilson by accident: "That was really embarrassing. I was completely topless. It was meant to go to Rick Astley." That's all right then. This wasn't the first time Lily had sent images of her boobs to surprise her acquaintances, Guy Ritchie was also on the receiving end of such a text. "They're all in the same sort of set though, which kind of makes it OK," says a former colleague of Ritchie. "It's like the public-school thing, a kind of 'famous person' aristocracy that makes it OK to do stuff like that, and everyone just laughs it off…"

But none of these pranks could upstage the story that was on everyone's lips just days into the New Year of 2009 – her torrid romance with none other than the art dealer Jay Jopling, a close friend of Damien Hirst and her father. Jopling was 45, Lily was 23, and the press shivered with delight as pictures came in of the pair frolicking and embracing on a yacht in St Bart's in the Caribbean with friends. Just months before, Jopling had been still with his ex-wife, the artist Sam Taylor-Wood, and the three of them had greeted each other cordially on the red carpet premiere for the movie *Flashbacks Of A Fool*.

Taylor-Wood and Jopling had separated by the time Lily was gazing lovingly into his eyes and stroking his grey-flecked locks, but the public were somewhat outraged. Not that the *Daily Mail*-reading public's feelings even came close to how Lily's father, Keith, would react, particularly as he had to be informed by a national newspaper.

"It is a bit weird that Jay and Damien hung around with Keith when Lily would have been a child, and Keith was *not* happy when he was told that Lily was having an affair with Jay," chuckles a press insider. "*The Telegraph*, I think, had called him up about it, and skirted around it a bit until they said: 'And do you have any comment to make on this…?' He didn't know what they were talking about.

"He was stunned and then started screaming down the phone: 'You're telling me that my daughter is sucking Jay's cock?'"

Yes, now Lily was all grown up, she saw Jay in a different light, and the pair had seemed "close" at Jopling's Christmas party at the gallery White Cube. In a way, it was easy to understand the pairing. Lily loved the cultured older man, for a start. She adored art, Jay was an art dealer. She was minted, and so was he (a constant issue for Lily was trying to work out whether potential lovers would simply be after her because of her money or fame). Also, Jay Jopling was not exactly the type to film her with his camera-phone and then send the results to *The Sun*.

Unfortunately, however, it was all rather more complicated than that. Taylor-Wood and Jopling were, according to reports, amicably separated and had worked out a way to still live under the same roof for the sake of their children. However, when Sam saw the images of Lily and Jay, she was "devastated", especially when she learned that one of their daughters had heard about the affair from the other kids at school. Press reports of a "messy divorce" flew around the internet and news-stands. Lily just wanted someone to rely on, some affection and some stability. Who knows the exact reason why Lily and Jay didn't last, but something tells us that yet more scrutiny and pap-dodging was not something either of them would have wished for.

It was maybe no surprise that after all the aggro Lily had received over the past year, the ups and downs and the criticisms on the web that she couldn't resist reading, she felt it was time for a bit of an overhaul. She had already managed to do that physically – her toned new physique was testament to that. Now it was time to do it mentally, and she prepared to have some meetings with a therapist who was "going to try and help her get more positive". If nothing else, Lily was determined not to let her demons get to her, although it's hard to know who would be able to cope happily with the barrage of judgmental attention she came up against.

Still, at least she had plenty to do in the meantime to distract herself from what was being said and hashed over in the press (and at home). Clash guitarist Mick Jones had asked her to sing with him on a cover of Clash song 'Straight To Hell' for a charity album, *Warchild Heroes*, which would come out the following month. "It was intimidating," she told Canadian chat-show host George Stroumboulopoulos. "I've known Mick since I was young, but I knew Joe (Strummer) more, and I was a bit scared of going into the studio with Mick. It was all very Clashy, beer and spliffs going..."

Warchild, incidentally, would become a charity close to Lily's heart, and they were ensured fulsome support from her: "Every time the newspapers say something wrong about me, I sue them and give half to the Teenage Cancer Trust and half to Warchild."

Lily had her special *It's Not Me, It's You* gig to look forward to, the first concert to promote the new album and the first London gig she had played in 18 months. The gig was on January 28 at Camden's opulent Koko, the former Camden Palace, and it seemed that everyone who was anyone – in media terms at least – was there to support (and quaff the free booze at the after-party): Kate Moss, Jamie Hince, Mark Ronson,

176

Jaime Winstone, Miquita Oliver and of course Lily's family. It was a special night, and set the tone for the year ahead, the year of *It's Not Me, It's You*. Two weeks later Lily would be in New York, playing a secret MySpace show at the Bowery Ballroom, before playing dates in Tokyo and the UK.

On February 9, Lily's album was released in the UK, debuting at number one and going platinum. "I was going to call the album *Brillyallent*," Lily mused in an interview during her stint in the US. "But I thought I was leaving myself open to too much criticism: '*Not* Brillyallent.'"

Her *It's Not Me, It's You* idea (as we know) was inspired by the time she gave some advice to a friend who was considering breaking up with a girlfriend, but didn't know what to say – but it was validated when Lily's therapist said exactly that and, of course, it was just what she wanted to hear. "He said, 'It's not you, it's them.' I was like, 'OK! Thank God for that.'" Money well spent.

The album certainly displayed another side of Lily Allen, it was more ethereal, poppier and more contemporary and with a definite thread running through it melodically. And, as was the intention, there was a new maturity to Lily's work, although it still displayed the freshness that caught everyone's attention in the first place.

The second single, the country-tinged 'Not Fair' was scheduled for a digital release the following month, being physically released in May, when it debuted at 16 and rose to number nine. 'Not Fair' was Lily's naughty lament to an ex-lover who was perfect in every way other than the fact he always came first, and never hung around to satisfy her in bed. With references to "wet patches" and "giving head", it was no surprise when Lily was told to modify the words for TV appearances. ('I spent ages giving head' became 'I spent ages kneading bread', which, as TV presenter Graham Norton observed through peals of giggles, had the potential to sound even more dubious.)

The album was typically revealing – despite her promise that she would be leaving family matters well alone, the rest of the Allen clan were all represented on the release. 'He Wasn't There' was about Keith: this was Lily making it very clear that, while she adored her daddy, he, well, just wasn't there when she was growing up. 'Back To The Start' was a reconciliatory tune dedicated to the mellowing of a rocky relationship with her sister Sarah. (This track includes such revealing, stark lyrics as: "You always were and you always will be the taller and prettier one. People seem to love you, they gravitate towards you, that's why I started to hate you so much." Lily was speaking, singing the words that so many families stifle and never say.)

'Chinese' is about hanging out with her mum, Alison, missing her when she's away on tour, and how she loves nothing more than to snuggle up to her on the sofa when she's back home, watch TV and eat Chinese food. Plenty of people speculated on various men they believed this song was about, but no, it was definitely about and for her mum.

And of course there was 'Fuck You', formerly 'Guess Who Batman' (GWB), based around a sample of the Carpenters' 'Close To You'. This song would soon delight audiences the world over as they joined in the sweary chorus, middle fingers aloft against the BNP, George W Bush and fascists everywhere. Lily would even be presented on French TV with a video of lots of viewers singing along with the track, giving the middle finger. She said she found it rather moving.

The jaunty track '22', a song about a nameless woman whom "society" deems increasingly irrelevant as a result of her age, started off about a specific person, but ended up as a more general song about women who feel they have to rely on their looks, and when their looks start to fade, they realise life isn't quite as straightforward as they'd thought.

"It hits them that they're not doing anything with their lives and it's too late," Lily explained. The resulting video, filmed in the toilets of a Masonic temple (where else?), showed Lily and a gaggle of girls getting made up in the reflection of the bathroom mirrors, but Lily gets more dishevelled as the video wears on…

"'22' is about how everything is run by guys, and we all know what guys are fuelled by," Lily explained. "If you don't get on the professional ladder by a certain age, then your only other option seems to be getting married… it's a sad idea." The solution? "Kill them…"

Lily and Greg found themselves in their own George Harrison/'My Sweet Lord' situation when it came to the track 'Who'd Have Known', which was accompanied by a video of Lily pretending to stalk Elton John (especially amusing since the *GQ* Awards 'incident'). Inadvertently, they had written a cheery song that sounded exactly like Take That's recent hit 'Shine'. It's not unusual for this to happen – sometimes a songwriter thinks they are coming up with an idea, or that a tune has been rattling around their head that they have just invented, but the reason it's in their head is because somewhere they have heard the tune before, even if they didn't register it.

Having realised the faux pas, Lily was open about it, talked about it in interviews and fortunately Take That were cool with it. They turned down the offer of appearing in a video with her, however. (She was especially disappointed she didn't get to hold hands with Mark Owen. Maybe the whole debacle had just been a ruse to hold hands with Mark Owen after all...)

More scandalous than her accidental Take That rip-off was the furore surrounding her song 'Everyone's On It', about the casual drug use that is happening all around her all the time. This track was particularly interesting to some of the journalists sent to interview her about the new release, as it offered another opportunity to quiz her on her thoughts on drug use. As usual, Lily didn't disappoint.

"The only (newspaper) story is that drugs are bad and they will kill you," mused Lily in an interview with *Word*. "I know lots of people that take cocaine three nights a week and get up and go to work every day, no problem. But we never hear that side of the story."

As ever the unembellished truth about drug use from the mouth of someone with a degree of experience on the matter set middle England into a tail-spin, especially the *Daily Mail*, which translated it as: 'Lily Allen says you can live a normal life on drugs'...

A spokesperson for Lily had to dutifully respond by releasing the following statement: "Lily Allen would like to state unequivocally that she does not condone illegal drug use and has every sympathy with individuals and families whose lives have been blighted by drugs."

But Lily was plunged into more hot water when just weeks later she said to the Dutch magazine *Revu*: "Parents should say, 'Drugs might seem fun, but they do funny things to your brain. Some people react to it good, some don't. Try it and see what you think'... If I hadn't been famous I'd have taken loads (of ecstasy). Wouldn't be too wise right now." Well, as her song says, "Why can't we all, all just be honest...?"

It's Not Me, It's You certainly covered plenty of ground, from the sexual to the chemical, the familial and even the spiritual, including a song about God, 'Him'. Her favourite line: 'I don't imagine he's ever been suicidal, his favourite band is Creedence Clearwater Revival...' Not too happy-clappy then. Peter Robinson's popular website *Popjustice*, a longtime supporter of Lily, was impressed. "No doubt this song will be interpreted as being wildly controversial and while there's no doubt that Lily knows what she's doing it's all beautifully phrased. Its classic Allen, really – having a laugh then catching you off guard..."

Everything was going well, even the critics who had dismissed *Alright, Still* were grudgingly impressed by Lily's new release, and Lily herself felt that she "loved every track" and insisted it was time she was known as 'Fear singer Lily Allen' instead of 'Smile singer Lily Allen' in the papers – 'Smile' was the song she had sung until she was blue in the face, until the idea of singing 'Smile' again made her snarl. But references to her first opus also reminded her of how much she'd grown up, and she admitted to Radio 1 DJ Sara Cox that she "cringed" whenever she thought of *Alright, Still*. "There was a cockiness about me then that I don't have so much now, some of the lyrics, like: 'cos I lost my phone...' I'm like, 'Shut up Lily! What are you doing? It's not cool.' Maybe when you're 18 it's OK..."

Lily was growing up in other ways too, becoming less open and more guarded, which was important. There was one unfortunate occurrence that stopped Lily in her tracks, and marked the watershed that saw her start taking her privacy much more seriously.

Lily took the time to post up a lengthy blog, and at this stage, the days of long Lily blog-posts were rarer than they had been on MySpace, so readers knew this was serious. After being approached by the *New York Times* the year before with regard to a cover piece on Lily for its arts pull-out, Lily had agreed, getting on well with the journalist it had sent over (with whom she would later hang out at New York's Bowery Ballroom after Lily's 'secret' MySpace gig in February) and letting her guard down, conducting the interview in Lily's own flat after a photographer took some images of Lily in the intimacy of her own home. Lily admitted in the blog that she would never have normally done this, but she respected the *NYT*, and "it felt like special circumstances".

Lily explained in the post that she'd been getting more stringent, making sure that, after a photo shoot, the magazine signed a contract indicating that they would not sell on the photographs without Lily's consent. But unfortunately, that is exactly what the *New York Times* did – it sold its pictures of Lily at home to *OK!* magazine, which then touted the images as a "world exclusive" as if it had interviewed Lily itself. To say Lily was upset is putting it mildly, and she branded the *NYT* "cheap and disgusting".

The 'world exclusive' tagline aside, a former freelance reporter who worked with *OK!* admits Lily's tirade seemed like something of an over-reaction: "It didn't really explode in the office, magazines get sued all the time. I can see her point but personally I think her volatile reaction made it seem worse than it was.

"Sometimes she has this hard-done-by thing, I think that's why people can be resentful to her, she has been given so many amazing opportunities on a platter, and she's like, 'Poor me...' I remember when she was in *NYT*, and they took the photos in her apartment and *OK!* magazine bought them because *NYT* has a syndication department and that is what magazines do.

"She wrote this blog about how awful it was for her. I just thought she needed a reality check. She felt utterly betrayed... but she's a young girl and maybe overreacting in an emotional way. When she wrote that, it was like, 'Do you know how lucky you are that people want to photograph you in your home? And the *NYT* want to put you on the cover of their magazine, and *OK!* magazine want to publish those pictures and thinks that you will sell their magazine because you are so popular and fascinating?'

"Lily has kind of grown up in public, she says ludicrous things but she's just a kid. Because we're putting all this attention on her, it's like, 'Go on, say something stupid again,' and it's not fair, is it? She can be obnoxious and annoying and she doesn't live in the real world, but who can blame her after her upbringing?"

Even so, it was the principle – Lily Allen did not want to be seen to be consorting with tabloid magazines, she didn't want to be thought of as the sort of star who would "talk to anyone", it devalued her, in her opinion. But, as the pages of tabloid magazines and newspapers would eventually be lining the bottom of birdcages, littertrays and recycling bins anyway, hopefully Lily's ire did not eat into her enjoyment of the promo rigmarole for her smash hit new album – there'd be the usual round of world travel, glittering gigs with star-studded audiences, champagne flowing… But that would also mean exhaustion, hangovers, stories being blown out of proportion and Chinese whispers in the press. Maybe it was all just too much of a good thing.

One thing was for sure, Lily did not want to be doing this forever. She wasn't even sure if she wanted to continue beyond the following year. Her dream of living in the country in a beautiful home, perhaps near her father in the Cotswolds, having children with a man who loves her, rearing chickens, gardening and cooking for friends, seemed like a distant star, but it was becoming more attractive by the minute. Nobody would truly believe her when she said she wanted to retire by 30 and decamp to the countryside, Lily Allen says a lot of things, after all… but it wasn't hard to see that she was nearing saturation point.

CHAPTER 20

"I don't like baring my soul without a 'boom-tish!' at the end."
Lily Allen on the nature of her songwriting,
talking to *The Liverpool Echo.*

One of the main reasons Lily was starting to feel emotionally exhausted was, again, the fact that the very tool that had helped to catapult her to stardom – the internet – was turning in on her. She might have pulled back on MySpace but Facebook was proving just as addictive. At least on Facebook she could limit her friends to actual *friends*, but Twitter was proving a different story altogether, and a series of Twitter 'wars' kicked off, with seemingly no end in sight.

The most vicious of these was between Lily and Perez Hilton, the LA blogger formerly so besotted with Lily, but who had since turned bitter and started writing about her in less than flattering terms. Like the class bitch, he knew what would hurt Lily, having gone for the jugular by sniping: "If I wanted to be a fucked up Brit, I'd rather be Amy Winehouse," and claiming rather more seriously that she'd smoked during her pregnancy. Hatred was already simmering between Perez and Lily as a result of the 'stories' he had almost obsessively posted up about her, but he used Twitter to get at Lily directly.

Perez had expressed an interest on his Twitter page in bagging an appearance in Lily's next music video, but Allen shot straight back: "Oh I'm sorry, we've already cast the jealous and bitter lonely old queen role..."

Hilton: "Jealous of who? David Beckham, maybe. And if I wanted to be a fucked up Brit, I'd rather be Amy Winehouse, whose got talent."

Allen: "God you're so obsessed with me it's embarrassing."

Hilton: "Congrats on your album doing well in America though, It's really hard to sell copies when you discount it to $3.99. Desperate!"

Allen: "It's also number one everywhere else in the world, douchebag. Go away you little parasite."

Hilton: "Aw you can see I've lost weight! I'm a littler Perez. But I'm still a big fat cunt – just like you! That's why I love ya. PS Thanks for advertising on my website. I'll take your money anytime!"

Allen: "I know you will, and that's what makes you a cheap ass whore. Now leave me alone."

Hilton was duly blocked, which was quite a relief for everyone no doubt, but a spat between Lily and Mike Skinner, an artist presumed to be cut from the same cloth as Allen, would also ensue. After Skinner wrote on his page: "Now is not the time for dick-measuring..." Lily responded cattily: "Do they make two-inch rulers?" A low blow, but Skinner was more than capable of going lower, reopening an old wound in the process: "Men don't need big dicks around you, yours more than makes up for it."

That was the end of that. "At least she's not stalking me any more..." Skinner later quipped. Yes, social networking allowed us to strip away any mists of enigma that might have previously surrounded our stars and see them in all their ugly, bitching but often hilarious glory.

One 'war' that would reach a happier conclusion was the one that had broken out between Lily and Lindsay Lohan a year earlier, after Lohan had apparently turfed Lily and her friends off their table in a chichi club in LA because Lohan and her entourage wanted to sit down (cue an entertaining Lily Allen MySpace blog-post). This little power struggle was seemingly no more. Lily had kicked off her mammoth (just under a year-long) promotional tour in the spring of 2009 with a 14-date run in the US.

Touring would be even more taxing than usual, as Lily's show was now significantly longer and more work-intensive for the simple reason that there were more songs in her set. She joked that, previously, she had had to incorporate something of a "stand-up routine" in order to flesh out the evening. But, after thrashing out the perfect set list with her musical director (and bass-player) Morgan Nicholls, she didn't have to worry quite so much about throwing in lengthy anecdotes.

Almost as soon as Lily had touched down at LAX, so tired she was still clutching her pillow as if ready to hit the sack again at a moment's notice, she was taken under the wing of La Lohan herself, after the flame-haired firebrand invaded the stage at one of Lily's gigs.

It's Not Me, It's You had reached number five in the US album charts and Lily was making the most of her two weeks Stateside, appearing on the *Tonight Show With Jay Leno* and the *Ellen DeGeneres Show*, on which Lily and Ellen duetted a version of 'Womaniser' by Britney Spears as part of Ellen's 'bathroom concert' series, perched together on the side of a bath much to the delight of Ellen's audience.

Lily also appeared on Jimmy Kimmel's show, answering the same old questions about being famous… Lily explained that she doesn't mind being in the papers, she just doesn't like being hounded by 'animals'. Jimmy Kimmel simply grinned: "I like it when you punch them."

Inevitably Lindsay Lohan's stage-crashing was also on Kimmel's agenda: "That was a complete surprise," said Lily. "She's a friend of a friend (Mark Ronson) and I invited her to the concert and halfway through my encore I got a tap on my shoulder, and I was like, 'What the… Hi!' Then I got on with the show and she walked off." The fact that Lily was singing a Britney Spears song at the time sent Kimmel into paroxysms of excitement: "It's like Perez Hilton's dream came true!" he cried. Lily squirmed and glanced knowingly at the audience. Lily's fans, at least the ones who had followed the battle between Allen and Hilton, knew that the last thing Lily wanted was to make Perez Hilton's dreams come true. Plunge him into a nightmare, maybe…

Time was short and Lily's managers were keen to see their charge stay off the sauce and keep it as a work-trip, but she couldn't resist the prospect of painting the town red with Lohan, starting off with a drinking session at the superstar playpen Chateau Marmont and then slinking off to Shamrock Tattoos in West Hollywood at 2am to get matching ink on their hands – the word 'Shhh', in homage to the pop singer Rihanna who had exactly that tattoo. Now, every time they lifted their index fingers to their perfectly glossed mouths, the word 'Shhh' was displayed. Cute – and also tied in neatly with an idea Lily had toyed with in the past: she had talked about maybe getting a tattoo of the words 'Shut up' on her hand so that when she was drunk and talking too much, as her hands gesticulated, she'd spot the stern instruction and put a sock in it.

Predictably the press went wild when they saw Lily and Lindsay's matching tattoos, but Lily already had some artwork on her wrists: including some religious symbology, a communist symbol and a picture of Homer Simpson. She had also talked about the possibility of getting a Keith Haring tattoo to add to her collection, to reflect her love of the artist.

Another who reacted with great interest to Lohan's new friendship with Lily was Lohan's father, Michael. Lindsay Lohan is not particularly known for her angelic qualities on nights out, and she doesn't seem to need anyone else's help to cause a stir, but Michael decided that Lily Allen was a bad influence on his little girl, and so another Twitter spat occurred. Michael ill-advisedly tweeted Lily: "Dear Lily, I think you have an alcohol problem that needs addressing. From Michael Lohan." "I was like, 'Leave me alone'," shrugged Lily.

Lily had better ways of using Twitter than just for defending herself against people's dads: organising treasure hunts, for example. Lily loved nothing more than leaving clues on Twitter for her fans after hiding free tickets to her shows in various places near the venues. Lily also made sure she was there to greet the lucky fans who found the tickets, but unfortunately it seemed that most of them were just interested in dashing off with the freebies rather than meeting the star herself.

"I've been hiding tickets in places and then sending out clues like an Easter egg hunt and then I just sit there and wait," she explained. "I did one in San Diego and I hid them in a sneaker shop under some sneakers and said, 'Go to this shop, ask this guy Eric,' and as I walked out of the shop, literally within two minutes, suddenly 10 kids just went flying past me.

"When I was in LA I hid some on the 'G' outside the Pacific Design Centre, on the sign. I sent out a clue and waited there for about 20 minutes and this guy pulled up in his car really casually, got out, got the tickets and then drove off!

"I hid some on a tree outside Victoria's Secret at the Grove… within 40 seconds they were picked up. This guy was on his iPhone and he looked up and he saw me and said, 'When did you write this?' And I said, '30 seconds ago.'"

After fighting jet-lag (and hangovers) on her two-week stint in America, she was whisked over to Japan (where she was presented on Japanese TV, slightly bizarrely, with a horse-head mask: she declined to put it on as she didn't want to "mess up her hair") before rushing back to England in time for her birthday celebration in May.

Not many girls can say that Damien Hirst had given them a huge oil painting, painted just for her, stuck with beautiful butterflies spelling out their name for their birthday. This year, Lily could (and she had to have the doorframe removed to fit it in her flat). She had also been given, by one of her cheeky friends, a doll of her dad (as the Sheriff of Nottingham). But her addiction to Twitter would mar her family celebration.

Lily was taken to her favourite restaurant, Nobu, by her family, but she literally couldn't stop tweeting. And the more she tweeted, the more angry her family became at having only a fraction of her attention. The mood clearly became more tense with every moment that passed, if Lily's tweet-fest was anything to go by. "Family birthday dinner…. Aaaarrrrrrrrrggggggghhhh !!! Does everybody feel like this?" she wrote. "OMG, I'm gonna hit someone in a minute. We just had a 10 minute argument about whether or not sake is better hot or cold. Cold obv."

And finally: "Here come the tears. I'm being told off for being on my BlackBerry." It seemed that the combination of Twitter and being with family had seemed to make Lily regress into a sulky little girl at the dinner table, retreating into silent preoccupation with her invisible friend. *The London Paper* was quick to print Lily's tweets that night in its showbiz section. It was not a great look. But Lily would soon be looking rather more 'mature' thanks to her special MySpace show the following week.

Lily felt it was about time she played a free secret gig for a lucky 300 of her devout MySpace fans in her favourite manor, Portobello, and the perfect venue was just waiting for her after having been closed for so many years. The Tabernacle in Notting Hill had just reopened, and not only was it geographically perfect, it was the place where Lily had her first stage debut as a child in the Portobello Panto, a festive if somewhat anarchic tradition started by her uncle Kevin, and since revived, as we know, by her sister Sarah.

And once again, despite her family involvement, any claims of nepotism regarding getting the plum roles can be easily refuted. As Lily had previously complained, she always played "something shit or a boy". That's showbiz. But soon she'd be the princess. The queen, in fact…

The theme of the night, she told fans on her blog, was London Tube Stations. Lily herself dressed as an elderly, lace-bedecked Queen Victoria, her grey-haired look being the perfect contrast to the show, which started with dazzling, flashing white lights as Lily opened with 'Everyone's At It'. A dubby drum and bass version of 'Smile' was also part of the set. She had to reach some kind of compromise after all – the fans wanted to hear it, but she needed to find ways of making it more interesting for herself as well as them. Lily closed her hour-set with her rendition of Britney Spears' 'Womaniser', clearly a song she couldn't get enough of covering.

Fans were thrilled – plus the owners of the 'best' costume won the opportunity to hang backstage at a "special meet-and-greet", Lily was exhilarated and happy on her home turf and the Tabernacle was well and truly relaunched. "Obviously it was pivotal for Tabernacle's rebranding," said Idea Generation's Andrew Soar, who worked on the press campaign to get the newly reborn venue into the limelight. "It gave them blanket press and helped to reintroduce the venue to the public. It had resonance and did not seem like being a publicity stunt as it was truly the site of her first stage role as a kid. And she obviously enjoyed it…!"

In her role as queen (who says she stopped being queen just because she eventually had to take the costume off?), Lily naturally had politics on her mind, not least because of the spiralling economy, which, by the way, Lily often joked she was "single-handedly keeping going. I haven't lost any money, because I'm terrible, I spend, spend, spend. There are loads of Chanel jackets in my wardrobe."

A general election was just a year away, the most important, arguably, for generations, and it would be one that had many reconsidering their usual choices. Tories are the popular choice for the moneyed and the privileged, and they were becoming more popular by the day with those who didn't fit the above categories – people were desperate for change. But Lily openly declared that Gordon Brown, then Labour's leader and England's unelected Prime Minister, would still have her vote. Lily's decision would not be swayed by flattery from David Cameron, the Conservative Leader, who claimed his daughter was mad about Lily's music (although he wasn't too keen on the swearing and sexual innuendoes) and even handed a CD of hers to Barack Obama. No, the lady was not for turning...

"Of course I'll still vote for (Gordon)," she told *The Times* (owned by right-wing newspaper mogul Rupert Murdoch, clearly keen for the chance to gloat about a celebrity Tory-convert; they would have no luck here) as she sat in her dressing room at the Tabernacle before the gig. "I can't not vote Labour."

Lily's ever-flourishing relationship with Twitter meant that everyone knew who she was voting for in that other important national event, the TV talent show *Britain's Got Talent*. News that she was "in love" with the comedic Greek-London dancing duo Stavros Flatley whizzed around the internet, and Lily was probably more lambasted for her statement that she believed the angel-voiced, blue-stocking singer Susan Boyle was "overrated" (Lily was quick to add she was not, however, saying Boyle was no good) than her political stance.

The previous year Lily's comments in support of powerful *X-Factor* contestant Ruth Lorenzo, and particularly her criticism of Lorenzo's rather more fey rival Diana Vickers, famed for her 'claw'-like hand gestures while singing, were also trumpeted within the TV columns of the red-tops. Even Miquita Oliver had to pick Lily up on her disdain of Vickers. "She had charisma!" argued Oliver. "She had a *hand*..." Lily shot back wickedly. One thing was for sure: now more than ever, whatever Lily Allen gave her attention to was hot property, and people were keener than ever to attach themselves to her for a glimmer of that reflected glory.

No one knew that better than Lily's protective management, and they were charged with the job of keeping people at bay so that Lily wouldn't be too overextended to do what she had to do. But Lily was horrified when she heard that she had nearly lost out on the chance to appear on *Neighbours,* her favourite Australian soap and the programme her day used to basically revolve around when pre-fame Lily was just killing time at home.

"Poor Todd, my manager, always has to kind of like pass on things. People will send him requests and, you know, he runs them past me sort of every couple of weeks. He went, '*Neighbours* called, they wanted you to go and be in a scene for the day, so obviously I passed.' I said, 'What are you talking about? Why would you do that? *Neighbours* is brilliant!'" "I'm not sure who was more eager, Lily or the cast," said the series' executive producer Susan Bower.

Amusingly, given Lily's well-known penchant for the more mature gentleman, her scene was set on the 'radio station' with show stalwart Dr Karl Kennedy (played by Alan Fletcher). Lily performed an acoustic version of '22', and the character of Dr Karl, somewhat star-struck much to his younger companion's embarrassment, admits to being a big fan of Lily's, to which she responds coyly: "It's nice to know older men have an interest in my songs…"

The hotly anticipated episode was aired that November, but Lily's fans were already privy to a few choice details thanks to her constant stream of excited tweets from Ramsay Street itself. "OK, so I did my scene. Me and Doctor Karl get our flirt on. Quite funny."

Lily admittedly *was* getting overextended again, however, and she probably could have done with some of Dr Karl's expert medical attention and TLC – summer was here, which meant festivals, which meant seemingly non-stop touring. Lily had been looking forward to performing at the Spanish festival Benicassim on July 19 alongside some of her favourite contemporaries, such as Kings of Leon and Oasis. But her immune system was yet again paying the price of her lifestyle, and a bad bout of gastroenteritis forced her to pull out. "Wish I was at Benicassim," Lily tweeted. "Got a bug and been vomiting all day. Thank you to the lady who gave me a bag to vomit in at Gatwick this morning…" In the end the festival had to shut down anyway due to extreme weather conditions and strong winds.

Just a few days later, however, Lily was all better in time for Japan's own Glastonbury, Fuji Rock, and she would have her chance to hang out with Oasis after all, as well as appearing on the same stage as the legendary Patti Smith. Lily was certainly in fine company.

Fuji Rock also has some resonance for Lily, not least because the organiser, Masa Hidaka, had enjoyed Glastonburys with her father, Keith, and basically based Fuji Rock on the Somerset festival itself. For the first year, Masa even flew Keith Allen, Joe Strummer and their Glasto campfire cronies out to Japan so they could recreate the Glastonbury vibe there and then. Masa also recruited Jason Mayall, brother of Gaz (à la Gaz's Rockin' Blues, one of Lily's favourite Soho haunts) and a fellow West London face to run part of the festival, so there was always a family vibe there up in the Japanese mountains.

For better or worse, on the 11-hour flight to Japan, Lily Allen found herself on the same flight as Liam Gallagher, the Mancunian knight in shining armour who had rescued her from what could have been a miserable night after the Brit Awards in 2007. Liam, who is obviously fond of Lily having known her since she was a child ("her old fella used to bring her round to Supernova Heights. Good kid…"), again brought out the lairy rock star cliché in Lily, unfortunately for the other passengers in the upper class cabin that day.

The pair glugged champagne like it was going out of fashion, apparently bellowing and swearing happily as their entourages presumably rammed in the earplugs. Rumour had it that both Gallagher and Allen's camps had warned cabin crew to "keep those two apart" but to no avail. The prodigious bender continued long after the plane had touched down.

"At *Lost In Translation* hotel in Tokyo," tweeted Lily, settling in after her appearance on the Green stage, and a DJ set during which she proudly, and appropriately, wore a Strummerville T-shirt. "Had an extraordinary amount of fun the past few days…"

CHAPTER 21

"I really feel this is the year of the girl, with La Roux and Little Boots and Florence Welch of Florence and the Machine…"

Lily Allen, 2009.

It wasn't just the year of the girl, it was also the year of the more unusual girl, the less girly girl, the stronger, more characterful, more questioning girl – and part of that was thanks to Lily crashing into our consciousnesses in 2006, not being told what to wear, not being told how much she should weigh or what she should say.

This is part of the reason Lily is seen as a 'role model', a title that has never sat comfortably with her. The part she played in emboldening this generation of very individual new female singers – La Roux with her androgynous persona and retro quiff, Florence and her wild Pre-Raphaelite image and almost pagan leanings, Kate Nash of course and VV Brown – left her nursing mixed feelings.

Lily had always felt that girls like her were not catered for properly by the music industry, but this raft of singers who were, in some ways, cut from a similar cloth, seemed to leave her feeling slightly threatened, rather than empowered or flattered. It seems no coincidence that Lily, with her touch of the tomboy and ever determined to shun the overt sexualisation of acts like Girls Aloud and Sugababes, had started to take to the stage in low-cut basques, hot pants and vertiginous heels. Was she feeling she had to compete for attention? Who can say? She certainly loved to get a reaction from how she looked, and admitted that she "gets it", it's fun to look a bit foxy on stage, and maybe she felt she should use the arsenal of her looks in a way she defiantly had refused to before. And Lily definitely preferred the company of men to women, with the exception of Emily, her friend and assistant, and she liked nothing more than feeling that her "boys" – the band and crew – were at her beck and call, the less females around the better.

"It probably sounds bitchy but I like being on tour because I know all my boys, my band, their priority is looking out for me and I like that," she told *GQ*. "I like being in a room and four fucking bimbos coming in and they're all drooling after them, but I know that, really, the one they care about is me. That makes me feel comforted."

At least La Roux, aka Elly Jackson, was boyish enough not to step on the perennially flirtatious and often competitive Lily's toes, and they were different enough to appreciate each other.

"I get pangs of jealousy when I hear people like radio presenters getting really excited about new music. I kind of feel like, 'Oh, I'm just fading,'" Lily told *Elle* magazine. "Who I really love is La Roux. She's a friend as well. I find it quite difficult getting on with a lot of my female competitors but I really, really like her."

Elly has been equally fulsome in her praise of Lily, whom she would tour with later that year – her own brand of Eighties inspired synth-pop perfectly complementing Lily's new sound. Lily had taken Elly under her wing and proved to be the ideal confidante for her. Elly was not interested in the trappings of fame, often wearing her usually bequiffed hair down when she went out to ensure that no one recognised her.

Another group of girls inspired by Lily were plotting a surprise for her – the Capital Children's Choir and its leader, Lily's former vocal mentor Rachel Santesso, were preparing an a cappella choral version of Lily's song 'Chinese'. Santesso had followed Lily's career closely, still feeling protective of her former protégée, and was very moved when she heard the track, dedicated to Lily's mother, on the album.

Rachel originally planned the recording, which she and the choir made at Abbey Road Studios, to just be a gift for Lily and her mother, Alison. Little could she have known the sensation it would create online after Lily posted up a euphoric tweet about it, directing her fans to the YouTube video where they could hear the angelically rendered song.

"Oh my lord, this is the sweetest thing ever. Thank you, Rachel Santesso (my mentor)," wrote Lily on her page. The choir's video for 'Chinese' has been watched by nearly half a million people to date, although the young singers were already quite high profile, even performing at the Spice Girls' reunion at the O2 in 2008 (which is ironic, as Lily had claimed she had been "blacklisted" from the gig and wasn't able to get in herself).

Lily was working hard, the tour promoting *It's Not Me, It's You* was continuing apace and she was thrilling crowds with her new electro sound, her sexy new look and Bjork-inspired silver space-vixen eye make-up. But disaster struck during her stint in Scandinavia, and all because she was trying to stay out of the way...

"I was in Scandinavia playing these festivals and I met up with these guys called Skream and Benga," she later explained to Absolute Radio DJ Geoff Lloyd, "I'm quite big in Scandinavia, and I didn't want to steal their limelight as they were DJ-ing so I was crouching behind the decks and I sort of fell on the back of the stage about 3ft onto my coccyx.

"I was in so much pain I thought I was paralysed, I thought I was going to have to have my legs cut off. I was running through how I was going to get on stage the next night. They gave me an epidural, it numbed my knees to my lower back to get through this gig, and halfway through the thing started running out."

Lily burst into "real toddler tears" and wailed to the crowd that they'd have to dance for her as she was in so much pain. She got through the gig though, despite having been seriously unsure she'd be able to do it at all. "Lily obviously was in a lot of pain," said an onlooker. "It was sad to see her suffering but she seemed to be bolstered by the warmth of the crowd in Finland that night." There's no people like show people...

It's little wonder that, by the time Lily returned to England, the idea of sitting in the sunshine for nine hours at a time seemed incredibly attractive, particularly if there were plenty of dashing-looking cricketers such as Andrew Flintoff and Graham Onions sauntering about in front of her. Yes, as the cricket season came into sway and England battled for the Ashes, Lily became slowly but surely, and very visibly, addicted.

She listened to the commentary for her "Ashes fix" as she drove, she even kept tabs on it while on stage during performances, whenever she could she was in the audience (titillating one and all – especially the press – with her see-through tops and general bra-lessness: for someone who professes to being shy and dysmorphic about her body, she seems to cope with it admirably), and, of course, she tweeted almost compulsively about it – although not always about the finer points of the game. "I think I fancy Graham Onions more than Freddie now, I've heard he goes for days…" she wrote. "Is Onions married? … I think I might try and get into cricket commentary once I've finished singing."

Thanks to the power of Twitter, and Lily's huge profile, *Test Match Special* commentator Jonathan Agnew himself, a fellow tweet-addict, was thrilled to see Lily take such an interest, and invited her to join him and try her hand at commentary.

This was an offer Lily couldn't refuse – it would be churlish, if nothing else, how many other people have every whim they happen to post up on their Twitter page immediately indulged and fulfilled? (She has also expressed great interest in appearing on *Come Dine With Me*, it's surely only a matter of time.)

So, on her way back to England from the Netherlands (still listening to *TMS* via the Internet), Lily, Ray-bans on to hide the dark circles, made time before heading onwards to V Festival in Chelmsford to dash to the Oval and hang out with Aggers live on air.

It was meant to be a bit of fun, and Agnew was clearly excited about meeting Lily. Previous celebrity guests had included Mick Jagger and Eric Clapton, so it was refreshing to hear a young female voice on *TMS*, not to mention, arguably, a bit of flirtation.

"You have to be quite brave to take you on, boyfriends and things," ventured Agnew.

Lily: "Let's not go there, Aggers."

Observer writer Will Buckley cringed when he heard the interview, accusing Agnew of "salivating", having "mid-life" issues, and of being something of a "pervert" around Lily, which understandably upset everyone concerned.

"As you can imagine, I have taken being called a pervert quite badly," Agnew complained. "I will tell you how (Buckley) described his readers if he fails to print a total apology to me and my family on Sunday."

Lily waded in on Twitter in defence of Agnew: "I really think this Will Buckley guy should apologise to (Agnew), he was nothing but kind and gentlemanly to me during our interview. I don't know one person that agrees with *The Observer* on this one. Maybe this is Buckley's attempt at creating a name for himself as the demise of the Observer Monthlys (including Sport) are imminent. Sorry @aggerscricket, I should have left you all alone."

Lily would be back at the cricket as soon as she had another opportunity, although this time she'd stay safely in the crowd and away from Aggers and another potential media mess. What the photographers were even more interested in was that handsome man sitting with Lily in the crowd, drinking beer with her, making her laugh and, crucially, kissing her.

Yes, Lily was rumbled – she had a new man in her life: a builder and property developer called Sam Cooper. He ticked plenty of boxes: a little older than her, stable and kind, and he'd known her for a decade thanks to being part of her social circle. Lily still had her eye on the prize of kicking back in the countryside with the ideal man, and it looked as if she might have found him. If nothing else, he wasn't afraid to stand up to Lily, keep her feet on the ground and help her put a lid on her spending.

"It's fucking disgusting some of the things I do," she laughed in an interview with *This Is London*, "like not batting an eyelid over spending two grand on a new pair of shoes, but it's difficult to hold on to reality... Being with Sam has really helped me with that because he's like, 'Stop! What are you doing? This money is your future!'"

Now the cat was out of the bag, everyone wanted to know that little bit more about Lily's new beau, but this time she was careful to control how much she said, otherwise nothing was sacred. "Some things aren't for public consumption," she told Chris Moyles firmly after he tried to wheedle some details out of her live on air. Lily was pulling back and keeping what was precious to herself. Sam was different, and unlike her relationship with Seb Chew, Lily insisted that she and Sam barely exchanged a cross word. "There's absolutely nothing about him that annoys me," she told *Grazia*. "He's not impressed by what I do."

Lily was evidently feeling calmer since beginning her romance with Sam, she barely complained when she was passed over for the Mercury Music Prize again (she registered surprise but was quick to back her friend La Roux. It was won by London rapper Speech Debelle).

And, unlike the year before, Lily retained her dignity and controlled her booze intake at the *GQ* Awards at London's Royal Opera House, where she was collecting a gong for being the magazine's 'Woman Of The Year'. She was in good company – her friend Dizzee Rascal was also collecting an award for best solo artist, Guy Ritchie was accepting the film-maker award and Elvis Costello was collecting the Outstanding Achievement honour.

Lily, looking gorgeous in a sheer Chanel gown and tumbling hair extensions, was accompanied by Kate Moss who presented her award. But even if Lily didn't cause a scene, remaining serene and lady-like throughout, she was on the receiving end of some extra attention when, after the award, Kate leant against the wall as Lily was photographed and interviewed, seemingly angry and ranting about something before storming out, Lily giggling slightly and looking embarrassed.

Even when she presented Lily's award, Kate seemed slightly out of sorts, smirking as she read the praise-filled introduction for Lily and holding up the paper on which her words were written as if to say 'it says here'... When Lily came to the stage to collect her award she appeared not to look Kate in the eye. Apparently the actor James Nesbitt had made a lewd joke on the mic about Kate, which she didn't find amusing, but whether that was all she was upset about or not, Kate Moss was not happy that night. After hurrying out, Kate then reappeared, interrupting a post-awards interview with Dizzee Rascal to announce that she had left her lipstick behind, and could someone find it for her? Dizzee Rascal naturally found the whole disturbance highly amusing, mock-chastising her for being "rude" before declaring: "Stop everything, Kate Moss has lost her lipstick..."

September would be an unforgettable month for Lily. It kicked off a heated debate that divided the music industry and everyone in it, and

Lily was at the forefront of the fight. The issue was file-sharing and distributing music for free. Artists and labels were already being affected by sites such as Limewire, which distributed music for free, and plenty of other sites that were illegally distributing music, ensuring that the artists and labels would lose out. To be fair, the consumer had been ripped off by the record industry for years for the privilege of buying a CD, but swindling musicians and songwriters was not the answer. This was someone's work, music that, in most cases, an artist had put their heart into. However, in a response to the situation, Radiohead broke new ground by announcing that their new album, *In Rainbows*, would be released on their website and fans could pay what they felt it was worth. Of course, in some cases people didn't pay at all. More people than ever were prepared to just take what they wanted for free.

This unprecedented move by Radiohead made the music industry sit up and talk about what was happening, particularly as the government was making a stand, having proposed that illegal file-sharers should have their internet access cut off. Radiohead, Billy Bragg and Pink Floyd's Nick Mason were among artists who disagreed with this move, insisting that file-sharing this way is just like making a compilation tape of your mate's music. But Lily Allen was horrified to see fellow artists supporting the illegal distribution of music, and for the first time in a while, wrote a lengthy blog on the subject.

"I think music piracy is having a dangerous effect on British music, but some really rich and successful artists like Nick Mason from Pink Floyd and Ed O'Brien from Radiohead don't seem to think so," she said, in reference to an interview Mason and O'Brien had given to *The Times*.

"You don't start out in music with the Ferraris. Instead you get a huge debt from your record company, which you spend years working your arse off to repay… You might not care about this, but the more difficult it is for new artists to make it, the less new artists you'll see and the more British music will be nothing but puppets paid for by Simon Cowell."

A stern warning indeed, and one that prompted a huge response from fans and fellow pop stars alike, including Just Jack, Muse's Matt Bellamy and Abba's Bjorn Ulvaeus. Some voices were in agreement, some were not, but Lily was serious in her intent to support emerging artists of any genre, any field, and two days after her first blog on the subject, returned to remind us that unless we put our money where our mouths are in supporting the artists we love, we're going to lose what this country does best. Lily is a voracious art buyer, book reader and vinyl collector (the record shop Honest Jon's in Portobello would often put aside stacks of records they thought Lily would like so she could just swoop in after returning from tour, buy them and take them home for a blissful afternoon by the record player). Again, Lily was finding that, while it was the internet that boosted her rise to fame, it was the internet that had the potential to turn sour, and she knew that there were plenty of people who had snapped up her tunes without paying anyone a penny.

A subject such as this deserved a blog of its own, which she set up and entitled 'It's Not Alright'. And on this blog she posted a bombshell, knowing that the eyes of the world would be on it: "Just so you know, I have not renegotiated my record contract and have no plans to make another record."

Supporters within the media were stunned by this announcement, and *Popjustice* got straight onto her spokespeople who simply batted back: "She is not quitting pop music and is still promoting her current album, which is why she said she is not thinking ahead to another record." But by now everyone didn't know what to talk about more – Lily's file-sharing fury or the fact that she looked ready to quit and run off into the sunset with Sam Cooper, which everyone knew she was itching to do anyway.

What followed was plenty of 'is she/isn't she?' speculation, great publicity of course. But Lily certainly wasn't enjoying the negative attention she was garnering from her 'It's Not Alright' blog. She was trying to stand up for what she loved, but the dissent she received was starting to wear her down, particularly when certain critics were quick to remind everyone that Lily herself distributed music for free when she sent out her famous mix-tapes to fans. The mix-tapes were still downloadable on EMI's Lily Allen website, but were quickly whipped down. Lily was also lambasted when it appeared that part of her blog had apparently been copied from the website *Techdirt*, without supplying a credit or link to the original post.

Lily was also on the receiving end of a somewhat unflattering 'open letter' from the rapper Dan Bull, a man who describes himself on his

Twitter page as a "geeky rap artist promoting logic, scepticism and political change through merciless teasing…" Bull had created a cheeky cover version of Lily's song '22', singing the words of his letter to the tune, giving his own take on the debate, and on where Lily fits within it as an artist who has borrowed samples from other artists. (All credited, mind.) He also warned that Lily's fans would find it hard to respect her if she was seen to be "desperate for cash"…

His lyrics include: "Now please don't be offended, Lily; I think your new CD's splendid, Lily. Everybody's at It and it's Not Fair, I Could Say, The Fear was Him but He wasn't There so let's go Back to the Start, before 22 – all music's in the public domain, so Fuck You…"

It came to a point where Lily could take no more. The internet was ruling her life, and it didn't feel like fun any more. Despite the fact it was so easy to be contacted and riled by potential critics, she was addicted to blogging, checking her messages and comments, googling herself, arguing, noodling on Facebook and fighting on Twitter. It took Elly Jackson, better known as La Roux, to prompt Lily into taking a good hard look at her internet use, and consider how important it was, and how much of her real life it was replacing ("I don't go on the internet, don't go on YouTube, Facebook, anything," Jackson told *You* magazine. "Lily's told me she's thrown her computer away. I don't blame her." Maybe Alfie had the right idea after all when he hurled Lily's laptop out on the street back in 2006).

It was no secret that Sam Cooper was no fan of Lily's constant tweeting, and it looked as if it might be time to go cold turkey. First the 'It's Not Alright' blog disappeared, then she stopped posting on MySpace, basic updates about live dates and so on were presumably posted up sporadically by an aide, and eventually, before September was through, Lily's Twitter followers saw the words they thought they'd never see, although it couldn't have been a surprise: 'I am a neo-luddite. Goodbye.'

"All those things were becoming a total addiction," Lily told *Grazia*. "I put my BlackBerry, my laptop, my iPod in a box and that's the end." Yes, Lily was going analogue and loving it. She rediscovered the joys of gingerly placing a precious 12" on the turntable, listening to an album the whole way through, rather than just scrolling flippantly through the tracks on her iPod. She remembered how rewarding it was just to be alone with her thoughts rather than feeling she had to post them up every five minutes for the world to see, and how comforting it was being with her loved ones without having the spectre of her BlackBerry pulling her focus away from them all the time.

"I've got more time, more privacy. We've ended up in this world of unreal communications and I don't want that. I want real life back."

CHAPTER 22

"I like collecting art, so I'll maybe open an art gallery. Maybe open my own florist. If I don't get picked up by the record company again for another record then I'll have to get another job, it's not really up to me, it's up to you."

Lily Allen talking on Absolute Radio.

Lily's (temporary) halt on all things online at least gave her a chance to smell the flowers, which is something she'd barely had an opportunity to do since 2006. And this space and new-found calm allowed her to appreciate her first award for music, which she was honoured with at the Q Awards. Lily, looking feline and sophisticated in a sparkly cream jumper dress and shiny black leggings, muzzed-up bed hair and kohl-rimmed eyes, picked up the gong for her track 'The Fear', and, visibly moved at the mic, didn't miss the opportunity to make it clear, as always, that she "had never won anything for her music before", and that this was particularly special to her.

Other winners at the Q Awards were White Lies, Spandau Ballet, Marianne Faithfull, Frankie Goes To Hollywood, The Specials, Sonic Youth, Robert Plant – music across the board was being celebrated, but, as the papers were only too thrilled to report, the winners were all upstaged by an embarrassing appearance by Amy Winehouse, "in recovery" according to her ubiquitous father, Mitch, and flaunting a brand new giant pair of football-esque boobs, spilling out of a tiny dress and heckling from the back of the room as Robert Plant picked up his Outstanding Contribution award. She also hadn't turned up in time to present, as planned, the Q Inspiration award to The Specials with film-maker and DJ Don Letts because she was "doing her hair". (How long does it take to put on a wig?)

Lily received another honour that October – one from the relaunched Nineties pop star Peter Andre. After his marriage to the glamour model and walking, talking business empire Jordan dissolved, Peter got stuck into working on projects he'd always wanted to develop. One of which, naturally, was releasing his own perfume. The scent was called 'Unconditional' (sounds familiar? P Diddy's signature fragrance is called 'Unforgivable', so there's clearly some subliminal marketing going on) and it smelled like, wait for it, "Lily Allen". Or how Peter imagined her to smell anyway. What would Jordan say if she knew Peter had been trying to imagine how Lily Allen smelt? Let's not go there.

"It's because she's fresh – she's kind of a fresh burst of summer," Peter explained to *Heat*. "There's something about Lily Allen that's really exciting to me." A Q Award, a homage in the shape of a perfume… whatever next? (Actually, the next gift winging its way to her would be her very own orange tiger-striped lily, 'The Lily Allen', courtesy of adoring Manchester radio station Key 103.)

Lily released the track 'Everyone's At It', her comment on the casually rampant use of drugs all around her, on October 23. Featuring such poetic lyrics as: "I'm not trying to say that I'm smelling of roses, but when will we tire of putting shit up our noses?", it was nothing if not straight to the point, as usual, and as 2009 edged towards 2010, it was clear that Lily's album *It's Not Me, It's You* had played an instrumental part in turning EMI's fortunes around. The label had more than trebled its earnings since the album had been released – the power of Lily was not to be underestimated.

The power of marketing and PR is not to be sniffed at either, of course, and EMI were working hell for leather at pushing their products to the four corners of the earth, trying to sniff out people who might, as yet, be unfamiliar with Lily or her album. (Hard to believe there might be anyone at all, but EMI was taking no chances.)

One of its PR tools was to create a viral game called *Escape The Fear*, in which people could play the part of Lily and try to dodge obstacles that might hinder her from fulfilling her dreams. The game was a huge hit, played millions of times and topping viral charts worldwide. The Lily Allen fairy-dust strikes again. And thanks to marketing tricks like this game, it was now impossible to escape 'The Fear'. Lily's music was working its way into everyone's consciousness.

In the meantime, Lily worked on her live shows, which would often feature her Nordic dubstep DJ pals Skream and Benga, the rapper Example (a self-confessed big fan of Lily's Cheryl Cole impersonations) and, increasingly, Hackney white rap artist Professor Green (simply one of her favourite people) in support.

Professor Green and Lily would perform a blistering cover version of The S.O.S Band's 1983 hit 'Just Be Good To Me', revived in the Nineties by Beats International ('Dub Be Good To Me') and reworked by Green into 'Just Be Good To Green', to be released in 2010. "We got chatting on Facebook and I mentioned the track," Green told *NME.com,* "which turned out to be one of her favourite songs. She suggested her singing the chorus. I didn't take much persuading! Lily's wicked."

The concerts were more glittering and fabulous than ever – cannons were positioned either side of the stage, exploding with sparkling confetti during 'Not Fair', a song about premature ejaculation – there were teams of dancers, outrageous sets ("I'd never thought, 'What would my set design be like?' before…") and the star of the show was looking more glamorous than ever – and wearing less than ever, something that seemed to many somewhat un–Lily, particularly as she claimed to suffer from body dysmorphia (where the individual agonises about being larger than they actually are). But Lily's humour was all over the shows, and the fans, who sang every word back at her, loved them.

Lily had to take a year's worth of clothes with her on tour because of the many costume changes, and as her ongoing touring schedule came to a halt in December, with a rip-roaring finale at Brixton Academy, Lily was bombarded with questions regarding her retirement. Was it still happening? Was it just a publicity stunt? Would she be back next year?

Fans were already in mourning, but deep down nobody really believed Lily would be gone for long, and she admitted that her announcement that she was taking some time out had been somewhat misconstrued.

"I'm not retiring, I'm doing that thing called life," she said, slightly archly during an interview backstage at her Liverpool show. "I've worked really hard to have a home and I'd quite like to live in it now..." Lily had also been missing Sam. They'd been "making it work", speaking to each other frequently on the phone, flying out to see each other whenever they could while Lily toured. But they wanted to spend some quality time together and not have to keep one eye on the time. Lily was also nesting. She'd just bought a duplex penthouse in Marylebone (as you do), and wanted Sam to live with her there.

The swanky pad near Great Portland Street, perfect for staggering home from Soho, wasn't all. Lily was ever closer to buying the ideal country pad in the bucolic Cotswolds, near her dad Keith and half-sister Teddie, and not far from where Damien Hirst and also Kate Moss have country retreats, much to the local curtain-twitchers' horror. The perfect spot, according to Lily, is Slad in Gloucestershire. But even for an all-powerful celeb, it was easier said than done snapping up a place round there. "It was Laurie Lee's valley and it's a very special place so when people move there they don't leave," she lamented. "I've already been looking there for a year now so I guess I'm just... waiting for people to die, really."

She could already visualise how her country abode would look, and she fully intended to inject a shot of Glastonbury into the garden. "My plan is to build a yurt (a Moroccan-style tent) on to the side of my country house," she told Q magazine.

"You have the house for traditional living and, of course, running hot water and toilets. But the yurt is full of old Moroccan rugs where you hang out. I want to feel like I'm at Glastonbury year-round, with a few home comforts next door." Sounds perfect. And very Lily Allen.

Even if she wasn't leaving the music business forever, Lily was clearly serious about taking time off – two years off, she insisted. She was already making plans for what she would do in her time not spent warbling into a mic. As well as all the home improvement, Lily was making plans to open her vintage fashion hire company 'Lucy In Disguise' in London with her sister Sarah. ("It's about making fashion democratic, letting people rent nice clothes for affordable prices so they can go out and feel like a million dollars and it won't cost them a million dollars.")

She was also in the process of setting up her own music label. "I want to bring a bit more reality to the process, to advise kids that if they sign an advance for £300,000 they have to be really careful or they will suddenly find themselves posing with Sony Ericsson phones. All because they've signed their rights away," she told *This Is London*. "I don't want to compete with big labels, but I want to support new artists."

It seemed that, with this great exciting expanse of something Lily was not familiar with – free time – Lily was determinedly filling it up, jam-packing it before she'd even got there. On top of this, fulfilling the live dates she still had in her diary and doing seemingly endless press as a result of her decision to take a hiatus, again, her health took a dive in the form of a chest infection, an ailment that, along with laryngitis and bronchitis, was something of an Achilles' heel for Lily.

She shelved two live performances on doctors' orders, and also cancelled her appearance on the BBC *Top Of The Pops* Christmas special. Fans desperate to catch Lily before her 'retirement' were starting to panic. There were just a handful of live Lily gigs until March 2010, when, supposedly, that would be it. She valiantly managed to honour her commitment to perform on Children In Need however, despite having fallen down the stairs struggling with luggage earlier that day. This made Lily go up in people's estimations, not only because she performed despite being in some considerable pain but also, probably, because everyone would have naturally assumed she had someone to carry her bags for her…

Showbiz columnists across the UK, who often seem to know what celebrities are about to do before they even know themselves, were not convinced Lily would be able to stay away from the limelight, but it was up to her to prove them wrong. "She's the sort of person who needs her voice to be heard. I can't believe she's going to stop doing stuff," said Luke Blackall, former showbiz editor of *The London Paper*.

"There'll be something, there'll be TV, there'll be writing, she'll continue to be in the public eye. I don't think she wants to be forgotten about. She seems to have a good understanding of what's cool in terms of culture, so I think she'll be here to stay. And she'll probably produce some famous children!

"The dilemma is not unique, celebs want the best of all worlds – they want the glamour and the freebies and the nights out, but they also want to go away and live in a quiet house with their families. It's naïve to think that it's possible to have all the trappings and also have a quiet life. And she's got herself trapped in it."

Blackall wasn't wrong. Almost as soon as the 'farewell gigs' were being planned, we were reminded that Lily Allen's "mainstream acting debut" was just around the corner in *Jane Austen Handheld,* a relatively low-budget spoof of the Jane Austen book *Pride And Prejudice,* directed by Tristram Shapeero of *Peep Show* and *Green Room.* Shooting had begun in 2007 and Lily would appear in the shape of Lydia Bennett with her old pal and fellow middle-England-baiter Russell Brand playing her lover George Wickham. Stephen Fry, apparently, would be playing Lily/Lydia's father. "It's a safe bet that this version will not be troubling the Academy voters…" surmised *The Guardian.* The film is still in production but scheduled for a 2010 release…

Lily was ready for a break somewhere hot to sweat out the last of her chest infection and have some R&R with loved ones. This Christmas, it was India that was calling her. The strict diet of yore went to the wall and she embraced curry like there was no tomorrow. We know that because something else went to the wall in January 2010: Lily's self-imposed Twitter ban. She'd managed four months though, which wasn't bad. The first thing she elected to tell us all was that she was heading to the gym as the "clarified butter has made its way from my tummy to my thighs". Lovely.

After her return from hot, sticky, stunning India, Lily was straight off to Australia for a short tour and the Big Day Out festival – and a bit of time out enjoying the Australian Open tennis championships with Sam and, it turned out, members of Muse, who were also on the Big Day Out bill. They were highly amused when they were photographed alongside Lily at Sydney Harbour, and the caption said 'Lily Allen with friends'… the picture editors hadn't even recognised the rock band. "None of us are interesting enough to be famous for anything else (than music) anyway," laughed Muse's Chris Wolstenholme, possibly somewhat relieved.

Lily loved being in Australia (even though she lost a bet to Muse's Matt Bellamy during the Australian Open, as photos of Bellamy leaping for joy as Lily handed over a stack of cash testified). It was baking hot, she had everything she could possibly want on a plate, Sam was with her – it was a far cry from where she was in 2005, still struggling to be noticed and suffering from a broken heart under a cold, grey, London sky. But she was getting tired; she was, maybe, a little demob happy, and her eye was on the prize of those precious two years 'off'. Support act and pal Professor Green's tweets showed that there was also, of course, plenty of boozing. Business as usual. Drunkenness and sunburn, but not quite a holiday yet...

"This is one of my last ever concerts," Lily declared during her gig at Flemington, Australia, as if they needed reminding. "So, I hope you are enjoying it..."

Maybe it was because she'd announced she was putting down music for a while, maybe it was those "nobody ever gives me an award for music" hints, or maybe, just maybe, it was because she simply deserved it, there would be a major event that ensured Lily's final months as a 'pop star' would go with a bang.

It was February, and February, in the UK music industry at least, can mean only one thing: the Brit Awards.

This year would be a particularly colourful and controversial ceremony – Lady Gaga would be there, and knowing how impressive her sets were bound to be, the British artists were not to be outdone. *The Daily Mirror* quoted an insider as saying that the set designs that had been submitted were particularly weird and wonderful this year.

"The bar has seriously been lifted. There are some amazing special effects, with pyrotechnics and new technology being introduced. Lady Gaga is usually the one with the flamboyant plans so everyone was braced for some outrageous feat with Beyoncé. But this time it was Lily who had the grand designs. She wants it to involve flying. At the moment the idea is to arrive on the stage in a model of an aeroplane."

Lily huffily denied this on Twitter. "For the record, I won't be flying in for the Brit Awards, nor have I requested to." No, she wouldn't be flying in on a model aeroplane. She'd be flown in on a model airship. Rehearsals were well under way and Lily was not going to be upstaged by anyone, Brit or not.

On the day of the Brits, Lily told *The Sun*: "I never win awards for my music ever," (getting a sense of deja vu?). "And I'm not holding out any hopes tonight. My chances are pretty slim because Florence (from Florence + The Machine) is obviously the favourite in the Best Female category.

"I don't think my album is the best album of the year, even though I've got more sales than everyone bar Susan Boyle…"

Whether she knew if she was going to get the award for British Female or not, Lily did know she was going to have a phenomenal time. So many of her friends would be there and were also up for awards – Kasabian, Oasis, Dizzee – it was, as she said, going to be a "big night". After a romantic Valentine's night at uber-posh Mayfair hotel Claridges with Sam, she headed over to get ready. Her red carpet outfit, a sleek, sophisticated floor-length black gown with an unusual crimson collar, belied the wild campery of the performance to come.

Reminiscent of Kylie's 'Showgirl' concerts, Lily's sequence featured armies of sexy military-style dancers with bright pink guns and designer prams, endless staircases to strut down and oodles of camp theatricality. Concentrating on her Brits performance at least took her mind off whether or not she was going to pick up an award. She would have to muster up the courage to float gracefully down on her 'airship' from the roof, 40 feet down to the stage. No wonder, when it was over, Lily looked as if she was almost about to collapse with giggles of relief into the arms of her dancers. The camera flicked over to Girls Aloud in the audience, there to support Cheryl Cole, who would be performing later in the show. If they were enjoying Lily's performance, they kept it to themselves…

Robbie Williams, at just 36, picked up the Outstanding Contribution award, much to the bemusement of quite a lot of people, Lady Gaga turned up looking suitably incredible to pick up the award for International Breakthrough Act, tea-cup in hand ("Don't forget yer brew, love!" quipped compere Peter Kay as she left the podium, keeping the celebs down to earth. Someone has to). Oasis were honoured for their album *(What's The Story) Morning Glory?*, also a bone of contention considering the release was being hailed as the greatest album in the last 30 years, and Dizzee Rascal, with whom Lily would be performing her final gigs in March, picked up the British Male Solo Artist gong. And so what about Lily? Did she finally win that Brit? Yes she did, and she took to the stage to collect it wearing a gigantic orange wig, supposedly so the photographers wouldn't know where to find her "and see my disappointed face" on the off chance she didn't win.

Dizzy with delight, Lily finally had her Brit. And ironically, she would later admit in an interview that it "meant nothing"... Maybe it had something to do with the fact that she was finally in a place, personally, of security and happiness she hadn't known before. The things she wanted now were her home in the country, time with her boyfriend and eventually, babies. The fripperies of fame were thrown into sharp perspective, which was right, it was how it should have been, rounding off her career nicely before she moved on to the next vibrant chapter of her life. But it's never that simple, is it?

Two weeks after the Brit Awards was another music industry calendar staple – the Shockwaves *NME* Awards at the Brixton Academy, the first in history to be presided over by the magazine's new female editor, Krissi Murison. It was an important new era, but while it would be nice to think that it would be "all sisters sticking together", the reality in the audience was not quite reflective of this.

Lily, who had just performed Carly Simon's 'You're So Vain' with her pals The Big Pink, left the stage and seemingly walked straight into an "exchange of words" with Courtney Love, a woman who used to think Lily was so sweet as a little girl...

The argument, which Lily later insisted was "NOT a bust up", was apparently regarding a Chanel dress that Courtney wanted to wear for the Brits, but, she claimed, Lily had "placed a lock on" it. *NME* also ventured that the argument between the pair was also connected to something Lily had said on Twitter about Courtney's teenage daughter, Frances Bean Cobain. An amicable chat turned "really nasty", *NME* reported, even claiming that the pair had to be separated by their respective entourages. Love was heard calling Allen a "little girl" before shouting, "welcome to the music industry".

Naturally, after seeing this report, Lily got tweeting. "She's upset because she has got it into her head that I put a lock on some dresses for the Brit Awards. She's made no secret of this and when I saw her at the *NME*'s she tried to talk to me, and I told her to shut up and stop spreading stupid rumours about me. And that's pretty much it. I would never fight with her, as a rule I don't pick on crazy old ladies… in other news, I'm slightly delaying my retirement till June. My last gig will be supporting Jay Z @Wireless (festival) in London." Yes, the hip-hop superstar whom Lily so admired personally asked for Lily, as he insisted he is a big fan of hers. How could Lily resist?

But it was hard to concentrate on the joys of Jay Z when Twitter war was being waged. Despite insisting she would never "pick on" or start a fight with Love, Lily then wickedly posted up an unflattering picture of Courtney that started a Twitter battle to end all battles. Forget Perez Hilton, this was serious. Lily immediately realised she'd done the wrong thing and apologised publicly, but it was too late as far as Courtney Love was concerned.

"Oh @lilyroseallen tweeted that pic?" wrote Courtney. "That's just baby brat nonsense… is there anyone who you haven't started a meaningless strop with?"

Ouch.

And that wasn't the worst of it. A torrent of insults ensued before Courtney then decided to take the moral high ground, claiming she thought Lily needed "help" and asked her followers to "send a prayer" to her, before promising never to contact her again.

Lily could never resist standing up for herself, and then going the extra mile if she needed to (and often if she didn't). But the constant 'feuds', or presumed feuds, generally stoked by the media, were becoming a drain, ever more proving why Lily wanted a break.

She might have "loved being me" back in the days of *Alright, Still,* but it's no surprise that in April 2010, she'd sigh to *The Times* quite simply that "I've had enough of being Lily Allen."

CHAPTER 23

"I started off enjoying all this, but if you went to Alton Towers every day for four years, it wouldn't be very fun, would it?"
Lily Allen to Hermione Eyre, *ES Magazine*.

Lily could think of no nicer way to say farewell to her fans than with two major UK gigs in London and Manchester – two cities close to her heart – with close pal Dizzee Rascal and Professor Green supporting. Dizzee and Lily would also both be nominated for Ivor Novello awards (Lily and her co-writer, Greg Kurstin, for 'The Fear' and Dizzee for the infectious 'Bonkers') soon after their headline gigs together, their destinies seemingly intertwined.

Manchester's MEN Arena and London's O2 were primed and ready for the mega-gigs, which were predictably packed to the rafters. Lily, again, was battling bronchitis as she took to the stage, apologising to fans in Manchester for being "a bit shit" because of her infection (but still sparking up a cigarette. Smoking ban, bronchitis, be damned!).

But the London gig, which was meant to be such a euphoric occasion as it was to be her final headlining show, was marred by violence. Lily, looking all grown-up in a long straight black dress, hair piled up à la Audrey Hepburn and wobbling, awkwardly high heels, had just dedicated the song 'Who'd Have Known' to Sam, who was in the audience, when she saw two men in the audience having a physical fight, worryingly close to where Lily's family were standing.

Lily burst into tears and left the stage immediately, or as fast as her towering heels could carry her. The audience rounded on the men with a chorus of boos as they were ejected from the gig. Allen stormed back on, holding a cloth to her face as she mopped up the tears and declared: "That's the worst sort of violence – it's fucking sick and you lot should be ashamed of yourself.... My brother and daddy were really close to it, and I got all scared. Are you all right, Pappa?" Her voice trailed off into sobs again. Keith, hardly a man unable to look after himself in these situations, was, of course, all right and the gig resumed with 'The Fear', and finally 'Womaniser'.

The scuffle had obviously thrown Lily, but, as *The Telegraph* observed in its review of the night: "The highlight came when she dedicated a song to David Cameron, pausing dramatically before adding, "It's called 'Fuck You'!" No doubt Lily was less than impressed when it turned out he'd be Britain's Prime Minister just two months later. (Interesting that the generally pro-Tory *Telegraph* should call this moment a 'highlight'.)

While Lily's 'retirement' remains in question, what will never be in doubt is her tireless energy and boundless enthusiasm for new projects and new ideas. There's the label (an office is being set up at the time of writing), the vintage clothes shop, planned for a September opening and Lily is becoming increasingly involved in green issues, not that this is anything new for her. She always votes Green in local elections and is anxious to try to record in ecologically sound studios wherever she can, but now she has more time and more control over her everyday life, Lily is taking on bigger projects, most recently taking part in a hands-on documentary about the rainforest in Brazil – the Sky Rainforest Rescue project.

OK, so the idea of celebrities wading into world 'issues' and becoming ambassadors can prove hard to stomach for many, but there is no doubt that Lily's profile can make the difference between an issue being ignored and an issue being recognised. (Why else would both Labour and the Conservatives try to woo Lily before the election and invite her to party conferences?)

Can Lily save the world, then? Maybe. She certainly took it over with alarming ease. Something tells us that, when it comes to Lily Allen, anything, and everything, is possible.

Sources, Bibliography & Acknowledgments

Bella Wolfson would like to thank everyone who helped and contributed in any way to this project. Special thanks to Omnibus Press' Chris Charlesworth, Charlie Harris and Jacqui Black. And as always, Baz Smythe, with all my love.

'What's up, Tiger Lily?' *Hot Press,* August 4th 2006, Steve Cummins;

'Me, my dad and Dumbo', *The Guardian,* September 22nd 2006, Chris Salmon;

'Lily Allen', *Pitchfork.com*, November 6th 2006, Scott Plagenoef;

'A bit of lip', *The Age*, January 28th 2007, Guy Blackman;

T4: *Lily Allen: Still Alright?* documentary presented by George Lamb, July 2007;

'How We Met: Lily Allen and Mark Ronson, *Independent,* July 2007, Guy Adams;

Glastonbury TV interview (BBC) with Phill Jupitus and Lauren Laverne, June 2007;

'Future Cut: The Logic behind Lily Allen', *Apple.com*, Jonny Evans;

'Cover Boy' (Mark Ronson interview), *Guardian,* October 6th 2007, Alexis Petridis

'Lily Allen's not really alright, still'. *The Sun* December 4th 2007;

'Lily Allen – Back To Earth', *The List*, February 27th 2008, Sylvia Paterson;

'Is this really the most hated man on radio?' (George Lamb interview) *The Guardian,* June 16th 2008, Laura Barton;

Lily Allen – Living Dangerously, Martin Howden, 2008 / John Blake publishing Lily Allen interview, *Attitude,* January 2009;

'Money? Drugs? Trousers? What did Lily Allen and Mick Jagger discuss over dinner?' *Word* magazine, January 2009, Rob Fitzpatrick;

'Lily Allen: uncertain smile', *The Telegraph*, January 16th 2009, Chris Heath;

'Lily Allen by Damien Hirst', *Interview Magazine* 2009'

'Lily Allen tries to keep her life private', *Liverpool Echo*, November 20th 2009; Sarah Owen interview, *Grove* magazine, November 26th 2009, Natasha Paulini;

'Capital girl: how we all fell for Lily Allen' *This Is London (Evening Standard),* December 11th 2009, Hermione Eyre;

'Brit Awards are always a big night' *The Sun*, Gordon Smart , February 16th 2010;

'Lily Allen has had enough of being Lily', April 25th 2010, *The Times*, Laurie Taylor;

Lily Allen interview, *Love* magazine, February 2010;

'Lily Allen swapped stilettos for wellies as she went on a trip to save an endangered rainforest.' May 3rd 2010, *Monsters and Critics*, Matheus Sanchez;

LilyAllenFans.com

And most importantly, Lily Allen's Myspace blog, and that of Del 'Strangefish' Greening, which Lily directed subscribers to while on tour, promising it would be 'vaguely interesting'…

Discography

DEMOS include:

Truth (featured in My Second Mixtape);
Sunday Morning (produced prior to Regal record contract. This would
be the B-Side to Littlest Things renamed U Killed It);
Friday Night (Remix) (also known as You're Gonna Get Burned);
Blank Expression (exclusive iTunes track 12 of *Alright, Still* album, a
Specials cover)
Naïve (cover of The Kooks track);

ALBUMS

Alright, Still
Smile, Kick 'Em Out, LDN, Everything's Just Wonderful, Not Big, Friday
Night, Shame On You, Littlest Things, Take What You Take, Friend Of
Mine, Alfie
Released July 14, 2006 (Regal/EMI), 3 x platinum in the UK, gold in
the US and Canada, and platinum in Australia, Ireland and the EU;

It's Not Me, It's You
Everyone's At It, the Fear, Not fair, 22, I Could Say, Back To the Start, never Gonna Happen, Fuck You, Who'd Have Known, Chinese, Him, he wasn't There.
Released February 9, 2009 (Regal/EMI), 3 x platinum in the UK, 4 x platinum in Australia, 2 x platinum in Ireland, platinum in the EU and gold in Canada;

SINGLES

Smile (2006)
Reached number 1 in the UK single charts

LDN (2006)
Reached number 6 in the UK

Littlest Thing (2006)

Alfie (2007)
Double A-side with Shame For You

The Fear (2009)
Reached number 1 in the UK

Not Fair (2009)
Reached number 5 in the UK

Fuck You (2009)

22 (2009)

Who'd Have Known (2009)

Back To The Start (2010)
Limited edition 7" for Record Store Day, April 17, 2010

EPS

FUEP (Fuck You Extended Play)
Released as a digital download March 31, 2009 (Capitol) exclusively for iTunes US.

Features Fuck You, Fag Hag, Kabul Shit and Womaniser

Paris Live Session r
Released as a digital download November 24, 2009 (Regal/EMI), iTunes only.
Features Fuck You, 22 (Vingt Deux), The Fear, Littlest Things and Everyone's At It

MISCELLANEOUS

Lily also featured on:

Lights Go Down
Basement Jaxx's *Crazy Itch Radio* (2006)

Bongo Bong, Love Light and Je Ne T'aime Plus
Robbie Williams' *Rudebox* (2006)

Oh My God
Mark Ronson's *Version* (2007)

Drivin' Me Wild
Common's *Finding Forever* (2007)

Wannabe
Dizzee Rascal's *Maths + English* (2007)

Never Miss A Beat and Always Happens Like That
Kaiser Chiefs' *Off With Their Heads* (2008)

Straight To Hell with Mick Jones
War Child Presents Heroes) (2009)

Beds Are Burning
Charity release for Global Humanitarian Forum climate justice campaign (2009)

Just Be Good To Green
Professor Green (2010)